Transnational Feminism

Transnational Feminism in the United States

Knowledge, Ethics, and Power

Leela Fernandes

NEW YORK UNIVERSITY PRESS

New York and London

UCD WOMEN'S CENTER/FDI

NEW YORK UNIVERSITY PRESS
New York and London
www.nyupress.org

References to Internet websites (URLs) were accurate at the time of writing. Neither the author nor New York University Press is responsible for URLs that may have expired or changed since the manuscript was prepared.

LIBRARY OF CONGRESS CATALOGING-IN-PUBLICATION DATA
Fernandes, Leela.
Transnational feminism in the United States : knowledge, ethics, and power / Leela Fernandes.
p. cm.
Includes bibliographical references and index.
ISBN 978-0-8147-6096-3 (cl : alk. paper)
ISBN 978-0-8147-7033-7 (pb : alk. paper)
ISBN 978-0-8147-6299-8 (e-book)
ISBN 978-0-8147-6052-9 (e-book)
1. Feminism. 2. Feminism--United States. 3. Transnationalism. 4. Women's rights. 5. Women's studies--United States. I. Title.
HQ1155.F47 2013
305.420973--dc23   2012038381

New York University Press books are printed on acid-free paper, and their binding materials are chosen for strength and durability. We strive to use environmentally responsible suppliers and materials to the greatest extent possible in publishing our books.

Manufactured in the United States of America
c 10 9 8 7 6 5 4 3 2 1
p 10 9 8 7 6 5 4 3 2 1

Contents

In memory of Clara Fernandes

Acknowledgments

THE IDEAS THAT have shaped this book have germinated over a long period of time and through the course of interacting with many students and colleagues. Many of the issues that I grapple with here are ones I have wrestled with as I have developed interdisciplinary courses and curricula at both the undergraduate and the graduate level at the various institutions I have worked at, as well as worked on designing the women's studies PhD at Rutgers. The process of working with students in the classroom and guiding them in their various interests, resistances, and commitments has enriched my own intellectual work on international perspectives on women and gender. In this process a number of colleagues and former students have helped sustain me and provoked me to think through the challenges of teaching about the world in the U.S. academy.

I have benefited at various points from intellectual engagements with a number of people, including Nikol Alexander-Floyd, Karen Barad, Drucilla Cornell, Ruth Wilson Gilmore, Wendy Hesford, Nancy Hewitt, Dorothy Ko, Wendy Kozol, David Ludden, and Asha Sarangi. Amrita Basu, David Ludden, Susanne Rudolph, and Linda Zerilli provided invaluable support over many years, which has helped me to move forward in productive ways. While at Rutgers, I was lucky to have met a number of people whose intellectual and personal friendships have far outlasted institutional location and affiliation. I am grateful to Jane Junn for her steadfast friendship and for being an example of how to live feminism. Prema Kurien has been a loyal friend and a neighbor I miss. Nikol Alexander-Floyd has been a dear friend who especially made my last year at Rutgers meaningful, fun, and survivable. Ruthie Gilmore has always been life-affirming and I am particularly grateful to her and Craig Gilmore for the blissful vacations in Lisbon. Caridad Souza gave me spiritual companionship and friendship at critical moments. My time at Rutgers has also been made meaningful by a wonderful group of students who are all now pursuing their own new and exciting research and activist agendas; my thanks go to Kate Bedford,

Melissa Brown, Carolyn Craig, Priti Darooka, Denise Horn, Stacey Hunt, Anil Jacob, Miduk Kim, Valsala Kumari, Karey Leung, Laura Liu, Simantini Mukherjee, Michele Ruiters, Yustina Saleh, and Undarya Tumursukh.

The University of Michigan has provided a congenial environment, and I appreciate the many new colleagues with whom I have an opportunity to engage and co-teach. I am grateful to the College of Literature, Science and Arts for providing me with a research leave that has allowed me to finish this book. I am also thankful to my research assistant Dashini Jeyathurai for her reliable help in tracking down citations and bibliographic materials. Ann Arbor has been a blissful place to finish this book, with fun visits and time spent with Ellie, Dave, Rosey, Natalie, Ian, and Dylan.

Over the years, I have learned from interactions at conferences, from responses to talks, and from conversations and workshops with many people both inside and outside of the academy and in a range of countries. These interactions have challenged and deepened my understandings of how knowledge matters. Finally, I am grateful to my editor, Ilene Kalish, and to NYU Press for their support of this project. Some portions of individual chapters have appeared in prior publications. Portions of chapter 2 appeared in "The Boundaries of Terror: Feminism, Human Rights, and the Politics of Global Crisis," in *Just Advocacy? Women's Human Rights, Transnational Feminisms, and the Politics of Representation,* ed. Wendy Hesford and Wendy Kozol (New Brunswick, NJ: Rutgers University Press, 2005). I first began thinking about *Bandit Queen* for an article published as "Reading 'India's Bandit Queen': A Trans/National Feminist Perspective on the Discrepancies of Representation," *Signs: A Journal of Women, Culture and Society* 25, no. 1 (Autumn 1999): 123–152. Some portions of chapter 3 appeared in this article. Finally, parts of chapter 6 appeared in "Unsettling 'Third Wave Feminism': Feminist Waves, Intersectionality, and Identity Politics in Retrospect," in *No Permanent Waves: U.S. Feminism,* ed. Nancy Hewitt (New Brunswick, NJ: Rutgers University Press, 2010).

1

Introduction

WHILE SIFTING THROUGH the mass of e-mails that accumulate at the beginning of a new academic year, I was struck by the subject heading of one message. The message line exclaimed, "Saudi Women Drive! NEW at Ms. in the Classroom." Upon opening the message, I found a generic informational advertisement recommending the use of a digital version of *Ms.* magazine for my courses. Buried at the bottom was a note that said, "P.S. The NEW Summer 2011 issue is available at Ms. in the Classroom, which includes Saudi Women Drive! Get the whole story on the fight for gender equality, including women's right to vote, in Saudi Arabia."[1] I was immediately struck by some of the contradictory implications of this small piece of feminist advertising. The use of an internationally oriented marker for a generic teaching-oriented advertisement seems to imply a widespread public interest and a presumed marketability of a sign of the "global" fight for women's rights. Yet this presumption is rooted in a mainstream national cultural symbol in the United States—the ability or right to drive. Driving and sociocultural identification with the car one drives are deeprooted cultural symbols in the United States that circulate widely in public discourses and popular culture.[2] The deployment of the global or international in this instance was thus firmly cast through a national framing of the feminist imagination. This kind of vision is particularly striking given the fact that academic feminists (to whom the e-mail ad was clearly addressed) writing about global issues have placed significant emphasis on the dangers of casting global or international gender issues through the subtle historical legacies of colonial images of inferior others. The message thus also underlines the disjuncture between advances in feminist theorizing within the academy and the more public, mainstream rhetoric of U.S. feminists. In this case, the symbol of Saudi women driving is presented in a message devoid of any description, reference, or context of the campaign, the country, or even the region. Saudi Arabia is presented as a site that has been vacated of any empirical, historical, or contextual depth. The idea of

Saudi women driving is thus emblematic of a U.S. national imagination. The geographic imagination at play here is defined by the borders of the nation-state rather than by a transnational perspective.

The complex issues and disjunctures that leak out of this example point to larger challenges that continually arise for feminists who write and teach about women, gender, and sexuality in locations that want to move outside of a national American narrative. Feminist scholars have increasingly sought to develop transnational perspectives in order to break from national narratives and decenter U.S.-oriented approaches. Yet, as this anecdote suggests, feminist efforts to invoke global or transnational perspectives are continually challenged by nation-centered narratives and visions of the world. In this book, I examine such challenges that arise in the creation of knowledge about the world. In particular, I examine the possibilities and the limits of the paradigm of transnational feminism that has arisen in interdisciplinary fields of study that have specifically been committed to breaking from nation-centric visions of the world. While I focus on the paradigm of transnational feminism, the issues I address speak to broader challenges of how to write and teach about the world in the current historical moment in the U.S. academy.

The anecdote that I have begun with captures some of the larger issues that continue to trouble the creation and dissemination of knowledge about the world within and outside the academy in the United States. In recent years, American universities and colleges have increasingly sought to expand the global dimensions of their curricula and academic programs. Institutions of higher education in the United States have long had programs focused on international studies, many of which evolved out of area-based programs that were developed during the Cold War period in the 1950s.[3] What is distinctive about the current emphasis on a global perspective is the attempt of new programs and avenues of intellectual inquiry to grapple with and move beyond the traditional borders of nation-states, regional areas, and disciplinary territories. The acceleration of economic globalization and the rapid global flows of people, capital, and cultural goods and information have intensified this search for global frames of analysis. The growing emphasis on global perspectives in academic institutions in the United States is in this sense partly an effect of globalization. Academics have sought to create programs of study that can make sense of the border-crossing flows that have been produced by or have intensified with globalization.[4] Meanwhile, the emergence and expansion of interdisciplinary fields of study within the academy (such as postcolonial studies, women's studies, and cultural studies) have produced a move away from older approaches to international studies that used the nation-state as a foundational analytical and political lens. Scholars writing in these fields have persistently called attention to processes of migration and diasporic identification that have unsettled the nation-state and produced new forms of cultural and political identities and practices.[5] The result has been a wide range of research and scholarship on various transnational political and sociocultural formations.[6]

As such formulations become institutionalized within the academy, the question that arises and that frames this book is one that asks how these paradigms shape the ways in which we produce, consume, and disseminate knowledge about the world within the United States. Such a question immediately becomes a fraught one given the contemporary historical and political context in which we pose it. The first decade of the twenty-first century has been marked by an intense confluence of intersecting local, national, regional, and international conflict, crisis, and change. Consider the key events that frame both public and intellectual understandings of the world within the United States. One of the overarching sets of events marking this period has, of course, been the post-9/11 U.S. "war on terror" and the ongoing wars in Iraq and Afghanistan. Hypernationalism in the post-9/11 United States has already unsettled romanticized beliefs in a deterritorialized postnational world that had begun to gain currency among some interdisciplinary academic avenues.[7] U.S. national interests have become further enmeshed with long-standing regional conflicts, including those between Israel-Palestine and India-Pakistan, among others. The twenty-first century has also been marked by the continued and intensified contradictions of economic globalization. On the one hand, states and international institutions continue to promote economic policies of liberalization. On the other hand, global economic crisis has served to reveal the continued significance of the state in structuring national and global economic activity. In both the United States and Europe, states have had to intervene to manage financial and political conflicts that have emerged over the nature of state intervention in the economy.[8] Meanwhile, the concurrent rise of China and India as growing global economic forces that has accompanied economic decline in the United States has produced new often fear-driven desires to know about these nations. The creation of "global" forms of knowledge that emerge on American campuses are thus often shaped by motives and affinities that are complex configurations of the instrumental (the need to know about regions and processes that affect individual, local, and national self-interest), affective (the emotional fears and desires that conflicts, crisis, and real or perceived threats create and that direct the will to know and understand), and the ethical (the desire to find responsible and accountable ways of engaging with the world).

Through this sketch of recent global events, I want to foreground the ways in which the framing of this global context is already a nationalized process. Thus, while large-scale events and processes are certainly transnational, they are perceived, framed, experienced, and negotiated in ways that are shaped by distinctive local and national contexts. The academy is one institutional site where such nationalized framings and negotiations are produced, disseminated, and consumed in important ways in the United States. Any interdisciplinary project that seeks to study questions that are comparative, global, transnational, or simply non-U.S.-centric emerges within a set of historically situated national discussions that have already been taking place both within and outside the academy in the United States.

The Rise of the Paradigm of Transnationalism

Consider some of the ways in which such national conversations and contexts have shaped the emerging paradigms of global and transnational studies in the United States. At one level, institutional resources and student interests have been shaped by the broad contours of these events. This is illustrated, for instance, by an increased interest in China and a continued and intensified interest in regions such as the Middle East that represent visible areas of conflict that are inextricably linked to U.S. governmental policies and state interests (particularly, of course, in relation to national security and economic interests). As students feel the impact of globalization on their own lives through their perceived threat of outsourcing of white-collar jobs and uncertain employment prospects, their interest in economic globalization and its effects has also grown. Intellectual paradigms have also been shaped by such events. Scholarly research agendas have been affected by the responses of both supporters of U.S. foreign and economic policy and critics of these policies (particularly in relation to war and economic globalization).

Meanwhile, processes of migration and the emergence of varied immigrant communities and forms of cultural identification have meant that students and faculty have also focused on both the countries of origins in regions such as Latin America, Africa, and Asia and the transnational ties between these regions and the United States. This has also intersected with the cultural dimensions of globalization as cultural goods such as film and media now routinely cross borders. Such cultural products are simultaneously local and transnational as they are consumed by multiple audiences in multiple locations. As scholars of cultural globalization have noted, this has led to new forms of cultural identification and new ways in which people and communities imagine their identities that no longer directly correspond to the territorial borders of the nation-state.[9] Some social theorists, for instance, have focused on the idea of cosmopolitanism as a way to break from nation-centric modes of identification.[10] These scholars have sought to identify ethical bases for identification and action that break both from territorialized nation-centric conceptions of the world and from state-centered ideas of citizenship. Meanwhile, the growth of studies focused on diasporic communities has produced a rich interdisciplinary body of scholarship on the intersecting identities of sexuality, race, ethnicity, and gender.[11]

Such approaches have consciously sought to dislodge nation-centric approaches to the world. However, the fields of knowledge that are produced through such paradigms often struggle to break from narratives that do not reproduce analytical frames or narratives that are implicitly associated with the U.S. nation-state. Ella Shohat, for instance, has cautioned against a kind of "submerged American nationalism" that permeates "a number of ethnic studies/women's studies/gender studies/queer studies curricula."[12] Meanwhile, writing about the field of Asian American studies, Kandice Chuh has provided an important discussion of such struggles to break from nation-centric frames of analysis.[13] Writing about the field, Chuh argues for a continual interrogation of "'Asian American' as the subject/object of Asian Americanist discourse and of U.S. nationalist ideology, and Asian American studies as the subject/object of dominant paradigms of the U.S. university" in order to ensure that the field does not reproduce the exclusionary dynamics of U.S. nationalism.[14] While Chuh is discussing the field of Asian American studies, she touches on a broader risk that also permeates fields of study that have explicitly sought to use transnational perspectives that seek to move outside of a U.S. frame. For instance, when transnational perspectives take liminal transnational identities of diasporic communities as unquestioned subjects, the generation and consumption of knowledge may inadvertently be located within particular kinds of U.S.-centered interests and concerns by centering transnational flows through the territorial space of the United States.

The emergence of the study of global and transnational processes in this context presses us to think of "the global" and "the transnational" not merely as a neutral geographic level of analysis but as conceptual categories that have emerged from specific political, economic, and historical circumstances. The kind of "global" or "transnational" perspective that has emerged is in many ways a national conception—it is shaped by the specific context of the U.S. academy.[15] A central argument that will unfold in this book is that interdisciplinary research on global and "non-U.S." locations is itself inadvertently nationalized. Such an argument may appear provocative to scholars who identify with such interdisciplinary paradigms, since much of the impetus of such theory and research (in crosscutting fields such as women's studies, postcolonial studies, and diasporic studies) is driven by an intellectual and political imperative of moving beyond the nation-state. In fact, interdisciplinary research (both feminist and nonfeminist) on transnationalism has identified itself with an ideological position that has been critical of nationalism and usually depicts the idea of the nation-state as an outdated or regressive political formation. Within the terrain of academic institutional practices, transnational interdisciplinary scholarship has also defined itself against older models of "area studies" scholarship whose origins lay within the specific geopolitical context of U.S. state interests during the Cold War. Certainly, the very "areas" that were carved out and institutionalized within the U.S. academy were derived from U.S. state conceptions of specific regional spheres of influence in which the U.S. state was competing with Soviet state power and influence. Transnational approaches have thus often explicitly attempted to dislodge such artificial boundaries that frequently created rigid institutionalized barriers to cross-regional, comparative, or transnational intellectual engagements.[16] Within such interdisciplinary sites, scholarship that takes the nation-state as the primary or foundational unit of analysis is now often viewed as an antiquated approach that has not kept up with newer understandings of the transnational nature of culture, politics, and economics. Yet, as I argue in this book, discarding the nation-state as a unit of analysis does not automatically dislodge a U.S.-centric epistemic project.

My argument is not, of course, that contemporary transnational and global intellectual or academic activities are explicitly shaped by nationalist interests in a self-evident or deterministic way or that such knowledge necessarily serves the interests of the American state or of U.S. foreign policy in any simplistic fashion—nor that individual writers and texts cannot or have not broken from nation-oriented visions of the world. Intellectual production is situated within and shaped by the historical compulsions of time and place but is never determined in a simplistic way by historical and structural conditions. Rather, the nationalization of interdisciplinary research and theory unfolds in more nuanced and indiscernible ways precisely because this research often normatively seeks to move beyond nation-centric perspectives. For instance, an overdetermined analytical and political compulsion to move beyond the nation-state often inadvertently transforms the "transnational" or "global" into a territorialized concept. Global and transnational research and theory are driven by the search for spaces and processes (whether they are cultural, political, or economic) that are not contained within the nation-state. The result, as I will illustrate in chapter 4, is that the space of the transnational becomes territorialized through the search for border-crossing activities and phenomena. The realm of the transnational in effect becomes a kind of derivative discourse that ironically mirrors the ways in which, as postcolonial theorist Partha Chatterjee has argued, postcolonial nationalisms became trapped by the discursive colonial models of thought they sought to oppose and replace.[17] Chatterjee has argued in his reading of Indian nationalism that core elements of the nationalist movement mirrored and reproduced the very categories of colonial rule they sought to displace. It is this kind of oppositional mirroring that is increasingly becoming codified within transnational/global research. Locked in opposition to the nation-state, transnational research often mirrors the borders of the sovereign, bounded form of the nation it seeks to move beyond.

The seductive danger of this nationalization of global and transnational research is intensified when we consider the ways in which the global and the transnational are not transcendent categories that simply empirically describe the broadest geographic or sociocultural scale of being and action but are categories that are constructed and operate within a specific historical and political context. In the case of U.S. transnationalism, the postnational imperative must be contextualized within and in relation to the ways in which U.S. national interests have been expressed through global claims of justice, democracy, and freedom. The postnational, in other words, is itself an American national concept in which (as I illustrate in chapter 2) the U.S. state has actively promoted its economic and foreign policy goals through challenges to conceptions of national and state sovereignty.

Consider, for instance, globalization theorist Arjun Appadurai's formulation of the postnational thesis of transnational processes.[18] Appadurai's groundbreaking work represented one of the first sustained theoretical arguments that contemporary forms of identity, imagination, and practice in a rapidly globalizing world are literally "trans" national—that is, they represent deterritorialized, border-crossing formations that exceed the nation. As he put it, "It is in the fertile ground of deterritorialization, in which money, commodities, and persons are involved in ceaselessly chasing each other around the world, that the mediascapes and the ideoscapes of the modern world find their fractured and fragmented counterpart."[19] Appadurai's arguments about deterritorialization and postnational globalization have been a foundational text in shaping emerging conceptions of transnationalism in a range of interdisciplinary fields, including cultural, postcolonial, and globalization studies. Indeed, Appadurai provides a rich analysis that seeks to disrupt static categories of the "West" and the "Third World" and explicitly addresses examples of global flows that are not defined by U.S.-centric definitions of migration. Thus, he discusses the complexities of postnational imaginations and identities of migrants from India to the Persian Gulf states—a migration flow within the so-called non-Western world." Yet, tellingly, when Appadurai identifies an ideal-typical site for the emergence of postnationalism, he turns to a discussion of the United States.[20] Thus he argues:

> We might recognize that diasporic diversity actually puts loyalty to a non-territorial transnation first, while recognizing that there is a special American way to connect to these global diasporas. America, as a cultural space, will not need to compete with a host of global identities and diasporic identities and diasporic loyalties. It might come to be seen as a model of how to arrange one territorial locus (among others) for a cross-hatching of diasporic communities.[21]

As he further argues, "But America may be alone in having organized itself around a modern political ideology in which pluralism is central to the conduct of democratic life."[22] This identification of the United States as an exceptional postnational space (rather than a typical nation-state) is not unique to Appadurai's work. The discipline of political science, for instance, has had a long-standing set of intellectual practices rooted in a logic of American exceptionalism. In this tradition, the United States (and American politics) has been analyzed as an ideal-typical site that is defined by democratic institutions, practices, and cultural norms.[23] However, Appadurai's arguments are significant because they represent a set of discursive narratives that have shaped interdisciplinary fields that have claimed to represent new and innovative conceptions, in contrast to more conventional disciplines that have produced narratives of exceptionalism.

The U.S. national narrative implicit in Appadurai's conception of a postnational United States is thus not simply an inaccurate or dated understanding of transnationalism. Rather, it is a discursive marker of the nationalized narratives of transnationalism that permeate and increasingly discipline interdisciplinary fields of knowledge. What has emerged in this process is a new set of disciplinary practices underlying such interdisciplinary conceptions of the global and the transnational. These normative practices have emerged at a historically specific moment that has been shaped as much by the national specificities of the United States as by the transnational and global processes that do indeed shape the world. In this process, there is a slippage between transnationalism as an ontological category (a real and complex material set of processes) and transnationalism as a normative paradigm that has increasingly become a disciplinary device within interdisciplinary research and theory. It is this slippage that is rooted in the historically specific discursive and material national context of the U.S. academy. Despite the extensive interest in the links between power and knowledge in interdisciplinary fields such as women's studies, cultural studies, and postcolonial studies and the strong influence of Foucauldian analyses of knowledge production, less attention has been paid to such national framings of interdisciplinary knowledge and the ways in which these framings produce "the world" within the United States. More significantly, this framing is a marker of a deeper trend toward the disciplining of interdisciplinary work.[24]

Thus, the essays in this book have two interrelated objectives. The first is to unsettle the nationalization of the paradigm of transnationalism. The second purpose of this book is to use this discussion of transnationalism to open up questions about interdisciplinarity and to find ways to unsettle the disciplinary mechanisms that sediment interdisciplinary fields such as women's studies. My intention is to specifically initiate a discussion about both the possibilities and the limitations of interdisciplinary knowledge on international, global, and transnational issues. The power of interdisciplinary fields of knowledge such as women's and gender studies, postcolonial studies, and cultural studies has rested on their ability to unsettle the complacency and rigidity of the traditional disciplines. In doing so, such fields have called attention to epistemological silences within the disciplines and produced new theories, methodological innovations, and political challenges that have simultaneously transformed and moved beyond the disciplines. Feminist scholarship began by pointing to the erasure of women from conventional analyses of historical, economic, and political life and soon moved toward transforming categories of analysis within all the major disciplines. Such scholarship, for example, transformed traditional conceptions of work by focusing on domestic labor and informal sector work, and challenged understandings of politics by focusing on the power in the private sphere. Meanwhile, interdisciplinary research on culture also produced methodological innovations by focusing on new sites of analysis such as film and the media that make up what Appadurai and Breckenridge have termed "public cultures."[25] As the impact of such vast and important contributions has spread, interdisciplinary scholarship increasingly falls into familiar patterns of research and analysis. The unsettling power of such forceful interdisciplinary challenges has begun to give way to interdisciplinary norms that increasingly discipline the forms of knowledge that emerge from these fields.

The paradigm of transnationalism is one case of this disciplinary impetus of interdisciplinary knowledge. It has, for example, become commonplace to use transnationalism as a framing device in many interdisciplinary fields. At a surface level, "transnational" has simply replaced "international" or "global" as a descriptive term meant to designate a move outside the territorial boundaries of the United States. At a deeper level, however, transnationalism represents a paradigm that explicitly seeks to move beyond the presumed parochialism of the territorial boundaries of the United States. Some scholars have already noted that the circulation of the term "transnationalism" itself can be problematic. Inderpal Grewal and Caren Kaplan examine some of the uses of "transnational" and caution against the loss of the "political valiance" of the term.[26] In line with a significant body of research on transnationalism, they call attention to inequalities and relationships of power that undergird the term and to the complex linkages between local, national, and regional processes that interact with transnational phenomena.[27]

Transnationalism is, in effect, both a category that captures particular kinds of processes and a perspective on the world that is embedded within relationships of power. Transnational knowledge thus functions in complex and multilayered ways. On the one hand, as I have noted, transnational knowledge in the U.S. academy arises in a specific location and historical moment within the national imagination of the United States. The political implications of transnational knowledge are contingent on the ways in which various American publics both within and outside the academy shape and respond to transnational processes. On the other hand, knowledge that is produced is itself a transnational product within a globalized intellectual marketplace. Transnational knowledge produced within a particular location thus circulates across national borders and may have different political implications in different local, regional, and national contexts. For instance, research that calls attention to poor working conditions that undergird China's economic boom may play a politically subversive role by challenging state power in China or India but may provide political comfort for American audiences increasingly threatened by outsourcing and capital flight to these rising economies.

Interdisciplinary paradigms such as transnationalism are located within and shaped by national imaginations in nuanced ways in U.S. interdisciplinary scholarship. Such dynamics have often been left unexamined because such interdisciplinary approaches are often located on the margins of national public discourses. Furthermore, scholars working in interdisciplinary fields are often located on the margins of intellectual sites in the academy as they critically respond to or disengage from the traditional disciplines and have often been at the forefront of calling attention to the relationship between power and knowledge. This has often prevented a closer examination of the ways in which interdisciplinary fields may themselves be shaped by national agendas and ways of imagining the world even though their intentions may be to disrupt these very agendas.[28] To pose this question that asks whether and how interdisciplinary fields are implicated in such national narratives is not to dismiss the significance of these fields but simply to interrogate the assumption that any set of knowledge practices can transcend the specificities of location and context. It is with this intention that an analysis of transnationalism must ask, in what ways is the dominance of this paradigm shaped by a national imaginary? In what ways is transnationalism an idea that is shaped by national publics in the United States as much as it is a concept that is grasping historical processes that have in fact unsettled the nation-state? In what ways has the idea of transnationalism begun to discipline research and writing in interdisciplinary fields of knowledge? These are the questions that shape the essays in this book. I seek to explore these questions through a specific focus on the paradigm of transnational feminism.

Transnational feminism has become one of the central paradigms in interdisciplinary women's and gender studies programs and curricula. The case of transnational feminism is a particularly fruitful case for analysis on a number of levels. Scholarship on transnational feminism has engaged with the major cultural, political, and economic trends associated with recent processes of globalization and has intersected with all the major disciplines and interdisciplinary fields that have focused on such processes. A theoretical focus on transnational feminism thus also provides an avenue for a critical engagement with crosscutting debates that span fields such as area studies, postcolonial studies, and the challenges of developing humanistic social science research agendas. Scholarship on transnational feminism has also paid close attention to relationships of power that shape knowledge production. Such work has engaged in self-reflexive knowledge practices in which feminist scholars themselves have examined the political implications and limits of categories of thought that have been used within this field. Transnational feminist thought thus comprises a rich and varied set of research and writings—both empirical and theoretical—that do not represent an easy target for critical analysis. On the contrary, the analytical tools for rethinking the concept of transnational feminism arise from within this set of scholarly writings. This set of essays thus represents an approach that both works within and builds on this body of writing on transnational feminism even as it simultaneously presents a critical engagement that interrogates the analytical terrain that increasingly structures this body of knowledge within a disciplinary field. Thus, in this endeavor I hope to engage in a theoretical project that is both deconstructive and constructive. In a deconstructive mode, I interrogate the limits of the paradigm of transnational feminism and use this case study to illustrate the disciplining of interdisciplinary research. In a constructive vein, I address the transnational as an ontological material and discursive formation and discuss ways to approach, analyze, and capture processes that do indeed exceed the nation-state (even if the nation-state has not withered away). This focus on transnational feminism thus provides both a set of theoretical debates that allow for this discussion and an empirical case study with which to analyze the links between power and knowledge that bind interdisciplinary theory and research.

The Case of Transnational Feminism

Transnational approaches to the study of feminism emerged in the 1980s through critical engagements with existing ways of addressing global feminism. These emerging approaches sought to move away from understandings of global feminism that ignored inequalities and differences between women.[29] Chandra Mohanty, for instance, specifically argued against models of global feminism that were based on apolitical understandings of universal sisterhood.[30] Writing about the then dominant version of international feminism that was rooted in a "sisterhood-is-global" model,[31] Mohanty argued that such a conception of sisterhood neglected the ways in which women's locations, identities, and political practices were embedded within transnational inequalities—particularly those linked to colonial relationships of power and structures of global capitalism.[32] The shift away from a singular "global" feminism to a more complex set of transnational processes pointed, for instance, to the ways in which women not simply were victims of their own particular systems of patriarchy but also were placed in complex historical and material relationships with both men and women in other parts of the world.[33] Scholars such as María Patricia Fernández-Kelly, Aihwa Ong, and Maria Mies analyzed the emergence of a new gendered division of labor where women in poorer Third World countries increasingly were tracked into manufacturing industries, often in "export processing zones" designated for multinational corporations.[34] As these groundbreaking works showed, the middle classes in "Western" countries (including middle-class women) were increasingly the consumers of products created by these women workers.

While a central dimension of this work was a focus on colonial and neocolonial relations of power between the Western (European and U.S.) and non-Western world, this work did not treat the West or the Third World as homogenizing or monolithic categories. Rather, such research sought to call attention to the colonial historical processes that have shaped contemporary transnational processes. Thus, for instance, Jacqui Alexander's seminal analysis of sexuality and the state provided a complex analysis of the layered intersections between colonial histories, contemporary global capitalism, nationalism, and the state. Writing about the nature of the postcolonial state in Trinidad, Tobago, and the Bahamas, Alexander showed that legislation designed to protect women from domestic violence in effect consolidated heteronormative marriage while criminalizing gay relationships.[35] Alexander's analysis of such heteronormative constructions of citizenship located these constructions of gender in relation to both historical and contemporary tensions between national identity and transnational processes. From a historical perspective, normative middle-class conceptions of black respectability emerged as a nationalist response to colonial rule and a slave plantation economy. In the contemporary context, the integration of the nation-state within a liberalized global economy through structural adjustment policies and the growth of the tourism industry have also fed into these tensions as they have destabilized the nation-state and produced new forms of nationalist, anti-Western sentiment. Sexual bodies provide a site for internal struggles of legitimation for the postcolonial state. The result, as Alexander notes, is that "as the state moves to reconfigure the nation, it simultaneously resuscitates the nation as hetero*sexual*."[36]

Alexander's essay served as an exemplary text that marks the emergence of a transnational feminist approach. In contrast to more singular models of global feminism, the analysis pointed to the complex layers of local, national, and state practices that interact with and are shaped by transnational processes. The construction of gender from this perspective is shaped by complex processes of sexuality, race, and class. As Chandra Mohanty argued, a transnational conception of a feminism "without borders" was one that was located within these intersecting structures of inequality even as it emphasized women's agencies, responses, and resistances to these relationships of power.[37] This normative interest in transnational perspectives was heightened by a growing body of scholarship that called attention to the gendered politics of nationalism and the modern nation-state.[38] Such work illustrated the ways in which nationalist movements invoked and reproduced gendered conceptions and sought to restrict or manage women's political participation. These studies thus pointed to the limits of nation-centric approaches to feminist struggles for equality.

Since the emergence of these approaches in the 1980s and 1990s, there has been an explosion of work on transnational feminism in the interdisciplinary field of women's and gender studies. This work has produced a rich and varied scholarship ranging from studies of socioeconomic and political processes such as globalization and migration to more theoretically oriented discussions of culture, power, and knowledge to discussions of feminist practice and activism.[39] Such work has marked a critical break from earlier understandings of a "global feminism." For instance, in lieu of a global feminist approach to women's movements as a unified movement against patriarchy, new transnational feminist approaches to women's movements have drawn on the intersectional analysis of local and global inequalities and substantially contributed to debates on how research, theory, and activism constitute the subject of feminism.

Yet the diversity and nuance of such scholarship have also been accompanied by a set of contradictory processes. This scholarship has had a significant intellectual impact within interdisciplinary knowledge. The proliferation of transnational approaches has meant that transnational-ism has now become a framing term for feminist knowledge of places (or people linked to places) outside of the United States. The result is that this framing device has been disciplined in troubling ways, and transnational perspectives are now disseminated and consumed in ways that reproduce the kind of U.S. national imagination I have been discussing. At the most basic level, the term "transnational" now often operates as a descriptive col-loquialism that refers to research or theoretical work that is not focused on the United States.[40] Used as a descriptive signifier, "transnationalism" does not differentiate between work that seeks to make sense of processes that have crossed or transcended national boundaries and questions, processes, and histories that are not necessarily primarily linked to transnational processes in significant ways. The consequence for knowledge production is the risk of reproducing the common ahistorical assumptions that all re-search must begin with or connect to a transnational frame.

Meanwhile, despite the fact that the origins of this paradigm were lo-cated in work that specifically called attention both to relationships of power and to the power dynamics of knowledge, transnational feminist knowledge is still distorted by a desire to consume issues linked to partic-ular representations of non-Western women such as veiling, female geni-tal mutilation, and other cultural issues. This is particularly true in public spheres within the United States such as the media, some activist sites, and classroom discussions within the academy.[41] These preoccupations are in fact markers of the national feminist imagination within the United States. Public representations of such issues in the media are perhaps to be ex-pected. Furthermore, given the driven ideological investment of the me-dia in representing non-Western, particularly Middle Eastern and Islamic, women as victims of cultural oppression, it should also not be surprising that undergraduate students in the United States also bring these imagi-naries with them to the classroom.[42] There is often a sizable gap between the breakthroughs of transnational feminist theory and research and the trans-/post-/interdisciplinary innovations that seek to push beyond bor-ders and boundaries, on the one hand, and students who are grappling with coming to terms with a world that they access through their own complex public spheres, often with very little factual knowledge, on the other hand. In many instances, this means that students latch on to visible issues that they gain access to within the confines of the public spheres that shape their imaginations. In other cases, students are often pressed into a purely deconstructive mode where they learn to express their inability to judge other cultures and remain mired in their own bounded and paralyzing self-reflection of their own power and privilege.

The limits of such framings of the transnational, of course, seem more readily apparent in ideologically charged spheres such as media-driven public spheres or in the case of younger students who simply have not had access to systematic or in-depth understanding of world histories through the secondary school system in the United States. Yet the incorporation of the "transnational" within interdisciplinary fields such as women's studies is also bounded by particular national understandings albeit in different and nuanced ways. Consider, for instance, a recent text that speaks to the cutting edge of interdisciplinary work and women's studies in particular, *Women's Studies on the Edge*, constructed by leading interdisciplinary feminist theorist Joan Scott.[43] The purpose of the book, as Scott puts it, is "to restore feminism's critical edge, even to sharpen it."[44] Thus, she notes,

> This impulse to self-critique has been present from the inception of feminism as a social-political movement. The critique I refer to is not the same as factional fights or different identity or strategic positions (difference versus equality, liberal versus socialist, straight versus queer, white versus women of color, first world versus third). Instead it is an examination of the very terms that organize our actions: What does it mean to make "women" the object of our studies? What are the exclusions performed by insisting on a homogeneous category of "women"? When inclusion is the aim, are there alternatives to the endless proliferation of specific (racial, ethnic, religious, geographic, national, sexual, class) identities? Is there such a thing as feminist theory or feminist methodology? What counts as emancipation and for whom?[45]

In the spirit of Scott's call for a continual process of self-critique, let us examine this text as an instance of the ways in which the project of interdisciplinarity becomes nationalized in subtle ways. *Women's Studies on the Edge* provides a useful example both because it is explicitly concerned with the risks of disciplining and institutionalizing interdisciplinary work (and its essays allude to or analyze a range of fields, including cultural studies, postcolonial studies, critical race studies, and transgender/sexuality studies) and because the text explicitly seeks to move beyond what Scott lists as the proliferation of specific identities including the national and geographic.

The text encodes the national and transnational through discursive practices that frame or attempt to disrupt the analytical lens of the nation-state—what Scott calls the process of "edging in" and "edging out."[46] There are three central discursive patterns through which Scott's framework of edging in/edging out delineates the national and transnational. First, the text makes an unstated analytical assumption that the theories and framings of feminism being discussed are those located within the U.S. academy. Second, the book makes an explicit attempt to speak to and to unsettle knowledge about spaces outside of the territorial United States. Finally, the text explicitly engages in a critical discussion of the limits of U.S. framings of interdisciplinary issues. While the individual essays that deal with these questions provide rich and complex analyses, taken together what we have is a subtle renationalization of the terrain of interdisciplinary and women's studies scholarship, despite the intentions of both individual essays and the volume as a whole.

Consider how this renationalization unfolds through the text. At a basic level, the discussions of the institutionalization of women's studies and the dilemmas this poses for the project of interdisciplinary knowledge focus on the U.S. academy.[47] This should not of course be surprising given that the text is addressing problems of institutionalization within the United States. However, this nationalization of debates on institutionalization becomes significant because the text claims to move beyond specificities such as nation and geography. The national space of the U.S. academy is rendered invisible even as it is foregrounded as the framing narrative for interdisciplinary work (including work that addresses contexts that are either outside the United States or transnational in nature). The U.S. nation-state in this narrative becomes the unmarked universal site, in contrast to the "endless proliferation of specific (racial, ethnic, religious, geographic, national, sexual, class) identities."[48]

In contrast to this unmarking of the U.S. nation-state, the second set of discursive practices seeks to explicitly address both the ways in which transnational identities and questions are addressed and the ways in which such representations are limited by U.S. conceptions of the world. The book contains two essays that address questions that explicitly unsettle the U.S.-based construction of women's studies. Afsaneh Najmabadi provides an important critique of the ways in which the "postcolonial" becomes a distorted signifier for all non-Western contexts.[49] She addresses the enforced unspeakability of her position as an Iranian feminist scholar as she is mistakenly characterized as a postcolonial scholar (when Iran did not undergo colonization) and as she is compelled to negotiate between rigid and bounded hegemonic identities of Islamic and secular feminism. In the second essay, Saba Mahmood presents a powerful critique of the ways in which the deployment of autobiographical accounts of diasporic Muslim writers has become a central ideological component of the U.S.-led "war on terror" that has been targeting the Middle East.[50] Mahmood illustrates that the representation of Muslim women as victims of cultural misogyny serves as a justification for the current U.S.-led wars in the Middle East. At a deeper level, as Mahmood notes, this ideological agenda is linked to both (neo)conservative political agendas and the secular norms and prejudices of liberal movements such as feminism.

The essays by Najmabadi and Mahmood provide powerful criticisms of the very U.S.-centered conceptions of feminism and interdisciplinarity that I have been analyzing. In different ways, both essays allude to the dangers of producing U.S. conceptions of the transnational. Najmabadi's analysis reveals the danger of reducing world history to U.S.-based understandings of postcoloniality. Meanwhile, Mahmood's analysis illustrates both how diasporic writers consciously address U.S. national audiences and how diasporic writings can be deployed and appropriated by both liberal/feminist and neoconservative American ideological agendas. However, while taken individually these essays highlight the national narratives embedded in interdisciplinary feminist knowledge practices, within the discursive frame of the volume in which they are located, they are disciplined by the reproduction of a nationalized conception of women's studies and interdisciplinarity that shapes the construction of the text. Thus the only representation of the transnational or of any context outside of the national borders of the United States takes place through the eye of U.S. institutional practices (whether those practices are of academic institutions or neoconservative think tanks). There is in effect no ontological existence—no reality or being—outside of this framing of interdisciplinarity and women's studies. Given the overdetermined attention to Muslim women and Islamic societies in the current U.S. political context, the fact that the only references to the world outside of the U.S. nation-state are indeed these very overdetermined signifiers only serves to accentuate this process of nationalization.

I have turned to this discussion of *Women's Studies on the Edge* precisely because it is a more nuanced and complex instance of the nationalization of interdisciplinarity and transnationalism within the U.S. academy. This instance of critical interdisciplinarity illustrates three central issues that I seek to highlight and address at various points in this book. First, the question at hand is not simply one of including or developing either critical perspectives on transnationalism or complex and rich knowledge about the world (whether in particular local, national, or transnational contexts). These perspectives thrive within the academy. Rather, the problem for interdisciplinary research and theory is how such knowledge is institutionalized, framed, and subsequently disciplined. This is not to engage in yet another sterile debate on the pros and cons of institutionalization.[51] The institutionalization of interdisciplinary knowledge has happened—the task at hand is not to bemoan or try to rationalize it but to address the concrete problems, responses, and negotiations that must be made in an ongoing and context-contingent process in order to allow interdisciplinary work to maintain a sense of dynamism. Thus, with the example of the Scott volume, the problem at hand is not the lack of inclusion of perspectives critical of U.S. nationalism but the ways in which these perspectives are disciplined when placed within a nation-driven narrative of interdisciplinarity, knowledge, and feminism.

The second issue that a text such as *Women's Studies on the Edge* foregrounds for us is the risk of rejecting ontology in the pursuit of purely epistemological projects—that is, the risk of rejecting discussions of historical, empirical, geographic reality as at best mundane "specificity" and at worst retrograde positivism. For instance, Scott dismisses nation, geographic location, religion, and race as specific identities that proliferate (presumably in contrast to epistemological generality). Geography and national identity are coded as specific, particular, and empirical factors (elements of ontology), in contrast to the deeper project of critical theoretical analysis (epistemological concerns with knowledge production). Yet the epistemological limits of Scott's discursive framings are precisely marked because of the ontology with which she marks interdisciplinarity and women's studies. Scott, in other words, makes specific empirical choices (that is, she engages in a method of selection) when she selects U.S.-centered debates on both U.S. *and* transnational questions. Scott's ontological grounding of interdisciplinary conversation is the United States even as she dismisses raising questions of location, nation, and geography as a set of subsidiary specificities. There is a double theoretical move in this nationalist framing. Such a dismissal renders invisible the marking of this U.S.-centered discursive approach even as it centers it. In this model of interdisciplinarity, the marked national geographic locations of other nation-states are simply particularistic identities that are checked off in a simplistic liberal model of multiculturalism, while the unmarked, overdetermined site of the U.S. nation-state serves as the ontological ground for conversations about knowledge, interdisciplinarity and feminism.

The third issue that my discussion of *Women's Studies on the Edge* seeks to foreground is an exploration of the tension between academic scholarship and the worlds outside of the academy. This tension is often mistakenly coded as a divide between theory and practice. Yet the problem of how to engage with the transnational that emerges within women's studies and feminist sites in the United States does not conform to a simple theory/practice dichotomy. At one level, both academic feminism and feminist sites outside of academic institutions have grappled with a similar dynamic in relation to engagements with women outside of the United States. This dynamic has produced a kind of Janus-faced feminist engagement with the world that oscillates between a missionary impulse, on the one hand, and a desire for transcendence, on the other. Consider, for instance, the conventional paradigms of global feminism that I have discussed. While postcolonial feminists and historians have analyzed the missionary impulse in the context of colonial histories of European feminism, this missionary impulse also resurfaces in more recent discussions of women's human rights and in transnational women's movements and activist agendas.[52] Thus, in a comparative discussion of transnational activism focused on Nigeria, states within the former Yugoslavia, and Afghanistan, Aili Mari Tripp argues that "outsider advocacy movements" (movements in which activists focus on women living in other contexts and states) are often characterized by what she calls "a 'rescue' mentality."[53] For instance, Tripp points to the highly publicized case of Amine Laval Kumara, who was sentenced to death by stoning in Nigeria in 2002 after being convicted of adultery. Nigerian activists and feminists involved in (eventually successfully) overturning the conviction repeatedly requested international advocacy groups to refrain from sending petitions (that Nigerian activists viewed as strengthening the political hand of Islamic extremists). Many international activists, especially those involved in Internet-based advocacy, ignored these requests and, as Tripp notes, circulated inaccurate and often racialized depictions. More recently, a similar international dynamic unfolded around the conviction and sentencing to death by stoning of the Iranian woman Sakineh Mohammadi Ashtiani. While, in this instance, Sakineh Mohammadi Ashtiani's children and lawyer initiated an international campaign for petitions and called for pressure on the Iranian government, the images and rhetoric of rescue circulated in a similar fashion—migrating through various blogs in the United States and popping up as an advertisement on social networking sites such as Facebook in rows with other commodities and websites being marketed. As one transnational activist organization's blog put it:

Last week a massive global outcry stopped an Iranian woman, Sakineh Momammadi Ashtiani, from being stoned to death. But Sakineh still faces hanging, and today, fifteen more people await execution by stoning—people are buried up to their necks and large rocks are hurled at their heads. Sakineh's brave children's international campaign shows that worldwide condemnation works. Let's turn this family's desperate appeal into a movement that ends stoning for good—sign the petition and send to everyone.

As with other such examples, Ashtiani and her family appear as lone victims being saved by international activists.[54] Indeed, the post-9/11 period in the United States has highlighted the persistence of colonial discourses on the need to save women through the resurgence of colonial stereotypes that academic feminist scholarship has long since deconstructed.[55]

If this missionary impulse is one side of and indeed the more familiar face of transnational feminist advocacy (and one that has been well criticized by feminist critics), the other face is what I have termed the desire for transcendence within the academy. At the most basic level, this need for transcendence is expressed through an impulse of moving beyond—whether it is beyond the borders of nation-states or the confines of old concepts. For instance, in one trend scholars argue for a move away from interdisciplinarity to transdisciplinarity.[56] In other cases, concepts such as race and nation are identified (as seen both in Scott's framing and also more broadly in the culture of interdisciplinarity that is increasingly practiced and reproduced on an everyday basis) as particularistic or regressive identity-based concepts.[57] In the everyday cultures (both written and lived through daily institutional and cultural practices) of "cutting-edge" interdisciplinarity, theories and research on race are critical only if they move us beyond the old-fashioned claims associated with identity politics. In this framing, questions regarding the politics of inclusion and exclusion and the structural, systemic reproduction of inequality are viewed as outdated normative questions. The nation, for example, is a central analytical and political category only when it is the site of critique (a space that should be moved beyond) rather than a valid analytical lens. In this mode, interdisciplinarity becomes contingent on a teleological sense of movement and of moving beyond.

My argument here is not of course that all feminist perspectives can be reduced to these two faces of the transnational. Rather, my point is that these are two of the dominant trends that shape transnational feminist work within and outside the academy. For instance, one of the needless tensions between "theory" and "practice" that permeates many women's studies programs and departments is in fact in large part about this opposition between the missionary impulse and the growing addiction to transcendence of feminist work within the academy. Thus, activist-oriented students often view "theory" as an elitist project and are resistant to any interrogation of the theoretical assumptions and political limits of feminist activist projects. Activism in this context becomes a missionary project in which feminists must go forth and act in the world on behalf of oppressed women without interrogating the theoretical and political assumptions (and limits) of their agendas. Meanwhile, theory increasingly becomes coded as a particular mode of deconstruction in which students must move beyond old paradigms and ways of thinking—often without pausing to consider how this addiction to transcendence itself is in need of interrogation. In the midst of these false binaries (between "theory" and "practice," between the missionary and transcendent faces of feminism) lies the world that feminism struggles to come to terms with.

The theory/practice debate and the anguish that often accompanies it are in many ways products of some of the specificities of public intellectual and political life in the United States. Intellectual and academic work tends to be stigmatized by a broader national public culture that valorizes anti-intellectualism. This has been accentuated by conservative political rhetoric that has effectively constructed colleges and universities as threatening sites that spread "liberal" values and effectively equated intellectual work with elites that are at best out of touch with real life and at worst representative of un-American values.[58] Meanwhile, the corporatization and professionalism of intellectual work has intensified this apparent separation between academic sites and activist-related work. While the project of connecting academic knowledge production to grassroots activism is an important one, the construction of an opposition between academic knowledge and activist or practice-related work often reproduces the misplaced assumption that academic sites are in some sense set apart from the real world.[59] Such an opposition misses the ways in which academic sites are central to the production, negotiation, and subversion of various relationships of power. For instance, as I will argue, academic sites are in many ways part of an institutional network that serves as a bridge between the state and civil society. Much as Antonio Gramsci argued, universities, colleges, and other academic sites serve as the trenches within civil society that enable the exercise of state power and that may be transformed as sites of struggle for counterhegemonic political projects.[60]

This conception of the academy as a network of institutional sites and practices that are fundamentally intertwined with state power holds important implications for interdisciplinary feminist research and theory— particularly in relation to international and transnational work. Given that interdisciplinary fields are located within such institutional webs, an adequate understanding of the relationship between power and knowledge must systematically address the relationship between interdisciplinary work, on the one hand, and state agendas, practices, and ideologies, on the other. At the most basic level, this institutional perspective cautions us against easy assumptions that interdisciplinary work (and a specific paradigm such as transnational feminism) has moved us past the nationalist imperatives of the state.

The primary assumption of this book is that *knowledge matters* and that discursive practices that circulate within the academy have real implications and effects. This book is thus not concerned with the question of dualistic discussions of bridging theory and practice.[61] Such discussions miss the ways in which institutions of higher education in the United States are central institutional sites within broader networks of power (linked to both the state and capital). Knowledge produced in the U.S. academy circulates in complex ways both nationally and across national borders. The assumption that academic knowledge is simply limited to private inaccessible debates within an ivory tower at best misses this complex relationship and at worst reflects anti-intellectual trends that permeate U.S. public culture.

Framework of the Book

My intention in this book is thus to unsettle this opposition between theory and practice and to take seriously the now well-accepted insight that knowledge itself represents a form of practice. My focus is thus broadly on the question of knowledge production and the complex apparatus of theoretical, practical, political, and cultural processes that make up this site. One of my primary goals is to unsettle the beliefs that often circulate among transnational and postcolonial academic feminists that a transnational feminist perspective marks a break from older regressive approaches that take the nation-state as their primary unit of analysis. In the current dominant culture of interdisciplinary feminist work, scholarship that locates itself within national historical frames of other countries is viewed at best as archaic or at worst as politically suspect. Yet the transnational frame that undergirds and polices such interdisciplinary judgments is it-self a product of the national specificities of the American academy. This is one of the central ironies of the transnational imperative of feminist scholarship.

Such contradictions necessitate that we ask, what does it mean to locate feminist research and theory within a transnational frame in the specific location and historical location that we live in?[62] At one level, this series of essays seeks to unravel some of these contradictions and to interrogate the limits of a hegemonic form of transnational feminism that erases com-peting understandings of international and comparative perspectives on women's and gender issues. However, and perhaps more important, this book seeks to be constructive as well as deconstructive. I thus wish to go beyond simply observing the limits of various approaches and point to ways in which "transnational feminism" can and has served as a produc-tive approach to feminist thought. I engage in this analysis through a focus on three major themes: (1) the growing significance of visual knowledge and its implications for comparative and transnational approaches, (2) the emergence of new forms of disciplinary regimes that shape interdisciplin-ary knowledge production within the academy, and (3) the relationship and contradictions between power, knowledge, and ethics.

Visual Knowledge: Representation and Public Spheres

One of the distinctive dimensions of transnationalism, and transnational feminism in particular, is a growing emphasis on the visual realm.[63] New technologies have led to the proliferation of various forms of visual rep-resentation. Such technologies, in an era of rapid globalization, have led to the rapid movement of media, film, television, and advertising images across national boundaries. This has led to changes in both cultural and political life. Thus, in her foundational work in interdisciplinary feminist cultural studies, Ella Shohat argued, "The global nature of the coloniz-ing process, the global flow of transnational capital, and the global reach of contemporary communications technologies virtually oblige the mul-ticultural feminist critic to move beyond the restrictive framework of the nation-state as a unit of analysis."[64] The spread of satellite technology has meant visual images of political events and conflicts circulate rapidly across borders. This has had destabilizing effects for states as dissidents have been able to use technology to publicize their struggles and agendas. How-ever, it has also allowed states to both use and control these technologies.

Meanwhile, cultural products such as film and television have also circulated through transnational circuits. As theorists of globalization have long argued, this has not led to simplistic forms of a homogeneous global culture or Westernization.[65] Rather, the Westernization of elites and expanding middle classes has been challenged by both secular and religious nationalist cultural representations, as well as by the persistence of local cultural practices and resistances and the creation of hybrid cultural identities and forms.[66]

Such processes have led to a growing literature on visual practices and the politics of representation. These new cultural products are often distinctively gendered. For instance, television series in comparative contexts often use particular models of family life and representations of women's roles to depict idealized cultural images that can provide a nationalist response to external cultural forces of globalization and Westernization. Writing about Egyptian television series, Lila Abu-Lughod has illustrated the ways in which particular images of family relations seek to produce a national identity that is distinctive from both Western and Islamist cultural forces.[67] In India, media and advertising firms have often constructed images of a "new Indian woman" with a hybrid modern-national identity to present the changes associated with India's globalizing economy through a nonthreatening image.[68]

The significance of such visual practices is not limited to a response to globalization. A growing feminist literature has also focused on the significance of gendered images in constructing narratives of war and conflict. In an insightful analysis of the Kosovo conflict, for instance, Wendy Kozol illustrates the ways in which racialized and gendered media images of the conflict in the United States produced support for U.S. military action. Kozol's analysis is representative of a broader set of feminist writings that have debated the implications of visual representations of women as victims of war, violence, and human rights violations.[69] Such writings have debated whether these visual depictions of women have been useful in promoting rights and justice or whether they have in effect transformed women into a spectacle to be consumed by various viewing publics and produced racialized and gendered nationalist narratives.[70] More recently, the focus on the politics of emotions, or what Sara Ahmed has called the "affective economy," has further enriched such analyses of representational practices.[71]

The significance of the visual realm means that feminists must grapple with the implications of gendered visual practices and representations. This is particularly the case given the ways in which inequalities of race, class, and nation have constituted such gendered images. A transnational feminist approach is thus presented with the critical task of examining the ways in which the cross-national circulation of such images produces and is shaped by such inequalities. Such visual practices, as cultural theorists have argued, are not simply reflections of such power relations. Rather, they are productive practices that help to create and reproduce these relationships of power. I thus begin these essays with a discussion of the significance and limits of a focus on visual representation. Given that this book seeks to foreground the locatedness of the paradigm of transnationalism within the United States, I begin with an analysis of the contemporary moment of the post-9/11 politics of the U.S. "war on terror." Feminists have paid much attention to the gendered, racialized representations in the post-9/11 period. I examine one of the central debates within transnational feminist scholarship—the uses and limits of languages of human rights in the post-9/11 period. Drawing on this case, I argue for an approach to representational practices that complements the lens of the visual with an analysis of the covert scripts that constitute the state's representational practices. In chapter 3, I extend this focus on representational practices by moving to a discussion of the power dynamics of the national and transnational production and circulation of cultural products such as film.

While these essays point to the importance of such representational practices, the visual turn of transnational feminist thought has had double-edged implications for feminist thought. An emphasis on the visual has often been collapsed into a preoccupation with issues that are readily visible. In other words, the visual has been transformed from a set of particular practices and sites of analysis to a realm of readily accessible border-crossing issues that are visible to academic audiences in the United States. The visible sites of analysis are in a sense those that such audiences can readily visualize in their imaginations. Chapter 4 thus looks at the challenges that this affinity for the visible has posed for interdisciplinary feminist research.

The Paradox of Visibility: Regimes of Interdisciplinary Knowledge

A discussion of transnational feminist approaches provides a useful case study for an analysis of the current trends in interdisciplinary theories and methods. The slippage between feminist preoccupations with the visual and the visible enables us to think through some of the discursive regimes that have come to shape interdisciplinary knowledge. In the case of women's and gender studies, the transnational feminist focus on visible border-crossing issues points to deeper issues and problems that arise with regard to the study of countries and regions outside of the United States. Much feminist scholarship has pointed to the epistemological problems that arise when we attempt to produce knowledge of "other" women, particularly those from marginalized locations.[72] Recent trends in transnational feminist scholarship have specifically responded to these criticisms, particularly by attempting to link local and global processes and by paying attention to the intersecting identities that shape women's subjectivities.

Despite the richness of such scholarship, there have been subtle disciplining trends within women's studies scholarship. At one level, such scholarship has centered around specific kinds of visible issues such as women working in export-processing zones, transnational migration, tourism, nongovernmental organizations (NGOs), and cultural practices (such as veiling and female genital mutilation), among others. This is the case even when such scholarship is paying attention to the complex power relations that constitute such issues. In other words, the critical discussions of Western feminist representations also inadvertently reinforce these trends because they preserve a focus oriented toward the West. At a deeper level, the focus on the transnational and the desire to address epistemological questions of power and knowledge have in fact not led to systematic discussions of how best to produce fields of interdisciplinary knowledge that enable students to systematically locate women's and gender issues within their own cultural, historical, and political contexts—contexts that are not reducible and sometimes not even primarily linked to transnational issues. These trends have produced a dominant model of interdisciplinary scholarship that rests on an excessively linear approach to the production of knowledge—an emphasis on new transnational processes and the use of new forms of language to represent such questions have become markers of an advanced interdisciplinary approach. Yet in reality most students (both undergraduate and graduate) come to interdisciplinary fields like women's studies with little basic empirical knowledge about specific places and contexts. The term "empirical" itself has become a marker of an outdated positivist approach. Yet students are often most in need of specific and systematic empirical knowledge. Without this knowledge, they turn in their research to visible issues that they can readily grasp. Meanwhile, self-reflexive discussions of knowledge production often stop at a familiar epistemological paralysis about the perils of writing and representing "other" women.

I analyze some of these kinds of pitfalls that have arisen with the institutionalization and expansion of interdisciplinary approaches in chapters 4 and 5. However, the essays in this book seek to move beyond criticism and deconstruction of such dominant trends and explore alternative possibilities and responses to interdisciplinary work. Karen Barad, for instance has argued for a theoretical understanding of knowledge that includes three realms: the epistemological, the ontological, and the ethical.[73] Barad's approach specifically urges us to consider the materiality of our knowledge practices. Working in the field of science studies, she conceptualizes a form of materiality that is ontological even as it is constituted by discursive processes, agency, and practice. Such an approach provides a useful path for moving beyond existing epistemological discussions of the power dynamics of transnational knowledge production. Further developing such an approach, I argue, requires that we consider more systematic discussions of the methods and practices that are used to produce transnational feminist knowledge. Taking the ontological dimension seriously, for instance, means that interdisciplinary knowledge must reconsider resistances to a systematic consideration of how we approach empirical research and teaching within interdisciplinary sites such as women's studies.[74]

Underlying these challenges is a need to disrupt teleological approaches to the question of knowledge production. This teleological approach assumes that successive new paradigms that emerge must move beyond and break sharply from preceding approaches and conceptions. There is no better example of this than the "wave model" that has become a canonical historical formulation of feminist thought. The kind of rethinking of transnational feminism that I am arguing for requires a critical rethinking of this formulation.[75] The paradigm of "third wave" feminism, for example, which has included both U.S.-based research on race and postcolonial/ transnational feminism, has been misrepresented through this linear form of temporality. Writings on "third wave" feminism, as I argue, provide us with an example of conceptions of border-crossing and difference in ways that move us beyond the disciplinary impetus of interdisciplinary research that produces binary oppositions between new and old paradigms and between epistemological knowledge and empirical reality.

Power/Knowledge and the Question of Ethics

Finally, the book addresses the question of knowledge production as ethical practice.[76] The question of ethics is of course always embedded within feminism. The feminist concern with addressing questions of inequality, power, and justice is itself an ethical project. Feminist debates on power relationships that characterize research practices are also implicitly questions about ethics. However, ethical questions, while linked to questions of power, are not reducible to such questions. A discussion of ethics enables us to move beyond the limits of a conception of power and knowledge that operates solely within the discursive-epistemological realm. A theme running through many of the chapters in the book is the way in which a focus on ethics can move us beyond the current impasse on what some adaptations of Foucauldian approach view as a circular and unyielding relationship knowledge and power.[77] This move requires a shift to an understanding of knowledge as a set of practices rather than a set of circulating texts or predetermined power relations. Taken in this way, the question at hand for scholars of feminist or other interdisciplinary fields becomes: What is the relationship between our knowledge practices and our ethical practices?

Ethics is itself of course not a neutral zone of activity. Much harm has been done through political projects that claim an ethical imperative. Historically, many forms of military intervention—ranging from the European colonial project of civilization to conflicts as recent as the Bush administration's wars designed to spread democracy—have claimed an ethical imperative. The question of ethics also raises debates over the question of whether (and which) ethical principles are universal or may be products of specific historical and cultural contexts. Simply reverting to the realm of the ethical does not provide easy answers that can escape the power-laden nature of knowledge production. As I argue, ethical formations and belief systems are not zones of exception that automatically move us beyond the problems inherent in knowledge production. In fact, ethical realms are themselves shaped by particular cultural, historical, and national circumstances. A focus on ethical practices thus does not provide a shortcut that can circumvent U.S.-centered philosophical assumptions or the power relations that stem from the state.

Yet a discussion of ethics brings with it two key issues that are of relevance both to feminist thought in general and to any transnational feminist approach committed to justice. The first is a practice-oriented approach to knowledge and an agency-centered understanding of responsibility. The second is a shift from the preoccupation with visibility that I have noted to a consideration of the often invisible practices, attitudes, and behaviors that constitute ethical action. The power-knowledge dyad, for instance, has led to intensive debates on strategies of representation, particularly in the case of texts and representations of marginalized women. These have ranged from Spivak's early argument against representation in her classic essay "Can the Subaltern Speak?" to a range of experimental strategies on how to present one's texts to various audiences.[78] The focus on representation is of course one that is concerned with the visible presentation of one's research and writing. A discussion of ethics allows us to build on these insights and also to include a range of practices that do not fit the domain of visibility. In other words, these ethical practices may be witnessed by small numbers of people but are not commercially visible on a mass scale through the public performative practices we use to display our knowledge products. This move toward the ethical also points us to a reconsideration of how we define and think of knowledge.

Outline of the Chapters

This introductory essay has laid out the central themes and structure of the book. I begin with a discussion of the ways in which visual practices are a central element in understanding transnational feminist knowledge. I engage in this analysis through essays that engage the circulation of knowledge in public spheres that include but are not limited to formal academic sites. In chapter 2, I examine how the U.S. "war on terror" has reworked the question of transnational human rights. Such processes, I argue, are not reducible to visual images. State practices draw on ideologies of race, gender, and nation in order to redefine (and narrow) the boundaries of civilian life. Chapter 3 moves from the realm of state practice to that of public culture. The chapter examines the ways in which different forms of knowledge (such as film and biography) circulate across national borders and have varying power effects in varying national contexts. Taken together, these essays examine the centrality of representational practices (both visual and nonvisual) in understanding the politics of knowledge production. Chapter 4 disrupts the conflation of the visual with visible border-crossing issues, presenting a critical discussion of some of the dominant trends in transnational feminism knowledge and the "regime of visibility" that increasingly disciplines transnational research and theory. The chapter then examines an alternative approach that incorporates the epistemological, ontological, and ethical dimensions of knowledge production. Chapter 5 continues this discussion through an examination of the ways in which the paradigm of transnational feminism has become institutionalized within the academy. Chapter 6 continues this discussion of dominant trends and alternative approaches through an analysis of the ways in which dominant U.S. models of multiculturalism such as the wave model of feminism have disciplined and distorted the insights of "third wave" feminism. The chapter then turns to alternative ways of thinking about the relationship between race and transnationalism. Finally, chapter 7 reflects on the stakes of transnational feminist scholarship for how we understand and engage with the world in which we live.

My concern throughout these essays is with knowledge as practice. While my focus is on women's studies and transnational feminism, the implications of my discussions are not limited to this field. Women's studies is simply a case study for analysis, and many of the discussions are pertinent to other fields. I draw out such connections whenever possible, particularly in relation to interdisciplinary approaches such as area studies and postcolonial studies. As with any series of theoretical essays, this book is a work of interpretation that draws on my own intellectual background and engagements. I thus draw on examples and empirical work from my own academic research and teaching on feminism, globalization, South Asian studies, and postcolonial theory in the United States. Taken together, these essays are thus an attempt not to reflect every trend or debate on transnational feminism but to provoke debates and reflections in ways that continue to unsettle the disciplining of minds that sets in even within the most productive interdisciplinary fields.

2

U.S. State Practices and the Rhetoric of Human Rights

ON JANUARY 13, 2009, during the course of Hillary Clinton's Senate confirmation hearings for secretary of state for the newly inaugurated Obama administration, Senator Barbara Boxer began her questioning by holding up large, blown-up photographs of Pakistani women who were the victims of an acid attack. Boxer's intention, as revealed in her exchange with Clinton, was to foreground Clinton's interest and experience in promoting global women's rights. Clinton responded to this opening with a strong statement. Linking the attacks in Pakistan with attacks on schoolgirls by Taliban supporters in Afghanistan, she asserted:

> They want to maintain an attitude that keeps women unhealthy, unfed, uneducated, and this is something that results all too often in violence against these young women. This is not culture, this is not custom, this is criminal. . . .I want to pledge to you that as secretary of state, I view these issues as central to our foreign policy not as adjunct or in any way lesser.[1]

This moment within the U.S. Senate encapsulates some of the central issues and contradictions that have shaped transnational feminist debates on human rights within the United States. The Boxer-Clinton exchange sought to mark a break from the past policies of the outgoing Bush administration. Clinton's declaration of her support for women's rights represented a central feature of a shift toward a broader conception of foreign policy that included issues such as economic development and women's rights and that was not founded solely on military action.[2] At a deeper level, however, this rhetorical exchange highlighted long-standing historical trends in which the question of women's rights has been intertwined with U.S. state and foreign policy objectives. This rhetoric, along with Boxer's use of the images of Pakistani women, also echoed a long colonial history in which non-Western women have been cast as victims who need aid from interventionist forces.[3]

Feminist scholars and activists have long debated the tension between the colonial imperative that underlies this interventionist state approach to women's equality and the liberal feminist investment in promoting women's rights as human rights. Much of the transnational feminist research on this debate on women's human rights has been shaped by a polarized framework. Feminist writers and activists have used the language of human rights in their struggles to compel states and international organizations to address questions of gender inequality and women's rights.[4] The creation of a global platform that rested on the call for a recognition of "women's rights as human rights" sought to elevate women's issues within global and international forums (particularly within the United States). This platform then fundamentally began to shape local NGO discourses and practices in comparative contexts as feminists in these contexts used the language of human rights to press their states for a range of rights.[5]

Critics of this approach to transnational feminism have sharply condemned the use of the universalistic language of global human rights. The primary criticism stemmed from postcolonial feminists who argued that this rights-based framework both imposed a homogeneous global language on complex local/national contexts and ended up intensifying the dominant position of the American state through the emphasis on global organizations such as the United States. In a sharp critique of the rise of the feminist global human rights paradigm, Inderpal Grewal, for instance, argued that the "women's rights as human rights" campaign could only be successful by ignoring geopolitical inequalities that shape relations between nation-states and that undergird the dominant global position of the United States. Thus she argued, "In the context of the U.S., the state and its related nationalist discourses of 'American' subjects are powerful enough to recuperate the progressive efforts of many individual women, dominant and non-dominant groups of women and also U.S.-based NGOs."[6]

Within this polarized debate between proponents and critics of the feminist human rights agenda, a range of scholars have sought to produce more nuanced analyses and have sought a middle ground that neither condemns nor romanticizes this approach to transnational feminism. This research has illustrated that the global human rights approach to transnational feminism has had uneven and complex effects. As Amrita Basu has argued, transnational feminist networks that have built on the NGO structures associated with the United Nations and global human rights approaches have been more successful under particular kinds of conditions. Thus, she notes that transnational campaigns have been effective in contexts "where support for a particular demand exists locally, but its expression is constrained where the state is either indifferent or repressive towards women; and where the violation involves physical violence and redress can be found by asserting women's civil and political rights."[7] Anthropological research has also shown that local activists often seize on global languages of human rights and effectively use such rights in the context of local struggles and through culturally specific meanings of rights.[8] Kay Schaffer and Sidonie Smith, for example, provide a compelling analysis of the complex and varied ways in which life narratives "bear witness to suffering and impact differently upon dominant and marginalized, subaltern and outgroup communities, [and] emerge in local settings that are inflected by and inflect the global."[9] Such research has sought to navigate between the danger of imposing a universalistic rights framework on cross-cultural contexts and the danger of minimizing the importance of the work that local activists and thinkers have done by strategically using rights-based frameworks to pursue very real struggles against cultural, political, and economic inequalities. In these endeavors, feminists have increasingly recognized the importance of taking the state seriously when attempting to develop a transnational feminist approach to human rights. Kamala Visweswaran's critique of human rights approaches to immigration asylum cases in the United States points to the ways in which U.S. immigration policies help produce a legal process in which lawyers and advocates tend to base asylum cases on culturalist arguments (that depict violence against women in terms of cultural factors) in ways that ignore both the role of the asylee's state in the violence and the U.S. state's role in shaping policies or supporting regimes that have enabled the violence. Thus, she quotes Saeed Rahman, one of the asylees she has interviewed:

> When lawyers use terms like intolerant, police brutality, Islamic fundamentalism, etc. images of the Third World, underdeveloped folks, backwardness and fanaticism are evoked. . . . However for some asylees this can be a difficult discussion. . . .We are also aware of the ways in which our histories are shaped by the U.S. For instance, in my case, I grew up in a military dictatorship in Pakistan which was strongly supported and maintained by the United States. . . .It would not have worked out if I gave an introductory class to my immigration officer on U.S.-Pakistan relations.[10]

The underlying thread of this narrative and the Boxer-Clinton exchange is a complex relationship between the state and practices of representation.

The question that we are left with is one that asks what kinds of work such representations of non-Western women do for the U.S. state when they cut across varying administrations and institutional structures within the state.

As I have alluded to earlier, much postcolonial and transnational feminist research has referenced the role of the U.S. state in shaping global human rights debates and representations of women from non-Western countries. Yet in such work the U.S. state generally appears as a static figure that stands in for colonial or imperial processes.[11] Liberal feminist approaches that advocate global rights approaches, on the other hand, usually render the U.S. state invisible.[12] The result is that transnational feminist approaches to the human rights debate tend to transform the U.S. state into a rhetorical flourish that is meant to signify imperial power and global relations of inequality.[13] The gap that exists in such an approach is a closer examination of exactly how representational practices shape the workings of the U.S. state. Within the field of American studies, Jasbir Puar, for instance, has well illustrated the complex ways in which U.S. state representational practices have both produced and been constituted by various formations of racialized sexuality in the United States.[14] Such formations, as Puar argues, have been reproduced within mainstream gay and lesbian movements in ways that have nationalized queer identities in the United States. Without such an examination of state practices, transnational feminist approaches at best risk reducing practices of representation to a reductive version of ideological manipulation or at worst leave the U.S. state unmarked within the paradigm of transnationalism.

This chapter provides an analysis of the ways in which state practices of representation in the post-9/11 period of the United States' "war on terror" have reworked the question of transnational/global human rights. In contrast to existing literature on war, violence, and representation that has focused primarily on the visual or visible forms of representations and narratives, I argue instead for an analysis of state representational practices that are not readily reducible to the visual/visible.[15] My concern is with the ways in which state representational practices within the United States attempt to reconstitute the civilian spatial-material realms in the regions with which the United States is at war—a process that is simultaneously national and transnational.

In the immediate aftermath of the 9/11 terrorist attacks in the United States, the gendered politics that unfolded in the public domain in the United States echoed a long history in which gendered ideologies, women's bodies, and racialized masculinities have served as central signifiers for nationalist agendas and international political conflicts. As feminist scholars have long argued, nationalism is structured in systematic ways through the politics of gender and sexuality.[16] As Nira Yuval-Davis has argued:

> Women usually have an ambivalent position within the collectiv-ity. . . .they often symbolize the collective unity, honor and the *raison d'être* of specific national and ethnic projects, like going to war. On the other hand, however, they are often excluded from the collective "we" of the body politic, and retain an object rather than a subject position. . . .In this sense the construction of womanhood has a property of "otherness."[17]

This gendering of otherness is intensified when it is constructed through international relationships of dominance and power. For instance, follow-ing the 9/11 terrorist attacks, during the U.S. military preparations and dur-ing the period of the military campaign against the Taliban and al-Qaeda in Afghanistan, media images and public discourses were rife with images of veiling and of the oppression of Afghani women. Such discourses did not require much ideological creativity given the very real repression of Taliban rule, which feminist activists had been working against long before the events of 9/11, and given the long history of colonial representations of veiled women as a core narrative of orientalist ideologies that have his-torically shaped Western approaches to the Middle East and the Islamic world.[18] Sensationalized reporting of the gender oppression of women in Afghanistan, on the one hand, was juxtaposed with new narratives of mas-culinized heroes in the depictions of the roles of firefighters and policemen in the context of the 9/11 attacks, on the other hand.

The deeper links between such gendered discourses of veiled women in the media and the interests of the U.S. military campaign are appar-ent when one considers how the social, economic, and political interests and rights of Afghani women dropped out of U.S. mainstream media dis-courses once the initial military campaign was carried out. In many ways the dynamics of this form of gendered politics have been emblematic of the familiar patterns in which women have been deployed as cultural signi-fiers that I have been discussing. The ways in which the Taliban's repres-sive gender regime sought to use women as the foundation for its politi-cal agenda of cultural purification or the ways in which mainstream media representations in the United States have presented veiled women as silent victims are quintessential instances of such dynamics.

The politics of representation of non-Western women, as I have noted, are part of a much longer history of colonialism that has been well analyzed by feminist scholars in a range of comparative contexts. These representations continue to play a powerful role in shaping hegemonic understandings of contemporary political conflict in what becomes a kind of national common sense in places like the United States.[19] However, such long-standing gendered colonial narratives have also been configured in new ways in the post-9/11 period. Feminist debates on the language of human rights and the politics of representation have been affected by shifts in national and global political processes in the post-9/11 period. Shifts in global political processes have complicated languages of human rights and languages of feminism in ways that draw both on older questions of global inequality and on newly emerging patterns of post-9/11 U.S. foreign policy. I employ a transnational feminist perspective on the U.S. "war on terror" and the human rights debate to deepen our understanding of the linkages between the state and the politics of representation. I argue that the politics of representation is central to new configurations of state power that have begun to connect discourses of terrorism and the language of human rights. This politics of representation is not centered solely on the proliferation of specific visual strategies such as the deployment of media images. Instead, I argue that the politics of representation are part of a more complex series of state practices that rework the boundaries of categories such as civil society and terror.

My analysis in this chapter draws on theoretical work that has questioned the assumption that there are predetermined or self-evident boundaries between state and civil society. Joel Migdal, for instance, has argued for a "state-in-society" approach that analyzes the state in terms of both the image of the state as a unified entity that claims to represent its people and a series of practices—"those routinized performative acts—that batter the image of a coherent, controlling state and neutralize the territorial and public-private boundaries."[20] This encompasses a wide array of practices, ranging from the ways in which state functionaries may use their official roles to pursue their own private business interests, to a Gramscian depiction of the ways in which "private" organizations within civil society such as schools, universities, and religious bureaucracies may represent sites for the extension and exercise of state power. The heart of state power in such a conception lies in the ways in which it is able to draw a series of social, political, and territorial boundaries that create what Timothy Mitchell has described as an appearance of a clear demarcation between state and civil society.[21] As Mitchell notes, "It is a line drawn internally, *within* the network of institutional mechanisms through which a certain social and political order is maintained."[22]

Drawing on the insights of such approaches, I analyze some of the representational politics of this process of boundary formation and examine the ways in which such forms of politics draw on intersecting ideologies of race, gender, and nation. Such representational practices, whether they are in the form of media representations, the rhetorical discourses of politicians' speeches, or new forms of legislation such as the Patriot Act, are an essential part of the contemporary politics of the exercise of state power, both within and across the United States' national territorial borders. As I argue, an understanding of the ways in which state practices centrally invoke and produce the boundaries of categories such as civil society, civilization, terror, and terrorism is critical for an undertaking of any political project that seeks to adopt a transnational feminist framework of human rights. On the one hand, the language of human rights is implicated in such power-laden projects of boundary production that mark the post-9/11 exercise of U.S. state power.[23] On the other hand, a human rights approach can also provide important understandings of and responses to these state practices.

A feminist analysis of arenas such as the state, foreign policy, and the language of human rights thus cannot be limited to the public visibility of women in visual images. While there are numerous examples of the use of specific visual images such as the gendered process of militarization in the depiction of the rescue of Jessica Lynch from Iraq and the depiction of veiled women in earlier phases of the war with Afghanistan, strategies of representation have also focused more on generalized discourses of national injury, security, and the threat of the racialized masculinity of Muslim/immigrant men.[24] This chapter seeks to analyze the linkages between such representational politics and state practices and interests. These state practices redraw boundaries between the public and private in ways that both produce new challenges for feminist political strategies that draw on a human rights–based approach and make a feminist analysis crucial for an understanding of U.S. state practices and contemporary global politics.

The U.S. "War on Terror" and the Politics of Human Rights

Feminist critics of a global human rights approach to women's activism have called attention to two central issues. First, such critics have noted that feminist human rights approaches have often inadvertently engaged in questionable representational practices that have depicted mainly non-Western women as victims of essentialized cultural traditions and have paid less attention to questions such as state power or economic rights.[25] Second, feminist critics have argued that feminists using a global human rights approach have often paid less attention to inequalities between nation-states and the dominant global political-military role of the United States and to the ways in which such inequalities permeate global or universal languages such as the discourse of human rights. Such insights are of particular significance in the aftermath of 9/11 and the initiation of the U.S.-declared global "war on terror." In particular, the "war on terror" has set in motion political processes that rest on the expansion of state power both within and beyond the United States' national territorial borders. This has involved the use of both conventional forms of state power, such as military power, state surveillance, and law enforcement, and more subtle forms of disciplinary power through new normative constructions of citizenship. These political processes inform and further complicate the question of human rights.

In many ways, the U.S.-declared "war on terror" marks a new period in international relations and global conflict that is distinctive from earlier forms of war and conflict. A distinctive aspect of this "war on terror" is that the United States, by declaring war on a phenomenon such as "terrorism," both invoked the role and responsibility of nation-states and simultaneously sought to transcend the relevance of sovereign national borders. On the one hand, George W. Bush's warning to the world that "you are either with us or against us" invoked the requirement that nation-states cooperate in the war against terrorism or risk being defined as terrorist states for supporting or harboring terrorists. On the other hand, the transnational and hidden nature of al-Qaeda terrorist operations and networks has provided an ideological basis for the United States to define its "war on terror" as one that by definition must transcend questions of national borders and state sovereignty. The U.S. state reserves the right to transcend national borders either through small operations in cooperation with the governments of specific nation-states (for instance, in the Philippines, Pakistan, and Yemen) or through overt military campaigns as in Afghanistan and Iraq. This policy, I argue, marks a shift in the American conception of the global order to a situation where questions of state sovereignty are contingent in more overt ways on the interests and requirements of the United States' perceptions of its national security.

This global expansion of U.S. state power has had important implications for activist strategies and discourses that seek to draw on global or transnational frameworks.[26] Consider the case of a global feminist approach that seeks to draw on a human rights approach to activism. One underlying political and philosophical assumption of a global feminist approach is that local women's organizations can either transcend or pressure their own states by appealing to international organizations and pressing for global norms regarding women's rights. The feminist adoption of a human rights framework has been one specific model of such an endeavor, which has sought to press for the application of global human rights norms to women's issues. Implicit in such an approach is the notion that women in local situations will benefit from a global framework that makes state sovereignty subservient to an overarching framework. Indeed, such an approach has enabled local women's organizations in comparative contexts to use languages of human rights to press their governments for rights at the local level. The question at hand, however, is one that addresses the ways in which inequalities between nation-states affect the deployment of such global languages and norms. In particular, the transcendence of state sovereignty through such forms of transnational feminist practice is complicated by the exercise of U.S. state power in the post-9/11 period of global politics.

Consider the ways in which U.S. state and public discourses that have emerged in the post-9/11 period have sought to produce linkages between the languages of human rights, Western civilization, and U.S. national security and military action. The association between just wars in defense of humanitarian ideals and civilizational defense has a long and complex history in European and U.S. military and national culture.[27] As Peter Fitzpatrick has argued, an association between war and human rights that characterized earlier conflicts has been extended to the current "war on terror."[28] For instance, political and public discourses in the United States sought to represent the military attack on Afghanistan as a "just war"—a part of the broader "war on terror" that would preserve the democratic rights of the "civilized" world. As Fitzpatrick argues, the "war on terror"

> takes the idea of a human rights war to something like its ultimate extent. That is, the exemplary espousal of human rights along with the values taken as sustaining them—values of civilization, freedom and democracy—are operatively combined with their extension throughout the globe through the waging of war on those who are deemed in terms of a protean terrorism to be opponents of such rights and values.[29]

In the post-9/11 period, such strategies of representation can be seen in numerous examples, ranging from President Bush's references to the protection of freedom and civilization to media discourses that have constructed U.S. military activity in the "war on terror" through languages of freedom and liberation. The most overt instance of such strategies during the Bush administration was seen in the representation of the military attack and occupation of Iraq as a U.S.-led war of liberation for the Iraqi people. This military campaign represented a quintessential example of the construction of war as a human rights project.[30] Such a construction occurred through two central sets of discursive strategies. Prior to the start of the military campaign, U.S. and British state discourses and mainstream media representations constructed Iraq as a critical threat to global peace through its alleged possession of weapons of mass destruction. In such discourses, this potential use of weapons of mass destruction was constructed as a generalized threat to global security; the question of human rights was implicit in the associations between security and the protection of freedom and civilization. However, it was only during the subsequent period of U.S. occupation, and in light of the failure of the United States to find weapons of mass destruction, that the state's discursive strategies shifted to justify the war and occupation in the explicit terms of Iraqi human rights, through representations of the actual and severe human rights abuses of Saddam Hussein's regime. Consider, for instance, the following depiction in a speech made by George Bush to the UN General Assembly:

> Because a coalition of nations acted to defend the peace and the credibility of the United Nations, Iraq is free, and today we are joined by representatives of a liberated country. Sadaam's monuments have been removed and not only his statues. The true monuments of his rule and his character, the torture chambers and the rape rooms and the prison cells for innocent children are closed. And as we discover the killing fields and mass graves, the true scale of Sadaam's cruelty is being revealed. The Iraqi people are meeting hardships and challenges, like every nation that has set out on the path of democracy. Yet their future promises lives of dignity and freedom and that is a world away from the squalid, vicious tyranny they have known. Across Iraq life is being improved by liberty. Across the Middle East, people are safer because an unstable aggressor has been removed from power. Across the world, nations are more secure because an ally of terror has fallen.

Our actions in Afghanistan and Iraq were supported by many governments, and America is grateful to each one. I also recognize some of the
sovereign nations of this assembly disagreed with our actions. Yet there
was, and there remains, unity among us on fundamental principles and
objectives of the United Nations. We are dedicated to the defense of our
collective security, and to the advance of human rights.[31]

The excerpt of this speech, which I have quoted at length, demonstrates
how the Bush administration sought to link three distinctive elements: (1)
specific U.S. state policies in its "war on terror" that have rested on conventional military campaigns against existing nation-states, (2) the question of
"collective security," and (3) the actual repression of authoritarian regimes,
such as that of Hussein, that violate international norms of human rights.

While the repressive nature of the former Iraqi regime is undebatable,
the deeper question at hand for an understanding of the politics of representation in the post-9/11 period is one that addresses this linkage between human rights, security, and U.S. state policy. This linkage rests on
two paradoxical processes. First, the case of the war and occupation of Iraq
demonstrates how both the language of human rights and the language of
security form significant discursive/ideological strategies of representation
that are deployed by the U.S. state and dominant public discourses; in this
process, human rights and national security become intrinsically linked to
the interests of the U.S. state and to current state policies. Second, the distinctiveness of the contemporary political form of U.S. state power is such
that it necessarily transcends both the sovereignty of weaker states and the
constraints of international law. Thus, for instance, mainstream political
discourses (particularly visual media depictions) in the United States portrayed the war on Iraq as a war defending both human rights and global
security despite the absence of a UN mandate for the war. It is this simultaneous promotion of the interests of a single dominant nation-state and the
transcendence of state sovereignty and international law that has spurred
some scholars to distinguish the current world order in terms of a political
form of empire rather than in terms of international or transnational global
order.[32]

This political and analytical distinction between empire, on the one
hand, and internationalism and transnationalism, on the other, poses critical challenges for feminists concerned with both global forms of activism
and the use of a human rights framework. In the contemporary moment,
for instance, the formulation of a global, international, and transnational

feminist human rights approach must navigate within the representational terrain that I have been outlining. The point at hand is not to dismiss the possibilities for feminist activists and thinkers to rework the political terms of security or human rights but to point to the representational strategies and political discourses that complicate this project in critical ways. If feminist narratives of justice and human rights are to circumvent the risks of being appropriated in such hegemonic fields of meaning, they will need to confront the role of the U.S. state in explicit terms and move away from a preoccupation with static understandings of cultural tradition. This dynamic was already evident in the ways in which U.S. media and political discourses were able to deploy narratives of oppressed Afghani women to help mobilize public opinion in favor of its military attack on Afghanistan. As I have noted, such dynamics in many ways echo much older historical processes that have been well analyzed by feminist scholars and activists. Thus, for example, in the case of nineteenth-century European colonialism, the gendered and racialized representations of uncivilized "natives" provided a critical foundation for the justification of colonial rule. Images of veiled women in the Middle East and the burning of widows in India serve as symbols of both the barbarity of the "East" and the necessity of the civilizing mission of colonialism.[33]

Feminist scholars writing in the field of international relations and security studies have shown that such gendered rhetoric has a long historical precedent within militarized discourses, institutions, and strategies in the United States and Western Europe.[34] Helen Kinsella has shown, for instance, that chivalric treatises of the medieval Catholic Church (that in turn drew on Roman traditions of war) shaped the emergence of Western conceptions of the "just war."[35] This chivalric code of conduct, Kinsella argues, was incorporated into newly professionalized armies in the eighteenth and nineteenth centuries.[36] As she notes, "The concepts of chivalry and honor still infuse the formal codification of the laws of war in the military training manuals used by the United States, Canada and the United Kingdom."[37] Thus, as Lauren Wilcox has illustrated through a comparative analysis of military rhetoric leading up to World War I, "The chivalric codes in vogue at the turn of the century identified the vulnerable female body as the main cause for war. The enemy was cast as an inhuman sexual predator."[38]

The gendered politics of representation point to clear continuities between earlier historical processes of war within Europe, European colonialism and expansion in the world, and the contemporary politics of U.S.

state and global power. The question that arises, then, is whether and how such political processes are reconfigured by the postcolonial specificities of the contemporary world order. I argue that rather than assuming that contemporary global politics are merely a reproduction of older colonial historical processes, we need to recognize that the specificities of the post-colonial period require a deeper understanding of the relationship between the current global order and the modern postcolonial nation-state. The postcolonial nation-state is thus an integral part of the strategies of representation that shape the unfolding politics of U.S. global power. At an immediate level, for instance, this can be seen in the ways in which the occupation of Afghanistan and Iraq was constructed in terms of U.S. state rhetoric of nation-building.[39] However, this politics of representation is not simply limited to such forms of explicit ideological or visual images that represent U.S. troops as liberators or protectors of freedom and civilization. At a deeper level, such strategies of representation engage in a series of boundary projects, producing the boundaries between state and civil society both in the United States and globally in ways that provide a critical foundation for the U.S. "war on terror." The representational politics of the state engages in the production of a distinction between "civil" and "uncivil society," where the latter becomes a site of potential terrorism and a legitimate target of U.S. state intervention. Such processes, as I will demonstrate, can be seen in an array of practices, including media representations, political discourses, and legal and police action through the use of the Patriot Act. This representational politics redraws the boundaries between the public and private and builds on a series of gendered and racialized ideologies in ways that are of critical significance for a feminist understanding of global politics.

Civil Society, the "War on Terror" and the Representational Politics of the State

One of the central dimensions of the representational politics of the state centers on how the construction of terrorism operates in the proliferation of public discourses in the aftermath of 9/11. At one level, the definition of terrorism appears clear-cut, as it involves intended violence against targets that are clear civilian sites in order to produce terror and disrupt the lives of civilian populations.[40] At a deeper level, however, the question that the current "war on terror" raises is how the boundaries of civilian space are defined. In other words, any understanding of the "war on terror" is linked to political constructions of what is counted as civilian. State practices, as I will argue, have been engaged in the narrowing of the boundaries of what counts as civilian space both at a global level and within the United States.

The narrowing of civilian space can be seen in a number of instances. One significant example is the lack of official or public accounting in the United States of the number of civilian deaths that have occurred since the beginning of the military campaigns in Afghanistan and Iraq. Scattered news reports have noted the death of civilians in Afghanistan and Iraq. For instance, during the initial military campaign in Afghanistan, mainstream news provided some reports of particular events, the most visible being the mistaken bombing of an Afghani wedding party. Given the emphasis that social scientists place on data, particularly quantitative data, this absence is a noteworthy one. An early exception to this was the study by Marc Herold, who compiled data on civilian deaths.[41] Drawing on well-known international media sources, he estimated the number of civilian deaths to be more than 3,000 following the initial phase of the military action against Iraq, a figure substantially higher than estimates by mainstream news sources such as the *New York Times*. Mark White, a computer programmer in Georgia, has compiled the deaths of coalition forces.[42] However, his data do not address deaths of Afghans or Iraqis, and thus reproduce what Judith Butler has called a set of practices that differentiates between lives that are deemed grievable and bodies and lives that are rendered immaterial and invisible.[43] This absence of clear-cut data points to the question of when and where civilian spaces are acknowledged—a question that is fundamentally linked to the framing of the current "war on terror." Herold has noted that the absence of images of human suffering caused by the bombing created a war without witnesses in the United States; he has further suggested that the erasure of civilian deaths is fundamentally linked to racialized national ideologies that shape which bodies count in the context of global conflict.[44] More recently, Glen Greenwald has represented a lone public voice in the mainstream discourses calling attention to civilian casualties caused by the Obama administration's expanded use of unmanned drone attacks in the Afghanistan-Pakistan region.[45]

One discursive narrative that often unfolds in a discussion of civilian spaces implies that calling attention to civilian victims implies a defense or justification of the regime under attack, in this instance the Taliban regime. In effect, this narrative strategy invokes the very assumptions of the militarization of human rights in the form of a nationalized human rights war.

Thus, presidential speeches by George Bush consistently, as I have noted earlier, represented the war against Iraq as a project that simultaneously protected the national security interests of the United States and defended the human rights of the Iraqi people. The underlying result is that critics of the war risked being constructed either as antipatriotic or as defenders of repressive regimes. Examples of such processes range from the rhetoric of Far Right public commentators to more subtle processes through which political discourses are framed. For instance, an extreme example was seen in the rhetoric of a public figure such as Ann Coulter, a conservative commentator and syndicated columnist whose book *Treason* explicitly argued that American liberals have consistently adopted unpatriotic and "anti-American" positions throughout U.S. history. More subtle examples can be seen in the ways in which hegemonic political discourses in the United States have produced a national framework of meaning in which the act of invoking the devastating loss of life during the 9/11 terrorist attacks provided an effective rationale for U.S. military action. A striking example of this was the case of Iraq, in which constant invocations of 9/11 by state officials resulted in polls continually showing that a majority of Americans believed that Iraq was involved in the 9/11 attacks, despite a lack of factual evidence of such involvement.

The result was the creation of a nationalist common sense according to which regions designated as targets of the current "war on terror" became marked as symbols of terror and human rights violations devoid of civilian space. Consider, for example, the discursive construction of the phrase "Sunni triangle," which became part of the everyday national political vocabulary. The phrase refers to the Sunni-dominated area in Iraq that has been a source of that country's militant insurgency. The term reduced a complex socially stratified area into an objectified ethnic-territorial category, one that discursively transformed an entire community into a symbol of potential terrorists, insurgents, and members of Hussein's authoritarian regime. The result is that references to the "Sunni triangle" that permeated news reports, particularly on the twenty-four-hour news channels, depicted an area that appears devoid of civilian space. What is rendered invisible through such representational politics is that military strategies such as the encirclement of entire villages represented a systematic targeting of civilian spaces.[46]

The narrowing of the boundaries that constitute civilian space draws on longer historical processes. Helen Kinsella illustrates the complex shifting definitions of "combatant" and "civilian" in various historical periods ranging from the U.S. and Guatemalan militaries' construction of Native Americans and the Maya through discourses of collective guilt to the French construction of all Algerians as targets of suspicion during the Algerian struggle for independence.[47] As Kinsella argues, it was not until the period after the twentieth-century struggles against colonialism that the question of civilian protection was explicitly linked to discourses on human rights, "illustrated in the UN General Assembly Resolutions of 1968 and 1969 addressing 'Respect for Human Rights in Armed Conflicts.'"[48]

The post-9/11 period has in fact marked a systematic unraveling of this move to establish international humanitarian norms for civilian protection as part of an emerging set of global principles for the protection of human rights. The U.S. "war on terror" (and the corresponding deployment of a human rights language designed to protect civilian space) has narrowed the boundaries of what counts as civilian space. I argue that this is less a problem with the universalism of human rights language than it is with the appropriation of the language of human rights in the service of particular state interests.[49] For instance, from a human rights perspective, one of the most significant political and ethical implications of the 9/11 attacks is linked precisely to an understanding of the devastation and suffering produced by acts of violence against civilians in universal terms that transcend the interests of states and the ideologies of nationalism. The political/discursive assumption that links human rights and civil society with the national security of particular states is a problem of the particularization rather than the universalism of a human rights framework. In this process of particularization, human rights concerns are constrained through bounded understandings of civilizational identity and the erasure of civilian space, which reduces entire national contexts in non-Western (and particularly in Islamic) countries to the particular repressive or authoritarian regimes in power in those contexts. This tendency is specifically intensified during the period of military action—a time when civilian populations are at particular risk of turning into collateral damage. For instance, prior to the military campaign against Iraq, while mainstream political discourses engaged in a debate on the pros and cons of an attack, the question of the impact of bombing heavily populated cities in Iraq did not represent a significant factor for consideration. Instead, as Vivienne Jabri has argued, the exercise of U.S. state power and the simultaneous erasure of civilian life rest on the representation of these populations as "subjects of humanitarian concern. In the violent acts perpetrated against them, they are subjected as the embodiment of their tyrannical leaders and are hence absent as bodies in themselves."[50] State doctrines of humanitarian and human rights wars thus rest on the erasure of living civilian bodies; civilian deaths, indeed, cannot be acknowledged without the recognition of life.

This trend continued in the occupation phase of the campaign as no official or public systematic data were compiled on Iraqi deaths. Iraqi deaths and arrests were summarily depicted as an assault on terrorists without actual formal evidence of links between specific Iraqi individuals and acts of violence. Thus, for example, television news channels such as CNN, MSNBC, and Fox News ran continual captions and reports stating the numbers of suspected terrorists or insurgents being arrested or detained. However, with the exception of cases in which large numbers of weapons were found, such reports generally did not follow up with investigations or evidence that detained individuals had been involved in violent insurgency. Such public silences were fundamentally linked to the representational politics that effectively narrowed the boundaries of civil society and civilian space.

The most extreme instances of these practices have been the systematic violation of the Geneva Convention on the treatment of prisoners. Well-publicized cases of these violations have occurred at the Guantánamo prison and in the systematic torture of prisoners that was revealed at the Abu Ghraib prison in Iraq. The disclosure of the Abu Ghraib torture and abuses encapsulates many of the processes I am analyzing in this chapter. While the American mainstream public reaction appeared to be mostly one of shock (though a large segment of mainstream opinion, including mainstream culture shows such as 24, strongly support the use of torture), the graphic details of torture and abuse are an inevitable outcome of the political dynamics of the war against terrorism. Mainstream U.S. news reports portrayed the occurrences as a deviation from normal operations of the state and military, and politicians and news commentators used the investigations and hearing as proof of the superiority of American identity. Public congressional hearings held following the disclosure of the photographs of prisoner torture allowed the state to step in as a neutral arbiter of justice and protector of (Western) civilizational values of truth and human rights. Once again, what was concealed in the midst of most of the public discourses and self-criticism was the deeper implication of the U.S. state in these human rights abuses, that is, an acknowledgment that such human rights abuses have been an integral part of the U.S. state's policies in relation to the "war on terror" precisely because the "war on terror" has systematically rested on transforming entire populations into noncivilian and ultimately dehumanized people.

The U.S. state has sought to use liminal geographic spaces to circumvent both global human rights and U.S. law with regard to the interrogation of suspected terrorists. Thus, as one U.S. Navy source quoted in a *Newsweek* report put it, "The most interesting thing about interrogations is how the U.S. government and military capitalizes on the dubious status (as sovereign states) of Afghanistan, Diego Garcia, Guantanamo Bay, Iraq and aircraft carriers to avoid certain questions about rough interrogations."[51] Such cases caution against an easy dismissal of human rights as a useful framework for ethical and political action. A perspective that points to the violations of human rights in cases such as the post-9/11 detentions, and in analyses of civilian casualties and human rights violations caused by U.S. military actions, can provide important moments of contestation of the state appropriation of the rhetoric of human rights. The theoretical approach of analyzing state power as a series of practices contains within it the potential for such contestation. As Migdal has noted, "Through their practices, states lay claim to the collective consciousness of their population. Institutions *and* symbols have been at the core of the continuing reinvention of society. But, tremendous contestation prevails over who—the state as a whole, parts of the state, other social organizations—defines and taps into collective consciousness in society."[52] A feminist attempt at reinventing this sense of collective consciousness must simultaneously analyze the state's discursive politics of the representation of human rights and advocate for a human rights approach that is not constrained by the interests of the United States, given its dominance as a global power.

Consider, for instance, Catharine MacKinnon's analysis of the implications of the 9/11 attacks for thinking about women's rights.[53] MacKinnon presents a provocative comparison between international responses to the terrorist attacks and to violence against women. She argues that while both the 9/11 terrorist attacks and violence against women are propagated by "non-state" actors, the international community was able to engage in a vast effort to oppose terrorism but not to fight domestic violence. MacKinnon develops a powerful analysis of the gendered assumptions that enter into national and international classifications of what counts as systemic violence and war. As she puts it, in this war of violence against women, "no one is a noncombatant with protected civilian status."[54] Yet MacKinnon takes this provocative comparison and appears to argue for an international campaign against domestic violence that is at best analogous to or at worst modeled on the post-9/11 U.S. war against terrorism. She argues for a convergence of "civil human rights law with criminal humanitarian law" so that a "new humanitarian protocol to the Geneva Conventions to address the gaps on violence against women could be purposed, defining some widespread and grave forms of it as violent conflict under the law of war."[55] MacKinnon's analysis is devoid of any consideration of the national agendas and transnational inequalities that have shaped human rights rhetoric and the "war on terror," on the one hand, *and* the gendered politics of these wars and agendas, on the other. Her argument thus ends up marrying this feminist delineation of human rights to a U.S. national-imperial conception of women's rights and human rights. Consider, for instance, the familiar list of issues she presents as the substantive core of this feminist post-9/11 approach to violence against women:

> Women are incinerated in dowry killings in India or living in fear that they could be any day. They are stoned to death for sex outside marriage in some parts of South Asia and Africa. They are dead of botched abortions in some parts of Latin America and of genital mutilations in many parts of the world. Girls killed at birth or starved at an early age, or aborted as fetuses because they are female, are documented to number in the millions across Asia. If foreign men did all this inside one country, would that create a state of war? (Come to think of it, what does that make sex tourism in Thailand?) The nationality of the perpetrators has little to do with the injury to the women. While some of this is finally beginning to be seen as a violation of human rights, at least in theory, none of it is thought to constitute a use of force in the legal sense. On its own, it has yet to create what is perceived as a humanitarian emergency or to justify military intervention.[56]

MacKinnon's argument is both striking and mundane in its familiar list of "cultural crimes" (dowry deaths, genital mutilation) concentrated in the non-Western world (with only one potential and highly ambiguous gesture toward Western men in the reference to sex tourism). The only named regions and countries are within Asia, Africa, and Latin America despite the disclaimer that nationality is not relevant. One is simply left wondering which of these nations (most of which are former colonies) would be the appropriate target for justifiable military intervention.

MacKinnon's analysis is a striking but important reminder of the ways in which feminism can continue to support nationalist, imperial legacies in the guise of human rights agendas and hidden nation-centric conceptions of the world. Her analysis makes no acknowledgment of the now vast feminist scholarship that has addressed the histories and contexts (both colonial and postcolonial) of the places she lists. Her response to potential critics is to note, "Those who oppose international policing in this context might be asked whether they also oppose domestic policing."[57] This ironic challenge of course overlooks the feminist and civil rights movements and scholarship that have analyzed the emergence of a prison-industrial complex in the United States.[58] At a deeper level what is reinstated is a hegemonic national narrative that has been consolidated in the post-9/11 period in the United States. This post-9/11 national narrative thus becomes the underpinning for a "global" approach to women's human rights.

MacKinnon's arguments provide one example that reveals the challenges for feminists and how the boundaries of feminist agendas are drawn. While MacKinnon's post-9/11 model is a stark example of the dangers of recoding national and state interests within global or transnational feminist agendas, other aspects of the post-9/11 period pose more subtle challenges. For instance, human rights abuses I have described involve abuses against individuals by groups such as the Taliban, whose agendas are fundamentally antithetical to feminist concerns with human rights. Such representational and political dynamics of the "war on terror" challenge feminists to work with human rights frameworks that include male victims as a central focus rather than taking women as an exclusive focus of analysis. Such an analysis is particularly critical given the complicit role of female military personnel in human rights abuses, such as the abuse and torture of Iraqi prisoners. It is not enough to suggest that they were following orders from larger patriarchal structures. These events have demonstrated that feminists need more than ever to take account of the fact that women can abuse human rights and can participate in the sexual abuse of men. In other words, the category of woman is not simply a construction, it is a construction mediated by state power. Furthermore, feminist preoccupations with purely culturalist explanations of the oppression of non-Western women risk dehumanizing men of color in ways that may at best converge with state representational practices and at worst become complicit with such practices. An intersectional analysis of the politics of state power and human rights calls for a focus that addresses both how the intersections of race, gender, and the state shape women's lives and the construction of racialized masculinity. This construction is a central strategy of U.S. state power in the "war on terror," one that has broad and critical implications for both men and women at an international level.

Race, Gender, and the "War on Terror"

The assumption that authoritarian regimes are devoid of civilian space reflects older colonial stereotypes, which now intersect with contemporary ideologies of race and gender. Racialized constructions of masculinity play a central role in contributing to the narrowing of the boundaries of what counts as civilian space. This can be seen in the way in which the figure of dark-skinned men (who are assumed to be of Middle Eastern or South Asian Muslim descent) have operated as symbols of global terrorism. Such a construction is an implicit factor in how civilian populations are rendered invisible in discussions of regimes or regions designated as terrorist sites. However, such processes can also be seen unfolding within the United States. To take just one instance, current discussions about the need for racial profiling operate on an explicit assumption that it is acceptable to assume that individuals who fit this profile are potential threats to the safety of ordinary citizens in public arenas such as airports, spaces that are an integral part of civil society.

Consider, for example, the findings of an extensive Human Rights Watch report on post-9/11 detentions. The report notes that following the 9/11 attacks, "The decision of whom to question often appeared to be haphazard, at times prompted by law enforcement agents' random encounters with foreign male Muslims or neighbors' suspicions."[59] As the report goes on to document, "indications" of suspicious terrorist-related activity were often linked simply to identity markers of nationality, religion, and gender.[60] This is borne out by the fact that the approximately 1,200 detainees were almost wholly Muslim noncitizen men, most of whom, as the Department of Justice later acknowledged, were charged with immigration violations but were of no interest to its antiterrorist activities.[61]

What is significant here is how this construction of racialized masculinity, by designating particular individuals and immigrant communities as a threat to ordinary citizens, in effect places them outside the boundaries of U.S. civil society. The search for security in this situation is thus based on the narrowing of the boundaries of who merits the status of civilian— a process in which the status of citizenship itself is fundamentally altered by the politics of gender, race, and national origin. An important dimension of this process is how the state encouraged and relied on "ordinary citizens" to report suspicious activity (for instance, in the case of neighbors' suspicions mentioned earlier) and to serve as an informal part of the state surveillance apparatus. In other words, state practices of surveillance incorporated the activities of private individuals. Such practices exemplify Evelyn Nakano Glenn's discussion of the ways in which the racialized, gendered nature of citizenship in the United States has historically been produced through the everyday practices of local actors. As she argues:

> In some cases the actors are state, county or municipal officials, for example a welfare department social worker ruling on the eligibility of a black single mother for benefits. In other cases they are "private citizens," for example a movie theater owner deciding whether or not to allow Mexican Americans to sit on the main floor. It is these kinds of localized, often face-to-face practices that determine whether people have or don't have substantive as opposed to purely formal rights of citizens.[62]

This production of citizenship unfolds through the practices of racialized, gendered surveillance and suspicion that I have been discussing. Numerous qualitative cases of such practices have been documented by immigrant organizations and human rights groups such as Human Rights Watch. The Human Rights Watch report, for instance, describes cases in which Muslim men were picked up and detained "simply because spouses, neighbors, or members of the public said they were 'suspicious' or accused them without any credible evidence."[63] In many cases, such reports led to deportations of individuals who may have violated their visa terms, thus creating a situation in which everyday local practices of "private citizens" literally aided the state in its policing of the territorial borders of the nation-state, a task normally the prerogative of official agencies such as the Immigration and Naturalization Service. As we have seen through this case of the post-9/11 detainees, these practices demonstrate the blurring of the boundaries between state and civil society and enable the "private" realms of citizenship and civilian space to perform the "public" work of state authority.[64]

Such processes connect in important ways with existing research on a longer history of violence, imprisonment, and the intersections of race and gender that have historically shaped "racial profiling" of African Americans. Ruth Wilson Gilmore, for instance, has examined the ways in which a Los Angeles multiracial organization, Mothers Reclaiming Our Children, began to organize against an expanding prison system increasingly used by the U.S. state as a policy response to social problems. Her analysis calls on feminists to expand the boundaries of mainstream feminist activism and to engage in explicit ways with the racialized, gendered effects of the U.S.

state.[65] The implications of such an analysis are heightened in the post-9/11 period as the domestic politics of incarceration intersects with the global dimensions of the U.S. "war on terror" and targets vulnerable groups such as undocumented workers and immigrant communities. The most visible evidence of this is perhaps seen in the fact that reports have suggested that antiterror laws have increasingly been used to tackle domestic crime.[66]

Violence, Security, and the Boundaries of Terror

The gendered racialization of citizenship points to the way in which the U.S. "war on terror" that has been unfolding since the Bush administration years has effectively produced a culture of security that sought to redraw the boundaries of what counts as political violence. State strategies of representation have been particularly effective in defining political violence purely in terms of the threat of Islamic terrorism in ways that displace public attention from wide-ranging forms of political violence that include, for instance, gender-based domestic violence, hate crimes, and the structural violence of poverty and violence enacted by the state itself. Consider the U.S. "war on terror" from a feminist perspective that draws on long histories of addressing questions of violence and the relationship between the public and private. While the "war on terror" represented an expansion in terms of the breadth of the geographic areas it incorporates, it has in fact been defined by a narrowing of what counts as public political violence. For instance, feminist activists in comparative contexts have for decades been working to broaden the definition of what counts as human rights and, more specifically, of what counts as violence that demands state and international accountability. This has been manifested in a range of activities focused on addressing violence against women in ways that have sought to represent the household as the site of power dynamics and have sought to focus attention on the use of rape and violence against women as political violence that is used systematically in various forms of ethnic, religious, and national conflicts.

The "war on terror" has inadvertently begun to produce a discourse that increasingly defines public or political violence in terms of specific strategies of terrorism used by organizations such as al-Qaeda. Given the global significance of the "war on terror," the importance of U.S. discourses in shaping international agendas, and the ways in which women's rights are easily displaced from the public domain, the implications of the "war on terror" for how violence and violence against women in particular are dealt with represent an important question that requires further systematic examination. The most visible instance of this has to do with the ways in which the language of women's rights has been deployed as a symbol that highlights the backwardness of Islamic fundamentalists such as the Taliban. In this symbolic politics, the "war on terror" becomes synonymous with a war for women's rights. Yet little mainstream public attention in sites such as the news media or the rhetoric of political leaders has addressed the ways in which women gain access to real political or economic power in countries such as Iraq or Afghanistan. Nor is there significant public reporting on violence against women once the initial U.S. military campaigns have led to the presence of American troops in these regions. Despite the wealth of feminist research that has demonstrated the gendered specificities of violence that women face in contexts of war and occupation, such research has not entered public mainstream discourses in significant ways. Political discourses that often present a slippage between declaring a "war on terrorism" and a "war on terror" are a telling reflection of precisely this danger. The slippage seems to suggest that the terror of systematic violence against civilians is reducible to the activities of organized terrorist groups—a slippage that, as I have noted, counters the core of much feminist work on the nature of violence against women. If domestic discourses in the aftermath of 9/11 focused on a generalized sense of national injury, the ensuing "war on terror" has constructed a generalized discourse on the need to attack terror. Such a generalized conception of "terror" has become a naturalized national meaning, one that is then projected onto the international stage through U.S. state policy and rhetoric.

A more subtle form of the displacement of questions of women's rights can be seen in terms of responses to human rights violations within the United States. While the politics of racialized masculinity construct particular groups of immigrant men as hypervisible figures, immigrant women in such cases have often been rendered invisible. Thus, while some public discourses have called attention to the prolonged detention of immigrant men in the post-9/11 period, less public attention has been paid to the ways in which immigrant women have coped with, responded to, and survived in light of the detention of male relatives. Systematic data on the impact of detentions on family networks or on the coping strategies of female relatives of male detainees are limited. For instance, the Human Rights Watch report pointed out that immigrant detainees have not been granted the right to notify their families or receive regular visits with family members, and that no means have been provided for detainees to communicate with families that may be outside of the United States.[67] However, the report did not examine what such detentions have meant for female relatives of the male detainees—for instance, in terms of their immigration status, economic survival (with the loss of a wage earner in the family), and other social and cultural factors, such as language barriers, which may prevent them from gaining full access to legal recourse. Such questions necessitate a broader gendered understanding of the conceptualization of human rights, including the impact on female relatives as an integral part of any classification of human rights violations, which organizations such as Human Rights Watch have carefully documented.[68]

State Practices and the Specificities of Regime?

The analysis of the state and the politics of representation that I have been presenting thus far focuses on the particular case of the Bush administration's approach to and conception of a "war on terror." The specificities of state practices associated with this particular regime must therefore be weighed alongside the strong historical continuities in the strategies of representation that the state has used within the United States. This tension between specificity and continuity is evidenced in the challenges faced by the Obama administration. In contrast to the Bush administration, the Obama administration has shifted away from using the languages of terror and civilizational clashes that were a central rhetorical device of the previous administration. This discursive shift, along with a new emphasis on diplomatic engagement, marks an important shift that underlines the need for feminists to take seriously the impact of regime shifts and move away from the tendency to depict the U.S. state as a static or unitary formation.

However, even with such changes the long-standing effects of the state practices of representation that I have analyzed continue to remain central to state policy. Thus, the closure of civilian space remains a central strategy that now targets the border region between Afghanistan and Pakistan. As with the earlier representations of the "Sunni triangle" as a "triangle of death" reduced to insurgents and devoid of civilian life, the Afghanistan-Pakistan border regions are now depicted in both media discourses and Obama administration rhetoric as a lawless area that has been overrun by terrorist and insurgent networks. Aerial bombings of this region and civilians deaths (that are provoking outrage and protests in Pakistan and further radicalizing political forces in the area) are rendered invisible within the United States.[69] Such public consent has extended to support of targeted assassinations of individuals—now including American citizens—identified without evidence as terrorist leaders.[70] Such continuities echo the deeper continuities in state policy between the Bush and Obama administrations and underline the historical weight of such representations of non-Western and Islamic countries and the inextricable intersection between such representations and state practices within the United States. Consider, for instance, the Obama administration's expansion of the use of unmanned drones (an expansion well beyond the Bush era practices) in the Afghanistan-Pakistan border region. This expansion and the corresponding mainstream U.S. media silence regarding the civilian deaths caused by the drone attacks illustrate that the state practices I have analyzed are not unique to a particular administration but represent a deeper, historically salient dynamic within the United States and the stakes involved in national conceptions of the transnational. The Afghanistan-Pakistan border region, for instance, has been portrayed by both state officials and U.S. political analysts as a legitimate target for excessive and unaccountable attacks precisely because it is a "transnational" region and effectively not under the control of either the Afghan or Pakistani governments. The colloquial term "Af-Pak" to denote this region (commonly used by the military and by civilian policy analysts and advisers) illustrates this state construction of the transnational. This state-civilian construction depicts the transnational as a lawless, barren land devoid of civilian life—a construction that enables the media and other dominant public political discourses to overlook deaths caused by drone attacks and other military campaigns. More recently, this state ideological construction has increasingly been extended to the entire Pakistani nation. It is thus telling, as Juan Cole has cogently argued, that one of the most significant recent natural disasters to affect Pakistan, namely, massive flooding in the summer of 2010, was completely ignored by the U.S. media and went largely unnoticed by the American public.[71]

I have focused on U.S. state practices given that this book is concerned with U.S. conceptions of transnationalism. However, the practices that I have outlined have also begun to reshape other state practices in comparative contexts. I have been addressing the relationship between the "war on terror" and the question of what and who is included within the boundaries of civilian space in terms of the role of the United States. However, it is important to note that this relationship also has serious consequences for other regional conflicts, which have distinctive histories but are being linked to the global war on terrorism in new ways.[72] For instance, consider cases such as the India-Pakistan conflict over Kashmir, Russian policy toward Chechnya, the Israeli-Palestinian conflict, and the civil war within Sri Lanka. While it is not possible to address the complexities of these cases within the confines of this chapter, it is clear that the unsettling of state–civil society boundaries is a significant force that has reshaped each of these situations.[73] This has already been seen in the ways in which states in these conflicts have been able to use rhetorical strategies that erase civilian spaces to engage in ruthless state action against entire populations. In such contexts, how states define what counts as legitimate civilian resistance in light of the U.S. "war on terror" is also a critical question. If the narrowing of the boundaries of what counts as civilian space results in the foreclosure of legitimate nonviolent civil resistance, such a process will not only dislodge the potential for peace negotiations in ways that are already evident but also serve to fuel the very forms of violent political activity that the "war on terror" seeks to quell.

Conclusion

I have used a feminist analysis of the intersections of race, gender, and the nation to explore some of the implications that the current U.S. "war on terror" has for both feminism and human rights. In particular, I have sought to examine what I have called the representational practices of the U.S. state. In this endeavor, I have focused on an understanding of the politics of representation as a set of state practices. As I have argued, a critical dimension of contemporary U.S. state power lies in its attempt to engage in a series of boundary projects, demarcating the lines of what counts as "civil society," "civilian space," and "terror." Understanding such representational practices as a dimension of state intervention is particularly critical given the ways in which dominant media images in the United States have increasingly been interwoven into state and nationalist agendas. Perhaps the most vivid instance of this process was captured in the use of "embedded" journalists in the military campaign against Iraq. If the U.S. construction of the war in Afghanistan led to a form of "war without witnesses" in the United States, this process of embedding at the same time explicitly represented the war through the eyes of the state. Furthermore, as I have demonstrated, U.S. state practices have effectively appropriated the language of human rights in the current "war on terror." This process of incorporation curtails the universality of a human rights framework through the specificity of particular state interests. In this context, feminist strategies that draw on a human rights framework are compelled to address how universal languages of human rights are bounded through the territorialized interests of the nation-state.

What, then, are the implications of these political events and state practices for transnational feminism? At a basic level, the relationship between the current "war on terror" and the production of civilian space provides a paradoxical reworking of the relationship between the public and private realms of activity with which feminism has long been preoccupied. As feminist activists and writers have historically demonstrated, the private sphere has never been an innocent realm. Long-standing feminist work that has revealed the political nature of the private sphere provides the means to examine the ways in which the private sphere is intricately related to the exercise of state power. In the context of the U.S. "war on terror," what we have seen unfolding in fact is a redrawing of the lines between the public and private—in this case between what counts as public violence and what counts as protected, private, civilian space. As feminist scholars have long argued, the ways in which the boundaries between the public and the private are drawn have serious material and political effects.

What is of central significance for anyone invested in contributing to or understanding the paradigm of transnational feminism is both the centrality of the state in drawing these boundaries and the centrality of the U.S. state in particular. Scholars working in the field of transnational feminist theory and research have long called attention to the dominant role of the U.S. state. Indeed, in the aftermath of the 9/11 attacks in the United States and the run-up to the war in Afghanistan, one of the leading journals on transnational feminism devoted a special issue to critical political responses to these events.[74] Yet the debate on human rights requires more than a transnational feminist critique of the state—it requires an understanding of the ways in which transnational feminist knowledge within the United States itself emerges as a formation within a particular nation-state. The very fluidity of the boundaries between state and civil society that I have highlighted throughout this chapter compels us to understand transnational feminist theory and research that emerges within the United States as another site that also occupies a shifting field of knowledge within civil society that may merge with, coexist with, or contest various state practices. Such an approach unsettles any complacent understanding of U.S. transnational feminist knowledge as a site that is necessarily oppositional or external to the state.

It is with the desire to unsettle this complacency that I have begun this series of essays on the transnational with a chapter that focuses on U.S. state practices. The women's rights/human rights debate in particular and its points of convergence with state interests and practices highlight the need to locate the paradigms we produce within the specific contexts and conditions under which we produce knowledge. The "war on terror" and the intersecting regional crises and conflicts that it has affected are in this sense not just the object of analysis but also the context and conditions for the paradigm of transnational feminism that has now become institution-alized in the American academy. This focus on the contemporary moment is in fact meant to call attention to the need to interrogate when and why particular paradigms arise and what the consequences of these paradigms are. This rests on the assumption that educational institutions are sites within a public sphere—a public that rests at an uneasy boundary between state and civil society. In this vein, I turn in the next chapter to another dimension of the public sphere—the realm of cultural production.

3

Transnational Economies of Representation and the Labor of the Traveling Subaltern

ONE OF THE central features of contemporary globalization has been the transnational circulation of cultural products. Various forms of cultural representation (film, media images, literature, television programs) now move rapidly across borders. These forms of cultural circulation are no longer reducible to clear-cut geopolitical forms of movement. That is, the production and circulation of films do not move in a uniform fashion from what was once called the "East" or "Third World" to the "West." While global film and television programming is still dominated by U.S. industries, this dominance has been challenged by the rise of national programming and complex transnational cultural flows that are not limited to simple linear paths originating in the United States or Europe.[1] Cultural industries and corporations (such as the media channel Al Jazeera and the "Bollywood" industry in India) that have emerged in non-Western contexts now have significant global reach.[2] These shifting patterns of cultural circulation have been extended by the expansion of diasporic communities within the United States and Europe. Diasporic communities produce various cultural formations that travel back to and are consumed in their places of origin. Once again, this trajectory is not reducible to a linear movement from West to East. Meanwhile, writers, filmmakers, and other producers also increasingly target both their own national audiences and diasporic communities in the United States and Europe.[3] Furthermore, cultural production itself has become globalized with the rise of transnational joint ventures in the making of films, the publication of literature, and the production of news. The intensity of such cross-border movement has simply accelerated with the spread of Internet technological access.

In the face of such rapid changes spurred by globalization, there has been an expansion of work on transnational cultural production from cultural, feminist, postcolonial, and queer theorists.[4] Early feminist scholarship on transnational cultural production centered on the problem of representing difference. The question of difference posed a critical dilemma for feminists interested in engaging in transnational research. This dilemma turned on a paradoxical problem that arises with the politics of representation of various forms of difference. On the one hand, transnational feminism arose in part in response to calls to broaden the subject of feminism and to move away from the depiction of feminism through dominant forms of Western feminism. Feminists writing in the 1980s and 1990s interrogated the category "woman" and provided the impetus for the inclusion of differences such as race, class, sexuality, and nation in arenas such as university curricula, academic anthologies, and research agendas.[5] The task of feminist representation from this perspective was to combat the exclusion of difference. On the other hand, feminist theorists simultaneously began to argue that "difference" itself was being commodified in problematic ways. The problem with representation in this sense was with the nature of inclusion itself. Feminist scholars writing within the field of postcolonial studies in particular argued that the representation of difference was in effect reproducing colonial relations of power. In her classic essay, "Can the Subaltern Speak?," Gayatri Spivak argued that knowledge about the subaltern woman was entrenched in relationships of power in ways that made it impossible to recuperate her subjectivity or represent her voice. Thus, she argued, research and writing that sought to depict the subaltern as a subject that spoke in effect cohered "with the work of imperialist subject-constitution, mingling epistemic violence with the advancement of learning and civilization. And the subaltern woman will be as mute as ever."[6] While Spivak would later present more nuanced versions of her views, her conception of epistemic violence has had a lasting impact on transnational feminist research and theory.[7] Her challenge to any form of cross-cultural or comparative understanding of non-Western women provoked broader questions about the relationship between power and representation that feminist writers continue to address.[8]

The rise of diasporic forms of cultural production has complicated but not necessarily displaced such questions regarding the commodification and deployment of difference and authenticity. Gayatri Gopinath, for instance, has shown how diasporic South Asian films such as *Monsoon Wedding* and *Bend It Like Beckham* rest on a "splitting of queerness and feminism" that makes them palatable to liberal feminist and non–South Asian audiences.[9] The films, as Gopinath illustrates, deploy representations of queer sexuality in ways that reinforce heteronormative ideals of family and relationships even while appearing to be critical of patriarchal household structures. Or, to take a different example, as I have noted in chapter 1, in light of the U.S. "war on terror," Saba Mahmood has illustrated how the writings and autobiographies of diasporic Muslim women have been deployed in ways that have reinforced the orientalist constructions of Islam as barbaric—a process of demonization that has served as an important track for U.S. intervention and military occupation in the Middle East.[10] Such examples point to the ways in which the emergence of diasporic cultural production may in many instances be incorporated within older historical and geopolitical relations of power (albeit in distinctive ways and with particular claims of authenticity).

These discussions of representational practices have given way to what is now referred to as the affective turn in (poststructuralist) studies of cultural production.[11] For instance, Sara Ahmed has provided a rich analysis of the movement of emotions through the circulation of cultural objects (such as films, texts, and other discursive forms). This circulation constitutes what Ahmed has termed "affective economies" in which emotions are produced by the effects of such circulation.[12] In this process, according to Ahmed, circulating emotions "create the surfaces" of bodies and a series of boundary effects that mark differences between individuals, groups, and nations. The circulation of emotions thus materializes bodies and the relationship between bodies through processes such as the politics of fear, the witnessing of shame, and the performativity of disgust. However, while Ahmed provides a powerful argument for a recognition of the materiality of this circulation of emotions, what is left unspecified in her text, and in the affective turn at large, is a deeper understanding of how this circulation—this economy—is shaped or structured. Ahmed argues,

> Emotions work as a form of capital: affect does not reside positively in the sign or commodity, but is produced as an effect of its circulation. I am using the "economic" to suggest that objects of emotion circulate or are distributed across a social as well as a psychic field, borrowing from the Marxian critique of the logic of capital. In *Das Capital*, Marx discusses how the movement of commodities and money, in the formula (M-C-M: money to commodity to money), creates surplus value. That is, through circulation and exchange "M" acquires more value.[13]

Ahmed sets up this analogy between the circulation of capital and the circulation of the objects of emotion to illustrate the way in which "the movement between signs or objects converts into affect."[14] Thus, she concludes, "Signs increase in affective value as an effect of the movement between signs: the more signs circulate, the more affective they become."[15]

The cornerstone of this conception of the affective economy is thus the nature and extent of the circulation of signs and objects. Yet, it is precisely the nature of this circulation that is left untheorized in Ahmed's discussion. If, indeed, as Ahmed argues, it is an increase in circulation that increases the accumulation of affective value, then it is precisely the systemic and structural factors that shape the circulation of signs and objects that merit analysis. Without this analysis, the economic dimension of the affective economy loses its theoretical significance.

Indeed, much of the subsequent scholarship that has built on this line of inquiry has also left untheorized the relationship between affective economies and the transnational economies of cultural production.[16] For instance, there has been a lack of sustained theoretical discussion of how transnational and national political economies may structure this circulation of affective and representational economies or, conversely, how this circulation of emotion through various discourses and cultural objects in turn shapes national and transnational economies. What is left unexamined is how the affective economy interacts with, shapes, and is shaped by other economic formations in the domain of cultural production. Some scholars working on related questions on transnationalism and affect have called attention to the need for an understanding of the interrelationship between these economic forms. Writing about the emotional exploitation of children that is inherent in transnational adoption, David Eng illustrates how an analysis of a political economy of emotions is necessary for an adequate understanding of the global gendered division of labor that structures contemporary economic globalization.[17] He argues that the transnational adoptee performs a kind of ideological and consumptive labor that "consolidates the white nuclear family." As he puts it:

> We need to consider how the transnational adoptee might be grouped within Sassen's constellation of purchased "goods and services" precisely through the affective, though invisible, labor that she provides to suture the white middle-class family unit into a reified ideology of enclosed self-sufficiency. What does it mean to ask—indeed to demand—that the transnational adoptee function as an emotional guarantee, as a passionate laborer for her parents' access to full social rights and recognition in the United States public sphere and civil society?[18]

Eng's analysis provides us with a theoretical opening to begin to conceptualize how the affective realm constitutes an economic formation that interacts with and helps constitute transnational economic relationships. It is this theoretical understanding of the affective *economy* that needs to be deepened when addressing questions of transnational cultural production.

The dominant trend in feminist studies of transnational cultural processes—whether such studies are marked by poststructuralist and affective analytical lenses and/or ethnographic methodological practices—is to either explicitly reject or inadvertently turn away from specifying links between cultural production and systemic and or structurally oriented economic analyses. Consider, for instance, Grewal and Kaplan's concept of "scattered hegemonies" that marked one of the defining framing texts of interdisciplinary transnational feminism. Grewal and Kaplan are clear in their intent in calling attention to relationships of power (including capitalist relations) in their understanding of transnationalism.[19] Yet the concept of scattered hegemonies specifically reorients transnationalism away from any systemic understanding of the very relationships of power that Grewal and Kaplan seek to delineate. The connotations associated with the concept of scattering are in fact directly antithetical to the possibility that relationships of power are structured in patterns that may be rigid and enduring (historically reproduced rather than simply continually shifting). The concept of scattered hegemonies further dislocates the original Gramscian concept of hegemony from its explanatory force of how socioeconomic classes and the state enter in a political compact that historically sustains and enables the reproduction of structures of power in liberal democracies in systematic ways over time.[20] Grewal and Kaplan provide an important instance of the dynamic that I am discussing precisely because their project is to foreground relationships of power and to criticize conceptions of the transnational that evade such questions of power. Thus, the point at hand is not whether power (including the economic power of capitalism) is being addressed in such texts that have served as markers of transnational feminist scholarship. Rather, the problem is that these paradigms and their linguistic framings risk narrowing the conceptual tools and analytical understandings of transnationalism, cultural politics, and economic structures.

This trend in transnational feminist scholarship stems from a complicated set of historical-political and intellectual factors. At one level, the desire to find new paradigms and claim this newness as a defining mark of interdisciplinarity has contributed to the intellectual rejection of what are viewed by many interdisciplinary audiences as older categories that denote structural or systemic relationships of power. Categories that mark inequalities of political economy as structured and endurable formations such as the relationship between "First World" and "Third World," as well as the language of social structure, have declined in the languages of interdisciplinary study. More specifically, the poststructuralist turn within studies of cultural production and representation has meant that interdisciplinary cultural theory has been resistant to discussions of economic "structures" or attempts to analyze the relationship between economic and cultural processes in a systemic manner. Poststructuralist approaches to the study of culture presume that any such discussion of structuring economic forces necessitates a return to a reductive conception of "culture"— a conception that treats culture as a "superstructural" realm that is reducible to economic forces.

Such trends have been compounded by aspects of a divide between the humanities and the social sciences, which still resurfaces within interdisciplinary fields. There are two key elements of particular relevance in this divide. On the one hand, studies of cultural production and representational practices have been shaped largely by scholars working out of literary and anthropological traditions in which methods of discourse analysis—whether such discourses are textual or ethnographic—tend to conceive of the "economic" as a fluid, unstructured realm of practice, process, and identity (and where discussions of structures and systems are discarded as outdated structural-functionalist or modular approaches that lack complexity and texture). On the other hand, the dominance of particular models of positivism within the social sciences has meant that feminist social scientific critiques of interdisciplinary work have reified assumptions that what is needed is mainstream "social science" approaches that rely on particular *methods* of quantitative analysis or conceptions of causality.[21] However, this reassertion of the need for social science perspectives within interdisciplinary fields such as women's studies seeks to reassert dominant (and contested) paradigms within the social sciences.[22] The call for social science approaches within women's studies in effect rests on a homogenized construction of the social sciences. Thus, there is an ironic parallel between the method-driven definitions of interdisciplinarity that often characterize both ends of the humanities–social science divide and that surfaces within women's studies debates.

My concern is not to resuscitate this dualistic opposition but to open up the conceptual space for specific kinds of questions and modes of analysis that slip through the cracks when interdisciplinarity becomes reduced to a series of false choices between structural and discursive analysis, "humanities" and "the social sciences," and between the "real" cutting-edge, deconstructive, cultural criticism and the "real" positivist empirical analyses of the economy. In this endeavor, I seek to provide a transnational perspective on cultural production that considers the systemic structuring of affect and representation within the context of both national and global political contexts, economic structures, and discursive-cultural regimes. Such a transnational perspective requires a consideration of several analytical layers. First, the production and circulation of these cultural forms are shaped by the organization of historically specific structures of political economy at both the transnational and national level. Global and national political economies affect the kinds of strategies of representation that are deployed within these cultural products. Second, since the production of cultural forms is now directed at both national and transnational audiences, this layered circulation complicates the representation of the subaltern—the subaltern figure must in effect be able to travel both within and across national boundaries. This traveling subaltern engages in forms of affective and ideological labor—producing value for the affective economy—in the various nations to which he or she migrates. It is an understanding of this form of affective labor that has been missing in the recent proliferation of writings on discourse, culture, and affect. Not only must this traveling subaltern speak, she must also be fluid in multiple languages that can address the desires, fears, and needs that are structured in distinctive ways in different national public spheres. Furthermore, this form of labor is both affective and ideological precisely because the affective economy is both shaped by and serves to support national and global structures of political economy. The affective economy, while a distinctive sphere, also constitutes a central ideological structure necessary to reproduce these political-economic structures. Cultural production harnesses the affective labor of subaltern groups and transforms it into what Gramsci termed the "trench system" within civil society that upholds the structures of liberal democratic capitalism.[23] However, the laboring bodies of subaltern subjects also exceed the representational frames that seek to contain them. As Rosemary Shinko argues in her discussion of visual representations of the "condemned body," the body "can be regarded as a textual site where meanings will be made, not a text that prefigures the outcome and which can be read as a self-identifying project of liberation, but as a text that exposes, considers and is provoked to respond to the 'material existence and material grievances that create suffering and struggle.'"[24] In such moments, as we will see, subaltern bodies are not simplistic figures of resistance but embodied subjects that exceed the texts and representational frames that seek to contain them. Thus, specifying the connections between structures of national and global political economy, on the one hand, and affective economies, on the other, does not mean that cultural forms are simply superstructural products of the economy. The implications and effects of these organizing structures are contingent on questions of context (who is listening to and viewing the representation), form (for instance, whether the cultural form is film, fiction, or music), and the nuances of the strategies of representation within the particular form. It is this combination of structural, agential, and cultural layers that can begin to lead us to a more comprehensive and systematic transnational perspective on cultural production.

I flesh out this transnational perspective on cultural production through an interpretative analysis of two sets of cultural products that take different global routes. The first set consists of the film *Bandit Queen* and the autobiography *I, Phoolan Devi*, both representations of the life of well-known Indian Dalit (outcaste) woman Phoolan Devi.[25] The second set consists of the popular film *Slumdog Millionaire* and the fictional book on which the film was based, *Q & A* by Vikas Swarup.[26] These two sets of case studies, which provide parallel but distinctive forms of the cross-national movement of cultural products, represent two different kinds of transnational collaboration between Britain and India. The representations of Phoolan Devi trace a specific (post)colonial route between Britain and India and are enmeshed both in the colonial legacies of this geopolitical journey and in the postcolonial specificities of the responses within the Indian public sphere. Meanwhile, the film on Phoolan Devi and her autobiography gained little public attention within the United States. Both *Q & A* and *Slumdog Millionaire*, on the other hand, were routed through the cultural-economic center of the U.S. film industry. The novel was widely reviewed by mainstream U.S. publications, and the film received significant commercial success and recognition at the Academy Awards. As with *Bandit Queen*, *Slumdog Millionaire* was widely debated in the Indian public sphere but in a distinctive way that was shaped by India's changing economic position in the twenty-first century.

Through this comparative interpretive analysis, I develop an approach to transnational cultural production that is centered around three themes. First, I analyze the ways in which the historically specific contexts of national and global structures of political economy shape cultural production. As I will illustrate, this occurs in terms of both the structures that shape the production and consumption of such cultural products and the substantive strategies of representation that are deployed within the particular cultural forms. Through this analysis I argue that such trans/national processes are contingent both on older historical processes and categories that have long distinguished First World and Third World and on distinct changes that have been brought about by more recent processes of globalization. Second, I demonstrate that the effects of such cultural products are shaped in distinctive ways by the dominant discursive regimes that structure the national public spheres in which they are received. Finally, I illustrate that an understanding of cultural production is also contingent on the complexities of cultural form and the tactics of representation that are shaped but not simply determined by national and global political and economic structures. In focusing on these three themes, my goal is to open up the conceptual space for a transnational feminist analysis that is deconstructive and constructive, discursive and structural/economic, transnational and national, and both concerned with the historically constituted inequalities between the First and the Third World and cognizant of distinctive changes spurred by globalization.

Global Economies of Representation: Bandits and Slumdogs

A comparative analysis of *Bandit Queen* and *Slumdog Millionaire* provides us with a view of the ways in which competing global political-economic orders shape the cultural politics of representation. While *Bandit Queen* was funded and produced by a British television company, the film cannot easily be classified as a "British film," since it was directed, produced, and shot in India with an all-Indian cast. This form of cross-national collaboration has become a significant trend in transnational cultural production (one that has been accentuated both by diasporic artists and filmmakers and by the travel of elite cultural producers across borders). At first glance this complexity of the cultural production process may appear to disrupt older transnational relationships of power between the "First" and the "Third" World. In fact, this process of collaboration simultaneously marks and seeks to conceal relations of power between postcolonial countries and former colonial European powers. As I will argue, the specific transnational circuit between Britain and India that is embodied in films such as *Bandit Queen* recodes historically specific colonial inequalities within these postcolonial cultural products. Such cultural representations in fact are centered on the reproduction of conventional colonial constructions. These representational practices rest on long-standing historical constructions such as the opposition between the modern (coded as Western) and the traditional (coded as indigenous cultural traditions of former colonies) and conceptions of "orientalist" despotic societies. Rooted in such colonial legacies, such representations temporally place the postcolonial Third World outside of the historical moment of postmodernity in the European West.

In keeping with British colonial preoccupations with authenticity and with ideal-typical figures of "native culture," the collaborative nature of transnational cultural production reconfigures this search for authenticity. Visual spectacle produces an authentic, realist representation of the "Third World subaltern woman." Furthermore, the establishment of a collaborative relationship of material production legitimizes this voice in two ways. First, a clear collaboration that can be traced back to India consolidates the local and particular authenticity of the text. Second, an acknowledgment of the boundaries of the Indian nation-state subtly conceals the possibility of the colonial historical legacies that lurk beneath the collaboration. Phoolan Devi cannot be transformed simply into the bandit queen; she must be represented as India's bandit queen.[27] Such representational strategies require the measure of Third World authenticity to signify a form of difference as otherness. However, this difference can only be produced through an implicit sameness between the First and the Third World, one that rests on a set of shared humanistic, universal values. This sameness in difference unfolds in the film *Bandit Queen* through the deployment of images of the modern and the traditional.

My aim here is not merely to rehearse a deconstruction of the modernity/tradition binary but to demonstrate how the deployment of "difference" in the film serves to recode colonial relationships of power. The film casts cultural tradition as the force that explains the caste and gender oppression that Phoolan Devi endures and marks this oppression as peculiarly Indian and "different" from that in the West. Meanwhile, the film continually juxtaposes this tradition with more familiar images that link Indian society with a failed attempt to reproduce universalistic narratives of democracy and modernity. While the sameness of Indian society is marked by such narratives of progress, this sameness is always constructed through difference as otherness (culture) and difference as inferiority (failed modernity).[28]

Bandit Queen casts Phoolan Devi's life story in terms of the problem of "Indian culture" through a series of images that portray the intersection between caste and patriarchy in the everyday life of rural north India. The film attempts to present an incisive indictment of the reproduction of caste and gender hierarchies in a series of social institutions, including marriage and family, community life, state (in the form of the local village government and police), and even the political structure of the dacoit gangs in the north Indian state of Uttar Pradesh. However, film director Shekar Kapur's depiction inadvertently draws its explanatory power of such social hierarchies from an essentialized conception of Indian tradition. The film highlights particular forms of traditional culture such as Phoolan Devi's child marriage, caste-based segregation,[29] and passive villagers, which conform well to the Western imagination of oppressive Indian traditions. The film juxtaposes such hierarchies with an individualized view of Phoolan Devi's rebelliousness. While the film casts Phoolan Devi as a heroic woman striving against her culture, the audience is not provided with any context in which to place Phoolan Devi's actions; her rebelliousness is depicted as an aberration within a society that otherwise consists of active oppressors and passive victims.

The difference of gender and caste that marks the boundaries between the First and the Third World in *Bandit Queen* is also carefully constructed through a framework of sameness that can be used to measure Indian society against the West. This sameness rests on a familiar narrative of modernity that is juxtaposed with the representation of "tradition" in the film. Images of idyllic rural scenery and the rough savage scenes of the ravines and desert where Phoolan Devi and other members of her gang are in hiding are juxtaposed with stereotypical urban images of crowds and chaos. Shots of Phoolan Devi bringing her lover and gang leader, Vikram, to a doctor in Kanpur, one of the major cities in Uttar Pradesh, present a chaotic city in the middle of a public festival, with burgeoning crowds and blaring music being played by a marching band. Moreover, the film also presents images that serve not merely as signifiers of the modern encroaching on a traditional India but as markers of a failed modernity. For instance, all characters representing the modern Indian nation-state, ranging from policemen to doctors to state government officials, are depicted as violent or corrupt. Phoolan Devi is raped by policemen, the doctor who treats Vikram asks for a bribe in order to pay for his daughter's dowry, and the politicians and government officials link their plans to allow Phoolan Devi to surrender alive to the fact that the lower castes vote. These images serve two related functions in the film. First, they serve as signifiers of modernity and democracy that are familiar to Western audiences and therefore facilitate the process of translation of Phoolan Devi's "Indian" experience into a language comprehensible to Western audiences. Second, the association of such images with corruption and violence clearly projects an Indian modernity marked by failure, that is, a failure to achieve Western standards of progress and democracy. This mark of failure brings us back to the circulation of cultural capital encoded within relationships of power between the First and the Third World, which I have argued shapes the international production and consumption of India's bandit queen. The film does not merely produce an Indian otherness (the traditional) that is dissociated from the West but implicitly reproduces a relationship between India and the West by presenting Indian modernity as a measure of inferiority and failure.

The failure of Indian modernity and democracy has specific political implications within the context of the British production and consumption of the film given the historical relationship of colonialism. In the world of *Bandit Queen*, Phoolan Devi is trapped by a nation that has neither been able to discard the remnants of its oppressive cultural traditions nor been able to live up to the modern democratic institutions and traditions that India inherited through the legacies of colonialism. This double bind is depicted in the film by a visual strategy that denotes critical stages of devastation in Phoolan Devi's life by images of travel. The pull of tradition is marked by a scene in which Phoolan Devi is being forcibly taken away on a boat, shot against idyllic images of village India. The journey by boat signifies the first tragic event in the film as Phoolan Devi is taken away from her home by her husband. Later in the film, when Phoolan Devi is kidnapped by an upper-caste dacoit, she is beaten and taken by boat to the village of Behmai, where she is gang-raped and paraded naked in front of the entire village in a public demonstration of the brutal, violent reprisal for her transgression of caste and gender hierarchies. Meanwhile, such rural images of travel are juxtaposed with shots of a speeding train, a classic symbol of modernity (and more specifically of British colonial rule in India), that signify the force of the modern nation-state weighing against Phoolan Devi. A shot of the train prefigures a scene in which she is arrested and raped by the police in her village after she is falsely accused by the village district head of burglary. Later in the film, when Phoolan Devi's own gang is being hunted down with the full force of the state government, the shot preceding her surrender to the government is marked by her lying in a crumpled state by the tracks as a train passes by. Such images of movement, whether "regressive" as she is captured and taken by boat back to the confines of oppressive caste and gender traditions or "progressive" as the train marks her coercive recuperation by the Indian nation-state, frame Phoolan Devi as a nonconsenting victim of the modern and the traditional. These movements, backward in time into the world of repressive tradition or forward into the chronological narrative of a violent, corrupt nation-state, are cast into a singular timeless model of violence and failure.

My analysis suggests that the transformation of difference into otherness and inferiority is linked not merely through the content of the images that Kapur deploys but also through the form of these depictions. The binary oppositions such as the modern/traditional, difference/sameness, and First World/Third World are specifically constructed and managed through a trope that interweaves a politics of gender with graphic visual images of violence. Mainstream Western representations in film, television, and newspapers have a long history of representing the Third World as a site of violence and disorder—whether in relation to ancient primordial religious, tribal, and ethnic conflicts or to revolution or state repression.[30] Such images link the production and consumption of Third World authenticity to the spectacle of violence. The violent, disordered, and repressive Third World is thus juxtaposed against the civilized, orderly, democratic West. As Rey Chow has argued in her discussion of U.S. representations of the Tiananmen Square massacre, this is the "cross-cultural syndrome in which the 'Third World,' as the site of the 'raw' material, that is, 'monstrosity,' is produced for the surplus-value of spectacle, entertainment and spiritual enrichment for the 'First World.'"[31] Chow's suggestion in this analysis that we confront "the complicity of our technology, which does much more than enable us to 'see,'"[32] points to the ways in which the realist form in cinematic representations can be located historically within the wider genre of the ethnographic film that reproduced relations of race and colonialism through representations of the "primitive," "savage," and "native."[33] Bandit Queen, of course, to some extent reworks this genre, since the depiction of violent rape also foregrounds personalized injury that may invoke empathy. Nevertheless, there is an interesting parallel between the empathy presumed between anthropologist and "native," on the one hand, and audience and victimized subaltern, on the other; more significant, in both cases empathy is not inconsistent with the power-laden questions of the context I am foregrounding. The convergence of specific strategies of representation in the film, the historical tradition of the genre of the ethnographic film, and the political economy of the production and consumption of texts compels Bandit Queen to recodify power-laden boundaries between the First and the Third World.[34] Such processes are of particular significance for feminist analysis when the spectacle consists of the image of violence against the "subaltern Third World woman." A feminist project of representing violence against women contains within it the potential for reinvoking orientalist narratives, in particular, by marking the Third World as the naturalized site of an unrestrained violence.[35] Such narratives represent long-standing patterns in cinematic and visual cultures. As Ella Shohat has noted, cinema emerged in the West during the height of colonialism between the late nineteenth century and the First World War.[36] In this context, as Shohat illustrates through her detailed analysis of cinematic representations, "Not only has the Western imaginary metaphorically rendered the colonized land as a female to be saved from her environ/mental disorder, it has also projected rather more literal narratives of rescue, particularly of Western and non-Western women—from African, Asian, Arab, or American-Indian men."[37] Such long-standing historical images continue to circulate through contemporary transnational productions. As we have seen in the previous chapter, emotions of disgust and aversion that are produced through such texts can potentially circulate in ways that produce the discursive and affective terrain for the imperatives of state foreign policy. The stakes of transnational analyses of cultural production thus extend far beyond the dynamics of an individual film.

In *Bandit Queen*, the representation of rape results in a gendered transformation of the Third World into a spectacle of violence. The power effects of textual representations are produced not just through representations of Third World women but also through particular constructions of Third World men and masculinities. The construction of sexual difference through the deployment of particular meanings of masculinity provides a central mechanism for the articulation of otherness and inferiority of the Third World. In *Bandit Queen*, the oppression of tradition and the failure of modernity in contemporary India are translated through the representation of the intrinsic violence and abnormality of Indian masculinity. Consider the parameters of "good" and "bad" masculinity portrayed in the film. The "bad" men in the film are either violent rapists (upper-caste men, dacoits, police) or weak, passive characters such as the rural villagers who consent to such violence. Meanwhile, the "good" masculine figures are depicted through two characters in the film. The first, Phoolan Devi's lover, Vikram, is a dacoit who has transgressed the boundaries of the normal in Indian society. The second, Phoolan Devi's cousin, who helps her at points of crisis in her life, is presented as a bumbling, comic character.

More significant, he embodies a deficient masculinity because he can neither fulfill his traditional role as patriarchal figure (he is bullied by both his
wife and Phoolan Devi) nor save Phoolan Devi.[38] This reading of *Bandit
Queen* shows how a critique of an oppressive culture based on gender and
caste hierarchy recodes colonial constructions of otherness and inferiority. In keeping with its primary transnational circuit between Britain and
India, the representational strategies of the film are dominated by legacies
of colonial constructions of barbaric cultural traditions and a failed Indian
nationalism embodied as a corrupt, violent postcolonial state. The historically specific representations of the British-Indian transnational encounter
did not tap into American imaginations or historically specific national desires. Thus, *Bandit Queen* attracted little, if any, public or mainstream interest in the United States.

In contrast, *Slumdog Millionaire*, a very different kind of British-Indian
collaboration,[39] captured the U.S. public imagination through both con-
sumer/audience interest and significant institutionalized recognition
through the Academy Awards (winning eight awards). The U.S. public response was located at a specific historical moment defined by the convergence of particular economic changes within the United States and broader
forces of economic globalization. In the context of economic globalization,
the U.S.-India relationship has been marked by an acute sense of fear and
anxiety within the American public national sphere. In the public American imagination, representations of India have moved from a cultural absence (very little public or, for that matter, scholarly attention was paid to
India in earlier decades) to an economic anxiety regarding the outsourcing
of white-collar jobs. Public cultural representations of "accented" Indians
taking calls from Indian call center workers are often thinly veiled masks
for anger and fear over job losses. Such emotions have been accentuated
as the national economic crisis has produced a collapse of the American
middle class and a wide-scale expansion of poverty just as global public
rhetoric centers on the expanding middle classes and rising growth rates
in India.[40]

In the context of these economic shifts and contradictions *Slumdog Millionaire* tapped into a particular conjuncture of anxiety, fear, and desire.
At one level, the depiction of stark poverty within narratives of survival
and the overcoming of extreme suffering in *Slumdog Millionaire* portrays
a form of modernist authenticity that parallels the representational strategies in *Bandit Queen*. As with *Bandit Queen*, *Slumdog Millionaire* satisfies
consumer desires for rootedness in a postmodern world that is fragmented

and, in this instance, in a state of economic chaos. However, in the case of *Slumdog Millionaire*, the colonial relationship underlying the creation of the First and the Third World is shaped by the specificities of contemporary globalization and the uncertain political-economic position of the United States in particular. In the United States, deepening economic crisis with rapidly increasing unemployment, homelessness, and a shrinking middle class has brought questions of poverty and inequality into public discourses in ways that represent a sharp contrast to the neoliberal political culture that had been consolidated since the Reagan era.

The film provides a safe and uplifting representation of poverty that allows American audiences to both mediate their own economic anxieties and also project these anxieties on an "other" country that can still be viewed as distant and inferior. Consider the narrative structure of the film that is built around the central character Jamal Malik, who grows up in Mumbai's slums and struggles to overcome a life of poverty. Two central narrative devices structure the telling of Jamal's story. The first is the series of game show questions from the Indian version of the television program *Who Wants to Be a Millionaire?* The show is in fact the pivotal framing device, since it is Jamal's unlikely success on the program that causes its host to throw him in jail, insisting that Jamal was cheating. This leads to the second narrative device, Jamal's explanations to his police interrogator of how he knew the answers to the game show questions.

Consider how these two interconnected narrative devices operate. The narration of Jamal's story through the structure of a game show that is an offshoot of an American show allows the account of his life to unfold through a familiar lens for American audiences. This process of "remediation" is one in which, as Jay Bolter and Richard Grusin have insightfully argued, "the excess of media becomes an authentic experience."[41] They argue that this process of remediation enables a kind of hypermediacy. As they put it:

> In an epistemological sense, hypermediacy is opacity—the fact that knowledge of the world comes to us through media. The viewer acknowledges that she is in the presence of a medium and learns through acts of mediation or indeed learns about mediation itself. The psychological sense of hypermediacy is the experience that she has in and of the presence of media; it is the insistence that the experience of the medium is itself an experience of the real. The appeal to authenticity of experience is what brings the logics of immediacy and hypermediacy together.[42]

This process of remediation and the access to authenticity it sets in motion have important and distinctive implications from a transnational perspective. Consider how this process operates in *Slumdog Millionaire*. Jamal's story is literally broken into segments that are made for American television. More specifically, the episodes of Jamal's life break up the game show in the way in which advertising segments break up television shows. Jamal's story in effect operates as the commodity that is being sold to the audience. Mainstream American audiences are thus positioned to identify with the film's narrative with the safety and familiarity of a consumer's perspective. Yet the process of remediation allows audiences to have a sense of access to the presumed authenticity of life and poverty in India. This familiarity tames the otherness—the violence and poverty of the lives of inhabitants of India's slums—through these frames of familiarity.

Meanwhile, this dynamic of difference and familiarity parallels the play on sameness and difference that I have analyzed in *Bandit Queen*. If the telling of Jamal's story through the game show provides a point of sameness and identification for public audiences in the United States, the use of a violent police interrogator as the second device for unfolding the narrative marks the difference of the Indian nation. As with *Bandit Queen*, the violent scenes of torture that Jamal experiences as the opening to this second narrative device once again marks the failures and inferiorities of Indian nationhood and democracy. As I will discuss later in this chapter, the use of a violent male police interrogator is a substantive shift from the original story in the novel. In *Q & A*, the second narrative device is a female lawyer who successfully removes Jamal from prison and then asks for explanations of his answers in order to defend him effectively. The switch from a feminized figure of legal democratic rights to a violent male interrogator provides a stark example of how significant the mark of national (Indian) inferiority is in the creation of transnational films such as *Slumdog Millionaire* and *Bandit Queen*. In both cases, the masculinization of this inferiority (and the failure of the other nation) also represents an important element of the gendering of the nation; racialized masculinity is a sign of national failure. As we see with such processes of transnational cultural production (and as we have seen with the human rights debates in the previous chapter), nationalist ideals of countries such as the United States and Britain rest on the conception of deficient and usually violent masculinities in "other" (specifically postcolonial) nations. What is critical here is that these gendered constructions of the other, postcolonial Indian nation implicitly enable a consolidation of the national identity of viewing audiences in the United States and Britain. What we have, then, is a national recoding of a transnational process. Yet as with the other transnational processes I analyze in this book (including the paradigm of transnational feminism), the American and British national coding of these transnational films can be consolidated while being left unmarked because the postcolonial nation becomes the explicit terrain for criticism and analysis.

Such representations of elements of failure of the postcolonial nation serve to ease the anxieties of the economic threat that expanding Asian economies in India and China represent for the American national public. Take, for instance, the scene in the film where Jamal works in a call center—the most overused (and distorted) symbol of India's expanding middle classes and economic growth. The scene taps into familiar U.S. conceptions of middle-class Indians working in call centers and serving American consumers. In the scene, Jamal works as a lower-class informal sector worker who brings tea to the middle-class employees in the call center. He accidentally is given a chance to make calls when one of the employees dashes off to watch the game show *Who Wants to Be a Millionaire?* This chance event allows him both to reconnect with his brother (whom he looks up in the call center database) and ultimately his love. It is thus the call center, the sign most familiar to U.S. audiences of India's economic progress, that allows Jamal to fulfill his destiny.

Slumdog Millionaire is a vivid example of how political-economic contexts and structures shape both the transnational circuits of production and consumption of cultural products such as films and the specific strategies of representation used within these products. The subaltern figures in such cultural products in effect engage in a form of labor that helps sustain these structured transnational economic relations. Conceiving of the representation of subaltern figures in this way moves us in a different direction from Spivak's well-known rhetorical question, "Can the subaltern speak?" By moving away from the question of authenticity that underlies this question (how do we know if the subaltern is "really" speaking in her or his own voice?) to the question of the work that the subaltern does through the realm of representation, we can begin to theorize the material dimensions of transnational cultural production. In other words, regardless of the truth or authenticity of the subaltern's speech, transnational cultural production harnesses the symbolic/ideological, affective, and material labor of the subaltern. I have already pointed to the symbolic/ideological and affective forms of labor that subaltern figures such as Jamal and Phoolan Devi perform as they are made to reconstitute the nationalist sense of superiority and comfort for British and American viewing audiences. The material dimensions of this labor are perhaps most readily apparent through momentary challenges to the relationship of extraction that structures such representations. In both of the cases that I have been discussing, the films were challenged by actors playing some of the central subaltern figures being represented by or in the film.

The directors of *Slumdog Millionaire* sought to capture the realism of poverty in India both by filming large portions in Mumbai's well-known slum Dharavi, and by using child actors who are actual residents of Dharavi. Public media attention turned to the fact that in spite of the film's major international financial success, the child actors continued to reside in the same conditions in Dharavi.[43] The living conditions for one of the children, Azharuddin Ismail, were reported to have worsened after the film as his hut was demolished by state authorities, and he was then sleeping under a tarp with his sick father. The controversy intensified as the parents of Ismail and Rubina Ali claimed that their children had been underpaid, receiving less than domestic workers in India. Fox Searchlight (the American distributor of the film) and director Danny Boyle provided two responses to such claims. Fox Searchlight, while refusing to disclose the children's salary, argued, "For thirty days work, they were paid more than three times the average annual salary an adult *in their neighbourhood* would receive."[44] The second response from Fox Searchlight and Boyle was that they were paying for the children's education and that a substantial trust fund had been set up for the boys "which they will receive if they are still in school when they turn eighteen."[45] Both responses offer a striking glimpse of the economic inequalities that structured this transnational venture. On the one hand, despite all the celebration of the transnational, border-crossing collaboration, it is ultimately the local labor market value of the slum that Fox Searchlight uses to justify the wages it paid the children. The children's labor market power is valued according to the standards "in their neighbourhood." Thus, two sets of economic structures are reproduced through this cultural form: first, the internal economic structure within India where the labor of slum dwellers remains at a lower level, in contrast to the drastic rise in wages that upper-class and some middle-class Indians have benefited from in the postliberalization period is reproduced; second, the transnational economic hierarchies between the First and the Third World in which postcolonial nations have historically provided a supply of cheap labor are reconsolidated as the measure of acceptable wages. More specifically, it is the organized system of outsourcing, the most recent development in the international division of labor, that structures this economic relationship. According to this logic, when work is outsourced to India, it is structured by the local labor market of "the neighbourhood." Meanwhile, this is tempered by a liberal middle-class attempt at reforming the children by ensuring they remain in school. What is noteworthy is not the attempt to provide the children with an education but the fact that their receipt of the money was contingent on staying in school until the age of eighteen. What was missing from this civilizing mission was how Boyle or the trust fund would address the realities of a life in poverty. In reality, family crises, illnesses (Ismail's father, for instance, was already suffering from tuberculosis), and economic distress mean that children are often significant wage earners for their families. The terms of the fund thus prevented the children from receiving money that could help them move out of poverty—conditions that would help them stay in school and receive an education. It was only after the film's Academy Award success (and its continued financial success) that Boyle purchased apartments outside of the slums for the two children and provided money for their transport to and from school.

The question of what the long-term material and psychic effects of the film will be on its child actors cannot be deduced from the short time span since they were thrust from their lives in Dharavi to the center of the Hollywood spotlight and back to a liminal space within the hierarchies of class, caste, gender, and religion that they must now return to navigate. Certainly, this is not to suggest that the actions of the families of Azharuddin and Rubina are without their own interests and internal conflicts. Yet this brief discussion reveals the necessity of linking questions of economic inequality to discussions of cultural representation.[46] It is through these glimpses of protest that we see the complex interaction between global economic relationships, the political economy of nations, and the representational and affective economies of cultural production. The central element linking these three systems is the affective labor of subaltern individuals and social groups. Thus, in this instance, we see that the devalued labor of socioeconomically marginalized groups within India (structured by particular intersecting inequalities of caste, religion, and gender) allows the transnational system of economic and cultural production to extract their labor. The labor is both economic and affective as the children both labor through their dramatic work in this particular industry (the film industry) and perform the emotional work of producing comfort and easing the social and economic anxieties created by the very structures that tracked them to the slums of Dharavi in the first place. The problem is thus not one that is intrinsic or unique to *Slumdog Millionaire* or to the motives of the creators of this particular film. Rather, *Slumdog Millionaire* illustrates how economic production, cultural representation, and affective economies all rest on corresponding forms of labor extraction.

It is thus not surprising that similar moments of protest interrupted the circulation of *Bandit Queen*. In the case of this film, Phoolan Devi specifically attempted to stop it from being screened in India. Her motives were interpreted and represented through widely varying media reports and speculations, ranging from whether she had been paid enough for the film to whether she had been sufficiently consulted during its production. The well-known Indian feminist writer and activist Arundhati Roy charged director Shekar Kapur with not consulting Phoolan Devi about the film's representation of her life.[47] A central trope of public debates in India was Phoolan Devi's reported opposition to the graphic portrayal of the rapes, as well as her opposition to ways in which the film distorted facts of her life (for instance, by portraying her as the lover of the dacoit Vikram). As with *Slumdog Millionaire*, such moments of contestation highlight the process of extraction that takes place through the representation and consumption of the lives of subaltern individuals. An adequate understanding of Phoolan Devi's objection to the release of the film within India requires a shift from the transnational to the national dynamics of the circulation of such transnational products, particularly within the nations that such cultural forms seek to represent.

Laboring Subalterns, the New Middle Classes, and the National Public Sphere in India

Both *Bandit Queen* and *Slumdog Millionaire* emerged from specific historical and political contexts in India and intervened in and sparked widespread national debates within the dominant public sphere of India's English-speaking middle classes. While this socioeconomic group represents a relatively small elite within the country, it has historically played a significant role in shaping national public debates and orienting state policies in particular ways. This influence has been intensified in the postliberalization period as these expanding middle classes have self-identified as the primary cultural-political agents of a globalizing India.[48] *Bandit Queen* and *Slumdog Millionaire* thus serve as flash points that illustrate the national politics of transnational cultural production. The distribution and release of *Bandit Queen* resulted in a sharp public debate centered on the representation of rape in the film. The film presents five incidents of rape, using increasingly graphic depictions of violence, beginning with the rape of the eleven-year-old Phoolan Devi and culminating with an extended scene of her gang rape in the village of Behrnai. Kapur's use of nudity in representing the rapes is particularly unusual in the context of existing genres of popular Hindi and regional cinema.[49] The controversy over the graphic images of rape was intensified with Phoolan Devi's own attempt to stop the release of the film. These contestations were further complicated by the Indian state's attempt to censor the film because it contained nudity. Following the film's release, the controversy continued, as reports of male audiences cheering during the rape scenes circulated in television and newspaper reports.[50] Yet, at the same time, the film was screened with special showings for women-only audiences, opening up spaces for the production of a women's public sphere.[51]

Within the context of the national debate over *Bandit Queen* in India, I argue that the film produced a set of contradictory effects that both disrupted particular hegemonic social codes regarding sexuality and rape within the Indian bourgeois public sphere and reproduced relationships of power that re/colonized Phoolan Devi through the appropriation of her life experiences. In response to the controversy over his representations of rape, Kapur argued that his intention had been to represent rape as a nonsexual act without any hint of sensuality.[52] For instance, the graphic depiction of Phoolan Devi being raped by the upper-caste dacoit Babu Gujjar is presented in daylight, and the only nudity shown involves the male actor. Kapur argued that although the actual rape had taken place at night, he depicted the scene in daylight to avoid any sensual connotations associated with darkness or nighttime. Furthermore, none of the rape scenes depicts any female nudity; the only nude shot of the actress playing Phoolan Devi occurs in the incident when Phoolan Devi is paraded naked in Behmai village after being gang-raped. Kapur's representation departs significantly from typical images of rape in popular Hindi films. Although rape scenes frequently occur in popular film, they are generally highly sexualized representations, even though they do not include nudity. The successive rapes in *Bandit Queen* form a narrative of spiraling violence. The last incident of the gang rape depicts Phoolan Devi beaten until she is barely recognizable and unable to speak. The representation of rape as a brutal act of violence disrupts public silence on rape and violence against women in India. This disruption is particularly significant given the ways in which public out-cries over rape are usually constructed in terms of the loss of honor of the victim and her community.[53] The film, in contrast, presents a disturbing vision of the violence the woman herself experiences. Although for Western audiences *Bandit Queen* reproduces the transnational power effects in conforming to realist strategies of representation, within the national context of India, it breaks from the conventional strategies of popular films.[54] The strategies of representation deployed in *Bandit Queen* contain counterhegemonic moments when the film is viewed in the context of the Indian national public sphere.

These counterhegemonic effects are reinforced by the film's representation of rape within a discursive framework that depicts violence against women in terms of the intersections of caste and gender. The film presents a series of images in which upper-caste men in Phoolan Devi's village make remarks that interpret her act of leaving her husband as a sign of her sexual availability and promiscuity. Indeed, these scenes set the stage for the events leading to the first rape after she has run away from her husband, setting in motion the subsequent events in her life. The film's narrative interprets Phoolan Devi's final transgression of the law as the bandit queen as stemming from the violent reprisals she faced because of her transgressions of gender and caste boundaries. In doing so, the film interrupts the naturalization of caste and gender boundaries within contemporary India. For instance, it calls attention to the ways in which single women are constructed as a sexual and social threat to the moral and social order. Kapur's representation also demonstrates that the construction of the boundaries of gender is always contingent on the politics of caste. Phoolan Devi is repeatedly assaulted not just because she has defied hegemonic social norms by leaving her husband but because of a caste-based construction of sexual accessibility in which upper-caste men often assert violent sexual access to lower-caste women. Such counterhegemonic effects of the film are also produced by a different subversion of sexual codes in a scene in which Phoolan Devi takes the sexual initiative with her lover, Vikram. The image portrays Phoolan Devi positioned on top of Vikram, making love to him in a sexually assertive manner. As several Indian feminists have argued, the scene represents a positive portrayal of Phoolan Devi's sexuality, one that moves beyond rape, violence, and victimhood.[55]

These counterhegemonic possibilities subvert a common narrative linking the middle classes, their consumption practices of cultural forms such as films, and the Indian nation-state. Scholars and media critics in India have called attention to the way in which cinema as "an institution of modernity" plays a central role in the nationalist imagination.[56] Tejaswini Niranjana, for instance, has argued that popular films have begun to cultivate "an audience primarily composed of the newly articulate, assertive and self-confident middle class that is also claiming for itself the spaces of nation and secularism premised on Hindutva."[57] Niranjana links the production of this new middle-class audience to several interwoven political processes. On one level, the middle classes are presented in a celebratory fashion involving images of new lifestyles and consumption practices associated with policies of economic liberalization in India. On another level, the "'ordinary' middle class person is suddenly inserted into a national conflict" and is then projected as the means for restoring or recuperating the modern, secular Indian nation-state.[58] In this process, the future of "India" is reimagined through a lens that rests on the interwoven paradigms of modernity, nationalism, state power, and consumer capitalism.

Kapur's *Bandit Queen* contests such narratives in a number of complex ways, disrupting the production of new hegemonic public cultural images of India's successful transformation into a consumer capitalist nation competing in a global economy.[59] By foregrounding economic and caste inequalities in rural areas in Uttar Pradesh, the film in effect disrupts the narrative that assumes the Indian nation has in fact modernized and is now synonymous with the urban middle classes. *Bandit Queen* marks the social fragments that have historically been excluded from the Indian nation as materially and temporally present within the "new" liberalizing Indian nation.

The film produces another narrative that is counterhegemonic in the Indian national context: the means for social justice in the film lie beyond the boundaries of the legal democratic institutions (such as the courts and police) of the Indian state. With this narrative, *Bandit Queen* departs from the conventional genre of popular crime films that, as Ravi Vasudevan argues, invoke middle-class anxieties regarding crime yet contain these anxieties in an "acceptable narrative of nationalist inspiration, familial re-location and class reproduction."[60] Phoolan Devi is unable to receive justice through such instruments of India's democracy. The intersections of caste, class, and gender hierarchy produce a situation in which social justice is contingent on Phoolan Devi's transformation into an "outlaw."[61] In effect, justice and democracy ironically become two poles of a binary opposition.

As with *Bandit Queen*, *Slumdog Millionaire* fit within and provoked a different set of issues within India than it did in other national and transnational contexts. In India, the film invokes a set of issues that are under sharp social and political contestation—the control over urban space. In the context of India's economic liberalization that has accelerated since the 1990s, this contestation has been spurred on by the privatization of land both through real estate developers' desires to take back large tracts of land from settlements of the urban poor and middle-class interests in "beautifying" neighborhoods through cleansing the urban space of street vendors.[62] Meanwhile, residents of such settlements and street vendors' unions have attempted to resist these efforts. *Slumdog Millionaire* thus has contradictory implications in the Indian context, capturing an issue that is of central significance both for India's rising middle classes and for working-class and poorer communities. The attempt to represent realistic and vivid portrayals of the urban poor appears to disrupt dominant national narratives that seek to depict India as a booming middle-class nation that has moved beyond older questions of poverty. However, it does so through a sanitized narrative that can be consumed by India's new middle classes.

The film casts the story as one of individualistic upward mobility narrated through a successful game show that itself represents the new media that have played a central role in recasting the Indian nation as one that has moved from a retrograde socialist state to a globalizing middle-class-oriented consumer nation. If the film depicts the starkness of poverty in a sanitized form of modernist authenticity for American audiences, it provides a sense of comfort for Indian middle-class audiences in different but parallel ways. It is thus not surprising that as the story comes to resolution with the final game show question being answered, the film cuts to scenes of domestic middle-class audiences watching the program. The process of remediation allows middle-class audiences access to this figure of poverty with a sense of comfortable detachment. Furthermore, middle-class audiences can watch this story of a poor Muslim boy with a sense of identification both with the consumable format of the game show and with the promise of social mobility in an age of globalization that the show embodies.

Of course, as with the *Bandit Queen, Slumdog Millionaire* provoked more nuanced and unforeseen effects and responses. For many members of the "slum" being portrayed, the film was a sign of the success and vibrancy of their communities. Some slum residents in localized areas in Mumbai protested the film, for instance, decrying the derogatory term "slumdog" as an objectifying, offensive characterization. Farther afield, in the United States,

Republican National Committee chair Michael Steele caused a minor controversy by sending his "slum love" to Bobby Jindal, a rising Republican Indian American politician, revealing the transnational potential for such objectification to travel in distinct racialized ways. Meanwhile, in India, the film was successfully cast in new middle-class nationalist narratives. The success of the film has itself been viewed by some in India as a kind of global recognition of India as an emerging global economic power. While some critics (such as well-known film star Amitabh Bachchan, who played himself in the film) noted with nationalist detachment that the American Academy Awards were not a significant measure of success for India, critics in India's mainstream English-speaking public sphere largely embraced the movie.

Slumdog Millionaire was constructed in ways that fit within India's new middle-class narrative much more than Kapur's *Bandit Queen*. At one level, this is related to the kind of film that each represents. *Slumdog Millionaire* consciously sought to place itself within the cinematic traditions of India's Bollywood industry. Director Boyle himself spoke about his conscious use of such cinematic strategies from three well-known Indian films (including adaptations of particular scenes of Mumbai's underworld, as well as more mundane strategies such as the use of song and dance sequences).[63] In this sense, the film provides a stark contrast to *Bandit Queen*, which disrupts any attempt at using conventional Bollywood cinematic strategies of conflict resolution or the glamorized depiction of violence typical of mainstream portrayals. The contrast provides us with a sense of irony involved in discussing "authenticity" when dealing with questions of transnational cultural production.

Authenticity, Representation, and the Contingencies of Form

The contrast between the types of film that *Bandit Queen* and *Slumdog Millionaire* represent points to a deeper question of how the form of representation shapes the effects of transnational cultural production. I consider this further by juxtaposing these films with the textual forms on which they were based—the autobiographical testimonial *I, Phoolan Devi* and the novel *Q & A*. This comparison allows for a contrast between visual and textual modes of representation and also provides us with a contrast between two forms of textual representation. Consider, for instance, the key substantive question in the film's representation of Phoolan Devi's life—the representation of rape. While *Bandit Queen* subverts hegemonic social codes in contemporary India in many ways, the film's oppositional endeavor nevertheless raised unsettling questions regarding Phoolan Devi's own location in relation to the representation. The fact that Phoolan Devi attempted to prevent the screening of the film in India raises the question of whether Kapur's counterhegemonic strategies of representation inadvertently re/colonize Phoolan Devi and position her within new hierarchies of power. Such questions require a focus on Phoolan Devi's location and agency within the politics of representation.

Phoolan Devi's effort to block the film's screening cannot be understood simply as a form of consent to the existing silence on rape in the hegemonic public sphere in India. On the contrary, her opposition to the film signals significant risks that arise from the representation of violence against women and the dangers of reproducing a paradigm of victimhood through this representation. The film's emphasis on rape shifts Phoolan Devi from a legendary figure within the Indian context—a woman dacoit, both heroic and notorious, who stole from the rich and distributed wealth to the poor—to the status of a rape victim. The film's presentation of rape as an explanation for Phoolan Devi's transformation into an outlaw identifies rape as the sole motivation for her subsequent actions.

This depiction presents a sharp contrast to the autobiography, which deals at length with a complex conception of social justice that motivated Phoolan Devi's raids on various villages. In her vision of justice, resistance was retaliation not merely against her own personal experiences of violence but also against the exploitation of lower-caste villagers by upper-caste landlords. Consider, for instance, the following passage, which begins with Phoolan Devi describing her method of castrating men who were rumored to have raped lower-caste women:

> I heard it often enough. That's why, whenever I heard it, I crushed the serpent they used to torture women. I dismembered them. It was my vengeance, and the vengeance of all women. In the villages of my region there was no justice other than the *lathi* [stick], where *mallahs* (boatmen caste) were the slaves of the *thakurs* [landowning caste]. I dealt out justice. "Who stole from you? Who beat you? Who took your food? Who said you couldn't use the well? Who stole your cattle? Who raped your daughter or your sister or your wife?" The guilty one was brought before my court. He was forced to suffer what he had made others suffer.[64]

In contrast, in the film the only depiction of social justice that does not involve Phoolan Devi's own personal revenge against men who raped her is a scene in which she gives a small girl a necklace for her dowry during a raid on a village. The film individualizes Phoolan Devi's conception of social justice by casting it within a singular personalized narrative of rape and revenge. Ironically, in its attempt to call for social justice by revealing the brutal gender- and caste-based violence of rape, *Bandit Queen* does so by silencing Phoolan Devi's own vision of social justice.

My intention in juxtaposing the film and the autobiography is not to argue that the autobiography presents us with unmediated access to the truth of Phoolan Devi's life. Autobiography is a situated and negotiated text that is constructed through particular strategies of representation.[65] Certainly, as feminist research has demonstrated, the decentering of a universalistic Western male subject through autobiography does not serve as a self-evident or transparent means of decolonization but may produce contradictory effects. As Sidonie Smith and Julia Watson have argued:

> On the one hand, the very taking-up-of-the-autobiographical transports the colonial subject into the territory of the "universal" subject and thus promises a culturally empowered subjectivity. Participation in, through representation of, privileged narratives can secure cultural recognition for the subject. On the other hand, entry into the territory of traditional autobiography implicates the speaker in a potentially recuperative performance, one that might reproduce and represent the colonizer's figure in negation.[66]

Such contradictions are particularly acute when the autobiography in question is characterized by the hierarchies of power inherent in transnational relations of the translation, production, and consumption of Third World texts.

I, Phoolan Devi lies in an intermediary space between the genres of autobiography and *testimonio*. While the book is marketed as an autobiography, it is in practice created through methods closer to the testimonial form. The book was based on taped oral narratives that were translated and transcribed by its editors. The book provides no detailed information on these methodological practices. Readers do not know, for instance, how the editors selected events or made decisions on the order of the narrative, whether all the tapes were transcribed, what the nature of Phoolan Devi's input was in the editorial process, or what the interaction between Phoolan Devi and the editors was during the interviews. Unlike a well-known *testimonio* like *I, Rigoberta Menchu,* Phoolan Devi's text does not contain a formal introduction by the transcribers/editors, nor does the reader have any information on the background of these "witnesses" of Phoolan Devi's experiences.[67] The book merely notes that each page was read aloud to Phoolan Devi and signed by her. This designation of Phoolan Devi's consent, nevertheless, only emphasizes the constructed nature of the autobiography. This textual representation of Phoolan Devi's life history, positioned between the genres of *testimonio*, autobiography, and ethnographic interview, highlights the performative nature of all representations of the "real." Meanwhile, this liminality of form also demonstrates the contradictory processes of the commodification of Third World women's testimonials, on the one hand, and the transgressive potential of testimonial, on the other.[68] The classification of Phoolan Devi's *testimonio* attempts to contain the representation of her life experiences within the more conventional, individualized form of the autobiography. However, Phoolan Devi's presentation of her experiences in relation to wider structural forms of oppression and to the experiences of marginalization of lower-caste and lower-class men and women from her community disrupts this containment. John Beverly has argued that "testimonio is an affirmation of the authority of a single speaking subject, even of personal awareness and growth, but it cannot affirm a self-identity that is separate from a group or class situation marked by marginalization, oppression and struggle. If it does this, it ceases to be testimonio and becomes in effect autobiography."[69] The genre of *testimonio* itself does not necessarily represent an uncontested, authentic counterpoint to autobiography. Kay Schaffer and Sidonie Smith, for example, discuss the controversy that erupted over *I, Rigoberta Menchu's testimonio* when an American anthropologist challenged the factual accuracy of the narrative.[70] As they note, the charges produced an intense public debate over issues related to "personal and collective forms of remembering, narrative authenticity, and juridical versus non-juridical understandings of truth telling."[71] *I, Phoolan Devi* rests within a liminal space between autobiography and *testimonio*. The text transgresses the autobiographical and in the process demonstrates that trans/national materially based structures of the production and consumption of texts do not predetermine the power effects of such textual forms. Thus, while the autobiography circulates in the same trans/national circuit of power as the film, the power effects of the representation are not identical.

Particular narratives in *I, Phoolan Devi* disrupt binaries such as modern versus traditional or oppressor versus victim that the film reinforces. For example, scenes in the book contextualize Phoolan Devi's resistance in

relation to her mother's actions and in relation to Phoolan Devi's own vision of social justice. This contextualization interrupts the process of commodification and consumption of Phoolan Devi's life as a form of individualized resistance set against a homogeneous oppressive culture. Phoolan
Devi's words in the book, for instance, "I was born with my mother's anger," move the reader away from an individualized vision of her rebellion
and compel the reader to view the rebellion in relation to her mother's
struggles with and critical consciousness of the socioeconomic hierarchies
in her everyday rural life.[72] Such forms of rebellion provide a contrast to the
film's presentation of social oppression as a static feature of Indian culture.

Consider another contrast between the film and the book. The film begins its narration of Phoolan Devi's story with her parents' arrangement
of her marriage at the age of eleven to a man three times her age. In this
bleak portrayal of a hopelessly patriarchal family structure, Phoolan Devi's
father takes the role of negotiating the arrangements while her mother for
the most part stands on the sidelines, watching sadly and silently. Phoolan
Devi's father protests weakly that his daughter is too young to be taken by
her future husband, Putti Lal, but he gives in, since he has already paid a
bride price for her marriage. Phoolan Devi is then taken to her husband's
house, where she is raped while her mother-in-law stands outside, listening passively to the girl's screams. The childhood rape scene is presented
before the opening credits of the film and serves as the foundation for the
events that unfold in the film's chronology of Phoolan Devi's adult life.
Like the film, the book also opens with a short description of the rape of
eleven-year-old Phoolan Devi. However, the early chapters of I, Phoolan
Devi contextualize the events leading to the rape in ways that disrupt essentialized notions of a static Indian tradition. The book clearly suggests
that Putti Lal's insistence on taking Phoolan Devi away at the age of eleven
was a violation of customary practice and, therefore, of Indian tradition.
Phoolan Devi states, for instance, that she was told at her wedding that she
would leave with her husband in three or four years,[73] and she indicates
that her older sister did not leave for her husband's village until the age of
sixteen.[74]

The representation of Phoolan Devi's childhood years and family life
presents a striking contrast to the film's depiction of her parental family
structure. In contrast to the film's images of Phoolan Devi's silent mother,
the book presents her mother as a dominant force within the family while
her father appears as a passive, weak-willed man who consents to his sub-
jugated social status. Phoolan Devi presents an incident in which she is

beaten by the village *pradhan* (village district head) because she asked him for a mango. Phoolan Devi describes her mother dragging her to the *pradhan*'s house and then screaming at him in rage, "'You think we bring children into the world just to be your slaves? Instead of hitting her like that you should have just killed her! Go on kill her! Then she won't ask you for any more mangoes. Kill her if you want!'" As Phoolan Devi goes on to describe, "When he came home and heard what happened, my father was ashamed. He said it was our duty to serve them. That was the way the world was." While *I, Phoolan Devi* implicates Phoolan Devi's mother in the reproduction of gender hierarchy in certain ways (her mother laments the fact that Phoolan Devi was born a girl and warns her of the danger of female sexuality and the threat of rape), her mother's resistance complicates this. At one point, for instance, Phoolan Devi describes her mother's rejection of God and religion: "She never prayed like my father. She preferred to wail about the misfortunes God had sent her. 'If he would even just give me enough food for all these girls....' Once she took a little statue of one of the gods from our house and threw it down the village well."[75] These anecdotes illustrate contradictory moments in the creation of her mother's social identity. On the one hand, Phoolan Devi's mother articulates a form of gendered ideology as she copes with the economic consequences of bearing female children in a patriarchal society. On the other hand, her rejection of God simultaneously reflects a form of critical consciousness as she rejects a religious order that reproduces her caste location and provides no relief from her class-based poverty. In the process, the reader moves away from an assumption that rural Indian society is characterized by a naturalized form of consent to tradition.

I, Phoolan Devi disrupts hegemonic narratives about Indian culture and society not because of a claim to authenticity through the voice of Phoolan Devi but because of specific types of strategies of representation. It is not simply the empirical fact of the first-person narrative that is at issue here but the way in which the "I" is presented. The effectiveness of such representation centers around the ways in which the translated narrative of Phoolan Devi's life presents her identity in terms of a complex, multilayered form, one that is emblematic of wider structural forms of social oppression. Throughout the book, Phoolan Devi's narrative of oppression and resistance links social hierarchies within her village to the social relations between landlords and landless peasants. She identifies the origins of her own and her family's problems as her uncle cheating her father out of his share of land because her uncle "wanted to be like the rich, like a *thakur.*"[76] In her description of her early childhood, her initial rebellions are targeted at her uncle and later her uncle's son as she continually witnesses their ability to use money and upward mobility to cheat her family. It is at this point that Phoolan Devi begins to transgress gender boundaries by openly expressing her defiance of her uncle and cousin. In one such confrontation with her cousin, she notes:

> Mayadin [her cousin] was learning how to use the power he had inherited from his thieving father. And all the cowering dogs in the village had obeyed him. But he had been red with fury, he was sweating in his fresh clothes and I had seen his eyes blink with disbelief that I had dared to attack him in the absence of my father. I began to calm down as I thought about his embarrassment. It must have infuriated him. He must have thought that I took myself for the head of our household![77]

This depiction of the unfolding relationship between class, caste, and gender differs from the film's presentation of caste and gender hierarchy in important ways. By depicting her relatives' attempts to improve their social location through land and money and illustrating the ways in which the lure of upward mobility produces class and status hierarchies within her extended family, Phoolan Devi's testimonial counters the notion of caste as a monolithic, unchanging hierarchy.

Phoolan Devi's narrative is also distinctive in terms of her continual references to the complex articulation of the relationship between caste and class in the social relations of everyday life in her village. Her focus on the politics of class is significant not only because it adds another social category to her discussion of oppression but because the category of class disrupts any presumed naturalized boundary between the modern and the traditional. This narrative contests urban middle-class representations of rural India as traces of the premodern lingering within the modern consumer capitalist nation. Phoolan Devi's discussion of the links between landownership and caste highlight the economic bases of power, contradicting the notion that caste is a form of social distinction intrinsic to Indian (Hindu) society. This complex articulation between class, caste, and gender resurfaces later in Phoolan Devi's description of her vision of social justice, which, she argues, guided the raids she carried out on villages once she had formed her own band of dacoits.

Phoolan Devi's testimonial constructs her identity and experience through a narrative of oppression, agency, and resistance that reveals the complex relationship between caste, class, and gender in contemporary Indian society. In contrast, Shohini Ghosh has presented an incisive analysis of the ways in which Phoolan Devi's agency is foreclosed in the film. Ghosh notes that Phoolan Devi's empowerment is always dependent on male outlaws so that "she is empowered only when she is 'allowed' empowerment by the men around her."[78] More significantly, pointing to a "recurring pattern in the film where oppositional speech is punished repeatedly by assaults on the body," Ghosh argues that "only speech remains her truly autonomous domain of agency and resistance."[79] In the film, Phoolan Devi's speech is defiant, yet her actions are individualized and are dependent on a masculine world; the displacements that produce her intersectional identity, in effect, also locate her in a position of disidentification either from the elites or from the male dacoits. In contrast, in the book, Phoolan Devi is able to represent the interests of other marginalized members of her social world—her agency is thus contextualized within, and subversive of, material structures of oppression; her interwoven identity of caste, class, and gender in this context serves as a potential source for wider social transformation. *I, Phoolan Devi* reflects the "critical practice of outlaw genres" that attempts to "shift the subject of autobiography from the individual to a more unstable collective entity."[80]

I, Phoolan Devi is more effective than *Bandit Queen* in disrupting hegemonic relationships between power and resistance because of moments of subversion within the text that prevent a commodification of Phoolan Devi's life into the figure of a victimized "Third World woman." Such moments allow the *testimonio* contained in the book to interrupt the trans/national power relations that shape the book's translation, marketing, and consumption. A striking example of this type of disruption is evident in Phoolan Devi's response to the public's desire to see her and capture her through visual representations. In the account of her surrender to the police and state government, she vividly describes the pressure from the press as journalists continually attempted to photograph her and her resistance. She says, "I would charge at them and tear their cameras away from them. I hated being photographed. Every time I heard the click of a camera, I turned into a tigress."[81] The most significant insight into the relationship between power and representation is perhaps captured in the book's short epilogue: "I had seen all kinds of bandits. Assassins had tried to take my life, journalists had tried to get my story, movie directors had tried to capture me on film. They all thought they could speak about me as though I didn't exist, as though I still didn't have any right to respect. The bandits had tried to torture my body, but the others tried to torture my spirit."[82]

In contrast to the representations of Phoolan Devi's life, the representational differences between *Slumdog Millionaire* and *Q & A* are less stark. The novel, *Q & A*, written by Indian diplomat Vikas Swarup, also represents a form that was clearly directed at a transnational audience—both Western and the English-speaking Indian middle classes. Indeed, the book was well received both by the dominant English-language press in India and by critics in the United States and Britain. The transformation of the form of the novel to the film of course holds fewer complexities than the attempt to represent the real life of a living figure in the case of Phoolan Devi. *Q & A* and *Slumdog Millionaire* also shared more explicit commercial economic links—the novel was renamed *Slumdog Millionaire* after the release and commercial success of the film. However, the ease of cultural translation in the case of *Q & A* lies with a deeper and shared ideological ground that connects this novel with *Slumdog Millionaire*. The novel (like the film) purports to depict the life of the poor in contemporary India that is accessible to and thus comfortable for the elite segments of the Indian middle class (as well as for a mainstream middle-class reading public in the West).

The middle-class construction of the poor in *Q & A* unfolds through specific hegemonic national narratives that have been shaping new middle-class conceptions of the Indian nation, particularly within the postliberalization period. One of the most striking markers of this conception (one that is not taken up by the film) is a homophobic marking of the life of the poor. The opening narrative of the lead character, Ram Mohammad Thomas (renamed Jamal in the film), that marks the source of trauma for both him and his friend Salim is not a generic description of his poverty or of the police abuse he faces after being arrested for winning the game show. Rather, poverty and trauma are coded through homosexual assault on children. The novel begins with two key events of homosexuality and child abuse—an opening that also specifically equates gay sex with pedophilia.

In the very first episode that Ram Mohammad Thomas describes in the novel (corresponding to the first question in the game show), he and his friend Salim are discussing rumors that the film star (Armaan) whom Salim idolizes is gay. Their discussion occurs during the intermission of a movie right after a graphic description of a heterosexual love scene between Armaan and the lead actress that the children have just seen. Salim angrily denies the rumors. As Ram narrates, "Salim's anger is white hot. And I know why. He hates gays. To tarnish his idol with the brush of homosexuality is the ultimate insult in his book. I, too, know of perverts and what they do to unsuspecting boys. In dark halls. In public toilets. In municipal gardens. In juvenile homes."[83] The movie then resumes and later, as the two children watch the climax of the film, an old man places his hand on Salim's lap and attempts to sexually assault him. Salim screams at the man and slaps him. Just as the man is getting up to rush away, Salim and Ram realize that the sexual predator is in fact Armaan himself, disguised with a beard. This scene in the chapter entitled "Death of a Hero" marks the beginning of Ram's (and Salim's) life of trials and struggles. It is this intertwining of homosexuality and child molestation that marks their loss of innocence. This representation of homosexuality becomes the marker of the naïveté of the poor that runs throughout the novel. Salim never breaks out of his naive worship of film stars and his pursuit of a role within the film industry. However, it is Ram's consciousness of this sexualized disillusionment—this "death of a hero"—that separates him from Salim and the other figures of poverty who remain trapped in ignorance and passivity.

The scene leads immediately to the second incident of homosexual assault. The next chapter (the narrative corresponding to the second game show question) documents the roots of Ram Mohammad Thomas's life and identity. He is abandoned by his mother, placed in an orphanage run by a Christian church, and then adopted by a Christian couple. His new father soon angrily returns the boy to the priest of the church, blaming the adoption for his wife's running away with another man. Ram then lives with the priest in what is the only peaceful and happy period of his childhood—the only period in which Ram Mohammad Thomas feels that he has a family (and a parental figure). However, this period of tranquillity is soon disrupted by the arrival of a new priest, Father John. Ram soon discovers that Father John is engaging in homosexual sex. The housemaid sniggers that the new priest was caught in the church with another man. Ram himself goes to Father Timothy and confesses (using the church confessional box for the first time in his life) that he peeped inside Father John's room and saw "magazines under the mattresses, the designs on the body, the leather-clad visitors at night, and the snorting of talcum powder."[84] These illicit sexual activities are represented as acts of desecration of the sacred purity of church and childhood; Ram's use of the confessional is a (failed) attempt at regaining this purity. However, the violation and desecration that are associated with these constructions of gay sex soon culminate in a final sequence of violent encounters. One night Ram wakes up, and on his way to the bathroom he peers into Father John's room. As he narrates:

What I see inside is frightening. Ian [an English boy staying with them who later confesses to being Father Timothy's illegitimate son] is stooped over the table and Father John is bending over him. His pajamas have fallen down to his feet. I am totally confused. I may be an idiot orphan boy, but I know something is wrong. I rush to Father Timothy, who is fast asleep. "Wake up, Father! Father John is doing something bad to Ian," I shout.[85]

This discovery leads to a violent argument between the two priests and ends with Father John killing Father Timothy and then committing suicide. Ram finds both bodies in pools of blood near the altar in the church—a final act of violent desecration caused by the gay priest. After this series of events, Ram is thrust into his life on the streets and in the slums of Mumbai, Delhi, and Agra.

As with the first episode, the depiction of gay sex is conflated and intertwined with pedophilia, child abuse, and an assortment of other illicit practices (cocaine use, tattoos, pornography). However, this second depiction of homosexuality provides an even more powerful turning point than in Salim's case. For Ram it sets into motion not just his loss of innocence but also his loss of any sense of stability or comfort—financial, emotional, or familial. This depiction provides two of the central elements of contemporary middle-class national identity in India. First, sexual transgression (and the need for the policing of sexual norms) becomes the marker of decline and decay. Indeed, such depictions of homosexuality and the corresponding reproduction of heteronormative family structures have been a long-standing pattern in cultural representations such as film and television.[86] This is in keeping with broader patterns in contemporary India, where social anxieties, changes, and conflicts intensified in the postliberalization period have often been displaced on the terrain of sexuality. The policing of sexual norms and women's bodies and the reproduction of the heterosexual family have been key markers of stability that have anchored the identity of India's postliberalization middle classes. Indeed, the novel is littered with this intertwining of sexual transgression and violence (including incest, domestic violence, and violence against the prostitute Nita with whom Ram falls in love).

These constructions of sexual transgression and violence are connected to the second key element of new middle-class identity, the rationalization of poverty as a cultural phenomenon for which the new middle classes (and their elite layers) have no responsibility. Thus, the graphic scenes of homosexual violence become the device that frames the poverty of Ram and Salim—a move that displaces a focus on class inequality to the terrain of sexuality. Sexuality, in this context, is not portrayed as the sole cause of their poverty. Rather, it is the representational device that forecloses the need to question the causes of poverty. Poverty thus becomes a condition that simply exists for the English-speaking middle-class reader, and the ability of the characters to move themselves out of this condition is linked to random episodes of sexual transgression, violence, alcoholism, ignorance, and organized crime—all forces that are at a sociospatial distance from the idealized norms of middle-class family life.[87]

In contrast to this superficial conception of poverty in contemporary India, *Q & A* provides a more nuanced conception of the Indian middle classes than does *Slumdog Millionaire*. Swarup's depiction of his characters' lives of poverty is not limited to the slums of Dharavi. He portrays the poverty of the segments of the middle classes that live in low-income housing (the *shawls*) with a very fine line of social capital (usually in the form of formal higher education or some history of work in white-collar industries) that separates them from the working poor. Indeed, Ram's story in *Q & A* is one of gradual though stunted upward mobility, culminating in his winning the game show and achieving prosperity. Through Ram's changing social experiences and awareness, Swarup captures the middle-class consciousness of consumption and the fine but rigid forms of stratification that exist between segments of the middle classes. Sitting with a group of rich college students in a five-star hotel, Ram reflects, "The sight of all of this opulence makes me uneasy. In Mumbai, Salim and I would gate-crash the weddings of the rich for free food, but we never grudged them their wealth. But seeing these rich college boys spending money like paper, I am gripped by a totally new sense of inadequacy. The contrast with my own imperfect life pinches me with the force of a physical hurt."[88] Ram's nuanced distinction between the older, traditional display of wealth through weddings and the conspicuous consumption associated with the new rich in postliberalization India captures a particular sense of middle-class sensibility and anxiety over consumption. Empirical research on the Indian middle classes has shown that middle-class individuals often display ambivalence toward conspicuous consumption even as they use consumption practices to demarcate their social status and distinguish themselves from both the poor and the wealthy.[89] It is this sense of middle-class identity that Ram gradually forms through the course of the novel. His narrative thus condemns both the very wealthy (the college students, the wealthy royal woman who discards her young son when he discloses her affair with her brother-in-law, the tragic figure of a wealthy film star who is a victim of domestic violence and eventually commits suicide) and the ignorant, passive poor (the domestic worker who steals money to pay for her sister's wedding but is caught because she leaves evidence of her presence by straightening up the room). *Q & A* is thus a story about the making of middle-class consciousness projected onto the lives of poor slum dwellers.

This gradual, emerging middle-class identity of Ram Mohammad Thomas in the novel is concealed in the film *Slumdog Millionaire*. In *Slumdog Millionaire*, it is Salim's embrace of liberalization, as he stands atop the newly built high-rise buildings in Mumbai, that stands in for the rise of India's aspiring middle classes. Jamal's journey is an idealized and transcendent one of love and destiny. In the film, "it is written" that he will be united with his love. In contrast, in the novel, Ram Mohammad Thomas's love is a prostitute with whom he has first sexual experience, continuing to pay for sex until they fall in love; she is not the childhood love he spends his life looking for and who is always marked by the celibate childhood purity of this initial love. This transcendent, romanticized move allows the film to cross borders easily. In contrast, in *Q & A* it is money that ultimately allows Ram to fulfill his dreams and to transform his prostitute-lover into his "lawfully wedded wife, with a proper surname" by paying off her pimp.[90] Thus, Ram reflects in the epilogue of *Q & A*, "I realized long ago that dreams have power only over your mind; but with money you can have power over the minds of others."[91] *Q & A* and *Slumdog Millionaire* are thus geared in subtle ways toward two different kinds of nationalized middle-class audiences in India and the United States and illustrate the nuanced ways in which transnational cultural production is framed through national narratives.

Toward a Theory of Transnational Cultural Representation

I have presented this interpretive comparative analysis of these varying cultural forms in order to unpack the complex dynamics of transnational cultural production and representation. Four key dimensions emerge as building blocks that can lead toward a general theory of transnational cultural production. First, I have sought to relink the interpretation of culture with a conception of the systemic economic conditions that structure relationships between groups and nations and that shape the circulation of cultural products and the affective and representational practices that make up these products. As I have shown, there is a fundamental relationship of economic extraction in which the labor of the subaltern—economic, cultural, and emotional labor—lies at the heart of transnational cultural production. An understanding of this extraction of labor (and the ways in which the political economies of both nation-states and economic globalization structure the extraction in the contemporary context) is necessary for an adequate conceptualization of how affective and representational economies shape the production, circulation, and consumption of cultural forms.

To speak of such mutually constitutive economies is not to return to a reductive or deterministic conception of culture (where economic structure determines cultural practice in a simplistic manner). To that end, the second dimension of a theory of transnational cultural production includes a nuanced and textured understanding of the complex interactions between the form of representation, practices of translation and understanding, and the complexities of reception. Such dynamics are not reducible in deterministic ways to the systemic economic conditions that structure the circulation of cultural products and are shaped by the contingencies of audience, context, and representational tactics.

The last dynamic that shapes transnational cultural production is the interplay between historical continuities and discontinuities. For instance, during the course of this analysis, I have at various points continued to use the categories West and Third World even as I have sought to complicate them by discussing transnational processes of production, distribution, and consumption. Such categories are no longer typically used in transnational feminist analysis. Indeed, they are often viewed as dated forms that either do not depict the complexities of contemporary global processes or serve to homogenize the complex histories and cultures that constitute West and Third World. Why, then, persist with the use of such terms? I have used these categories because they continue to hold analytical and political significance for understandings of transnationalism. The category Third World holds within it the legacies of political histories and cultural representation that continue to shape global processes and that anyone concerned with transnational feminism must continue to confront. This is particularly the case for U.S. audiences—the context in which the paradigm of transnationalism has emerged and now circulates through various institutional sites of the U.S. academy. Contemporary American political and cultural discourses have continued to be shaped by narratives that rest on the assumption of a clash of civilizations between Western and post-colonial Islamic societies in South Asia and the Middle East. Meanwhile, regions within Latin America and Africa are also still subject to long-standing representations of these nations as sites of poverty and violent disorder—representations that are conflated with anxieties over immigration and race. These depictions, of course, may take new forms, but more often than not they draw on older colonial legacies and hegemonic understandings of regions that were once termed the "Third World."

The Third World is thus a category that holds within it particular forms of historical memory and unsettles the tendency of feminist thought to continually drive toward the creation of new theoretical languages that replace older modes of analysis.[92] This tendency to assume that intellectual progress requires the replacement of old categories represents a linear mode of thought that is built into dominant modes of interdisciplinary knowledge, particularly those that have built on poststructuralist/postcolonial approaches. I examine the problems inherent in such teleological modes of thought that are built into feminist scholarship more systematically in subsequent chapters. For the purpose of the issues that this chapter seeks to unravel, what is of significance is a reminder that the categories of Third World and West compel us to confront particular legacies of both the histories that cycle through contemporary processes in new ways and the persistence of forms of cultural representation that continually reinvoke these histories through the practices of the imagination. The terrain of the "transnational" is not a transcendent space that can escape such historical legacies.

Consider, for instance, recent examples in mainstream American discourses. The well-known Internet news site *Huffington Post* (one that identifies with the ideological liberal-left and has a significant impact on mainstream American public debates) has published series of news reports on "Third World America." The reports, playing off the title *Third World America*, the new book by the Internet news site's founder Ariana Huffington, focuses on expanding poverty and the decline of the American middle class in the context of the ongoing U.S. economic crisis. Meanwhile, Michael Lewis has also depicted the global financial crisis through such symbolic codes in his much-publicized book *Boomerang: Travels in the New Third World*, which focuses on countries such as Ireland, Iceland, the United States, and Germany.[93] The Third World is coded as a symbol of poverty and crisis. Such rhetoric marks a deep national anxiety over the decline of the American nation, a decline that will take it from its old status of sole superpower to an economically "backward" Third World nation.

To speak of such historical legacies is not to assume or argue that all transnational processes are reduced to an interminable confrontation between two homogeneous entities such as Third World and West. Certainly feminist scholars have pointed out, for instance, that dominant conceptions of the West often erase or ignore the specificities of Europe, particularly in terms of the difference between Western European and post-socialist histories within Eastern Europe.[94] Furthermore, the expanding economic power and geopolitical importance of countries such as India, Brazil, and China are significantly reshaping contemporary international relations. Moreover, as my analysis has shown, the politics of representation is shaped as much by inequalities within postcolonial societies as by relationships between nations. Nevertheless, the categories of Third World and West are representational devices that compel audiences interested in U.S. transnational feminism to confront the historical legacies of colonialism that precede and live within contemporary American imaginings of the world. A careful consideration of historical discontinuities provides a crucial dimension of any transnational project of cultural interpretation. We have seen, for instance, the differences that emerge from two routes—an older colonial journey between India and Britain that *Bandit Queen* takes, and the globalized, hypermediated narrative of *Slumdog Millionaire*.

Conclusion

The dynamics of transnational representation that I have been analyzing become particularly important when we move from a focus on cultural production to a broader discussion of knowledge production. As with cultural production, the forms of knowledge we produce are created in particular places (nations, regions, institutional sites), for particular audiences, and with implications and effects that we often do not intend or foresee. India's *Bandit Queen* and *Slumdog Millionaire*, in this sense, are simply parables for the dynamics of our own creations within the academy. It is with the intent of calling attention to these questions that I have used the expression "U.S. transnational feminism." These questions stem in part from the kinds of discrepancies of representation I have analyzed in this chapter. However, they also challenge us to move beyond the realm of representation. Forms of knowledge that become dominant within the United States have complex and uneven implications that are discursive and material. I thus turn to a broader discussion of U.S. transnational feminist knowledge within the academy in the following chapters.

4

Regimes of Visibility and Transnational Feminist Knowledge

THE STUDY OF transnational feminism is a historically specific paradigm that has emerged in response to the intensification of transnational flows associated with the contemporary epoch of globalization. The study of transnational feminism specifically arose in response to a growing emphasis on the limits of territorially bound nation-states in a range of studies and theories that sought to make sense of the impact of globalization. The limits of the nation-state were apparent in a number of realms. In economic terms, the movement of capital across borders (and the growing scale and power of transnational corporations), the dependence of a growing number of nation-states on economic support from international organizations such as the International Monetary Fund and the World Bank, and the growth of economic linkages through rapid movements of finance capital all seemed to point to a growing set of limits on the power of nation-states. The expansion of new technologies of communication has meant that the idea of the "imagined community" was no longer confined to the territorial borders of the modern nation-state.[1] Meanwhile, social movements responding to global economic and political changes have used new technologies and transnational spaces of communication to develop new forms of transnational activism that built on but also exceeded local and national histories and practices of organizing. In the context of feminist research and practice, for instance, feminist activists crossed national borders to produce transnational forms of women's organizing, and feminist researchers produced a rich scholarship on gender, globalization, and transnationalism.[2]

Such scholarship has not ignored or displaced the study of the nation-state. On the contrary, transnational feminist research has sought to develop critical analyses of the nation and has sought to explore the linkages between the local, national, and transnational realms of analysis. Transnational feminist studies of the nation-state seek to address how these new and distinctive spaces are reconfiguring and being shaped by local and national forces. The analytical cut embodied in this kind of transnational perspective is framed by a critical engagement with the nation-state. This approach to feminism is distinctive in the perspective that it has brought to the study of such questions and the way it has begun to displace existing approaches to the study of international and comparative feminist issues. The dominant paradigm of transnational feminism that has emerged in the U.S. academy is thus associated with a more specific set of analytical, theoretical, and political concerns.[3] Comparative and international approaches to feminist research generally sought either to examine feminist questions within different national and cultural contexts or to address the relationships and interaction between women from various local and national backgrounds. In contrast, transnational feminist approaches rest on an assumption that there are new and distinctive spaces, sites, practices, and discourses that cannot or should not be grasped within the analytical lens of nations and states. Whether the analytical lens is framed in terms of the perspectives of local agents negotiating, resisting, or shaping such broader transnational forces, or in terms of an analysis of the transnational sites themselves (and their effects on local communities of women), what is consistent in such approaches is the identification of a distinctive transnational space or site around which such agencies unfold.[4]

The question that I address in this chapter asks, what have been the implications of this paradigm of transnational feminism for the nature and direction of feminist knowledge production? This question is particularly significant given the increasingly dominant status of transnational feminist perspectives. In interdisciplinary spaces such as women's studies, feminist intellectual norms generally rest on the assumption that transnational approaches to the study of cross-national, cross-cultural questions represent a new, cutting-edge approach to interdisciplinary work. The result, as I argue in this chapter, is that the paradigm of transnational feminism has begun to serve as a framing device that orients feminist research within a particular set of methodological, substantive, and conceptual narratives. The analytical impetus of transnational feminist approaches to delineate new spaces that have moved beyond older formations associated with the territoriality of the nation-state has begun to discipline this paradigm in particular ways. First, the production of transnational feminism has become entrenched in a regime of visibility that shapes its terms and conceptions. More often than not, the new spaces that transnational feminist approaches identify are associated with specific kinds of border-crossing issues. The old territoriality of the nation-state is thus implicitly contrasted with a new, often deterritorialized, border-crossing form of transnationalism. The "trans" in "transnational-ism" in effect becomes literally represented by movement across national borders. As a result, the definition of transnationalism becomes skewed by a set of methodological biases that are oriented toward particular kinds of visible border-crossing issues. Transnational feminist research becomes en-trenched in a particular regime of visibility that skews our understandings of and ways of knowing the world. Transnational perspectives themselves be-gin to embody a limited geographic imagination through which we inadver-tently see like the nation-state. Geraldine Pratt, for example, has eloquently argued that her work in Canada with Philippine migrant women has shown her that "feminist academics have the responsibility to scrutinize how their geographical imaginations have been shaped by their institutional and na-tional contexts, and the ways that they may (despite their best intentions) 'see like the state,' whether this be by reproducing Russian-doll models of care and responsibility, overgeneralizing the reach of knowledge developed in the global North, erasing the global South, or conceiving places outside the global North through tropes of poverty and underdevelopment."[5] Pratt draws on Doreen Massey's critique of a Russian-doll model of care and re-sponsibility in the West, where care focuses first on people and issues closest to home and then gradually expands outward.[6] Such a perspective challenges us to move further and interrogate the borders that may implicitly undergird our visions of transnational feminism.

To grasp the complexities of transnational feminist perspectives and to address both the limits and the possibilities of such approaches, we need a nuanced understanding of the practices and processes of interdisciplinary knowledge production. Interdisciplinary feminist knowledge has already been steeped in a long tradition of addressing the relationship between power and knowledge.[7] Such approaches often focus on epistemological questions that have addressed the long histories of power and inequality that are embedded in our ways of knowing about the world. Such work has been particularly powerful in illustrating how violent histories of race, colonialism, and empire lurk behind and within conceptions of knowledge of "other" countries, cultures, and worlds. While I build on the crucial insights of such scholarship, I also argue that an adequate understanding of paradigms such as transnational feminist must engage both with the materiality of the worlds we seek or claim to know and with the kinds of practices that we use in this process of knowing. A focus on knowledge as a purely epistemological process tends to restrict our discussions to a narrow, textual-discursive realm where practice then becomes restricted to developing new strategies of representation rather than new ways of engaging with the world. I specifically argue for a broader approach that can address the layered dimensions of knowledge production: the epistemological (how we know), the ontological (the materiality of knowledge), and the practical (the realm of ethical/political agency).

This kind of approach draws on a long history of scholarship that has sought to address knowledge production in nuanced ways. Consider, for instance, three influential but very different examples that have specifically combined epistemological, ontological, and ethical/political understandings of knowledge—works by Karl Marx, Gloria Anzaldúa, and Karen Barad. I draw on these three examples because each provides a distinct and important example of intellectual work that has sought to bridge the epistemological, ontological, and practical realms through very different interdisciplinary approaches. Such examples provide a historicized sense of intellectual context both within and outside the academy for a discussion of our contemporary concerns with transnational feminism. Marx's theoretical writings on political, economic, and sociocultural life represent an early example of a distinctively transnational analysis and are a useful reminder that the move to the transnational is not a new improvisation of the postmodern period of late capitalist globalization. His analysis of the operations of capitalism systematically pointed to the limits of the nation-state in ways that ironically would put him at odds with the actual rise of nationalisms in much of the colonized world.[8] Decades of Marxist and post-Marxist scholarship have pointed to and reworked the limits of Marx's conceptions of materiality. Critics have argued that Marx's conceptions tended to treat labor as a homogeneous category, missing the ways in which the material structures of race, gender, and colonialism were central to the workings of modern capitalism.[9] Nevertheless, Marx's systemic understanding of capitalism remains of continued significance in understanding dynamics within the global political economy of the twenty-first century that go well beyond the specificities of particular policies that are now characterized as neoliberalism and are applied in various ways in cross-national contexts.

In this endeavor, Marx specifically grappled with the epistemological, ontological, and ethical dimensions of knowledge.[10] Thus, he sought to interrogate our understanding of "value," pointing to the ways in which capital and the creation of value were in fact a materialization of the labor of the working classes. Marx's approach was both epistemological, as it sought to analyze categories such as "capital" and "value" (how these categories were known and misrecognized), and ontological, as he sought to analyze the material workings of modern capitalism. This epistemological and ontological approach was central to Marx's normative-ethical understanding of political action. For Marx, the discursive-material purpose of knowledge was fundamentally linked to a set of principles of social and economic justice. The point of knowledge, as his well-known ethical imperative noted, was not just to interpret the world but to change it.[11] Thus, his various writings cut across the boundaries between the ontological/ethical/epistemological realms and between the theoretical, normative, and political dimensions of his analysis.

Gloria Anzaldúa's work is of course strikingly different from that of Marx—in method, embodied social location, representational style, and empirical emphasis. Anzaldúa's classic text *Borderlands* is one of the earliest examples of transnational feminist scholarship in the United States. In her autobiographical-historical discussion of borders, she moves effortlessly between the material and territorial borders between the United States and Mexico that make her life and cultural history. For Anzaldúa, the borders of her psyche provide the psychic/political/cultural space for her to move beyond the violence of those territiorialized borders. As she puts it, "I know things older than Freud."[12] Like Marx, Anzaldúa seeks to keep in tension the ontological, epistemological, and ethical dimensions of knowledge. Her creative objective is both epistemological (as she engages in rewriting her cultural genealogy) and ontological (as she portrays a transformative rematerialization of her psyche-body). Yet it is also fundamentally ethical, as she discusses an approach that breaks from a praxis that rests on an oppositional form of politics that demonizes or acts in counterstance to the oppressor and as she seeks to provide a spiritually rooted conception of transformation.

In line with these early examples of work that has sought to capture the complex configuration of the material, discursive, and ethical-political realms that shape knowledge production, Karen Barad has more recently contributed to this endeavor through her theory of agential realism. In *Meeting the Universe Halfway*, Barad explicitly argues for an approach that incorporates the ontological, epistemological, and ethical dimensions of knowledge production.[13] Drawing on her disciplinary expertise in quantum physics and on the work of Niels Bohr, Barad demonstrates how our knowledge practices literally make material marks in the world. Our knowledge practices materialize the world that we seek to know in ways that make the ethical practices and principles that we bring to our work a core element of any discussion of knowledge production. For Barad, knowledge production—including the practice of theory building—is made up of material, embodied practices. As she illustrates through an analysis of a variety of physical phenomena (including experimental practices such as the measurement of light and the use of ultrasound technology), the cuts produced by measurement and observation materially shape the objects of observation in ways that break down a presumed divide between the agencies and objects of observation or between modes of representation and material reality.[14]

I juxtapose the approaches of Marx, Anzaldúa, and Barad to provide three examples of work that shows us the complex ways in which the three dimensions of knowledge production (the ontological, epistemological, and the ethical) interact in very different attempts to understand the world. An adequate understanding of the implications of interdisciplinary work on transnational feminism requires a nuanced approach that examines all three of these aspects of knowledge production. I argue in this chapter that this broader approach to knowledge production provokes us to understand transnational processes in ways that break from the regimes of visibility that shape contemporary transnational feminist research and complicates existing understandings of the relationship between power and knowledge that shape such interdisciplinary scholarship. The early examples of Marx and Anzaldúa, for instance, challenge us to return a sense of history to existing discussions of transnationalism—in terms of both the need to historicize the paradigm of transnationalism and the need to develop a fuller acknowledgment of the intellectual histories and genealogies of current approaches. Meanwhile, Barad's argument that "practices of knowing are specific material engagements that participate in reconfiguring the world" highlights the stakes involved in discussions of knowledge production and the effects of a paradigm such as "transnationalism."[15] However, the examples of Marx, Anzaldúa, and Barad also provide us with three very different ways of thinking about the interaction between the epistemological, ontological, and ethical practices that make up our knowledge of the worlds in which we live.[16] They seek to know and make very different realities despite a shared normative-ethical concern with the creation of a new and just world. These differences should caution us against assuming that there is any formulaic solution to engaging with or creating knowledge about the world or that anyone can foresee the consequences of the work that they produce. Knowledge production is a much riskier act than we sometimes realize.

It is with this set of challenges and cautions that I attempt in this chapter to examine the implications of the paradigm of transnational feminism that has emerged within the U.S. academy. My interests in this endeavor are both deconstructive and constructive. I begin with a critical discussion of dominant trends in the field and examine the regime of visibility that orients transnational feminist research. However, I also seek to examine productive practices that emerge from this body of scholarship and point to potential responses to some of the limitations of this body of knowledge. My objective in this chapter is to discuss the paradigm of transnational feminism by explicitly holding in tension the epistemological, ontological, and ethical dimensions of knowledge production in order to provide an analysis of the implications that this paradigm holds for feminist engagements with the world.

Regimes of Visibility and the Terms of Transnational Feminism

One of the overarching trends in transnational feminist research is the systematic attention to the emergence of new sites and spaces that move us beyond the territorial borders of nation-states. The development of a transnational feminist approach in feminist intellectual circles within the U.S. academy now presumes a perspective that moves beyond the analytical lens of the nation-states that are associated with earlier international studies. The result of this trend is an orientation of transnational feminist research toward two intellectual imperatives. First, transnational feminist research is largely oriented toward the study of border-crossing cultural, political, and socioeconomic phenomena. Second, this search for border-crossing sites has inadvertently led to an emphasis on empirical and theoretical work that extrapolates from sites that are characterized by particular markers of visibility.

The implications of this drive for the visible can be seen in the way in which this analytical orientation has shaped transnational feminist approaches to the study of political economy. One of the central areas of research in the field of transnational feminism is the study of economic globalization and the effects of globalization in various contexts. A review of the literature reveals that much of the scholarship that is associated with transnational feminism centers on the study of a recurring set of sites. These dominant sites of analysis tend to be export-processing zones, the impact of international aid regimes on women, new sites and practices of consumption, cross-national labor migration, and, more recently, gendered forms of outsourcing such as call centers. Consider, for example, recent trends in feminist research on labor and globalization. Transnational feminist research has produced important insights about the impact of globalization on labor, and on the reworking of identities of class and gender.[17] Such studies have provided rich, qualitative research on the ways in which transnational political-economic processes have reconfigured local, national, and state practices in ways that rest on material and discursive conceptions of class, gender, and race. Aihwa Ong's ethnographic study of women workers in export-processing zones in Malaysia became a classic text that marked a growing focus on the ways in which a gendered division of labor was producing a workforce of young female workers in comparative contexts.[18] Ong's work engaged in a careful analysis of the ways in which local constructions of gender and ethnicity shaped the construction of this workforce and in turn sparked local and culturally specific forms of women's resistance. Other central areas of feminist research on transnational political economy have sought to address specific forms of labor such as global sex tourism and sex work, and the rise of global care chains that have tracked female migrant workers into domestic work. Rhacel Parreñas, for example, has shown how complex interactions between the state in the Philippines and the global political economy have structured the migration of Filipina domestic workers to the United States and Europe.[19] Such global care chains have reshaped the community identities and lives of Filipina workers in complex ways and have also transformed domestic political dynamics within both the Philippines and the recipient countries in the West. Or, to take another example, Bishop and Robison examine the rise of the sex tourism industry in Thailand, analyzing the ways in which sexualized neo-orientalist desires of Western tourists converged with the Thai state's use of sex tourism to drive the tourism industry that has served as the country's primary export-oriented industry. Thus, they illustrate the ways in which racialized conceptions of gender and sexuality lie at the heart of the Thai state's economic development strategy even as the state and public culture within Thailand participate in a shared denial of the existence of sex tourism in the country. These examples point to the ways in which studies of transnational feminist political economy have expanded traditional analyses of political economy by making visible particular gender and racialized forms of labor and by contributing to our understandings of how transnational economic processes intersect with local practices and state agendas.

While such individual studies have enriched our understandings of transnational feminism, the continued replication of the theoretical and methodological orientations of this body of work has begun to discipline transnational perspectives in significant ways. Transnational feminist approaches are now shaped by an increasingly uniform analytical lens and a restricted set of empirical sites of analysis. Consider the routinized list of empirical sites that now generally constitute research on transnational feminist political economy. These sites tend to be empirical arenas (whether they are discursive, spatial, institutional, or practice-centered) that are characterized by some marker of a territorially based transnationalism. In other words, these sites represent a formation that embodies some aspect of a territorial border-crossing movement. For example, scholarship on economic globalization usually focuses on two types of issues. Such scholarship tends to analyze the politics of globalization in terms of an interplay between multinational corporations and international organizations, on the one hand, and marginalized social groups, on the other. Meanwhile, analyses of labor and globalization have tended to focus almost exclusively on patterns of employment within export-oriented processing zones or within other self-evident transnational spaces such as the sex tourism industry and migrant workers' communities. The underlying conception that shapes such research is one that equates contemporary globalization with sites of analysis that are already marked as spaces that transcend the nation-state. Multinational corporations, international aid organizations (such as the World Bank), and export-processing zones are all literally transnational sites as they are territorial or institutional zones that are partly or fully beyond the authority of the nation-state.

As I have illustrated earlier, such research has produced rich and often groundbreaking ethnographies and sociological accounts of changing class and gender relations. However, the internal richness of individual studies is flattened out when the entire field of transnational feminist research becomes associated with these particular theoretical and empirical orientations. The pitfalls of this territorial definition of the transnational lie not with individual studies but with the cumulative effects of a paradigm of transnationalism that becomes disciplined by the kind of transnational perspective that has become dominant in feminist scholarship.

Earlier feminist work has already called attention to some of the pitfalls of the politics of border-crossing in feminist knowledge production. For instance, in her essay comparing dowry murders in India and domestic violence in the United States, Uma Narayan cautions us to consider the ways in which depictions of particular forms of violence against women cross borders.[20] She specifically calls on us to pay attention to the "features of context that 'bring' particular issues onto feminist agendas, mold the information that is available on the issue, and shape as well as distort the ways in which they are understood when the issue 'crosses borders.'"[21] Narayan is discussing the ways in which dowry deaths in India are miscast in the United States as a kind of "death by culture" rather than as comparable to forms of domestic violence that are present in the United States. When recognition of these issues crosses borders, as she argues, this form of violence is decontextualized and becomes a visible, static mark of cultural otherness.

In recent years, the study of transnational feminism has moved far beyond such stereotypical kinds of border-crossing that Narayan criticizes. Indeed, much of transnational feminist and postcolonial work has in fact sought to call attention to and move beyond this very politics of othering by addressing the complexities of gendered and sexual subjectivities. However, the pitfalls regarding context and travel that Narayan expresses in this essay resurface in more subtle ways in current narratives of transnational feminism. More specifically, I argue that the problem at hand is that the question of border-crossing has itself become a deterministic intellectual foundation of transnational feminism. The result is that the study of transnational feminism is skewed toward issues that cross borders in ways that produce new forms of methodological and empirical biases.

Consider, for example, Grewal and Kaplan's attempt to critically rethink conceptions of transnationalism.[22] Grewal and Kaplan point to some of the limits of the ways in which transnational research is currently deployed in interdisciplinary fields. They note, for instance, that transnational perspectives often produce a divide between American studies and transnational studies of the rest of the world, and they also examine how the term "transnationalism" has often become a kind of shorthand signifier of global research that has become dislocated from understandings of colonial histories and transnational relationships of power. While these are important points for consideration, Grewal and Kaplan fail to recognize a deeper limitation in current transnational research that is not reducible to the political dynamics of the usage of the term "transnationalism." Rather, the deeper issue at hand lies with the ways in which the emphasis on the transnational has been framing and consequently disciplining what is included and excluded in our understanding of the world. Take, for example, the solution that Grewal and Kaplan provide in response to problems with the term. They conclude their analysis by pointing to possible future trajectories of analysis. In this endeavor they cite refugee asylum and human rights, travel and tourism, migration/immigration, and global policy responses to HIV/AIDS as examples of the kinds of research that should guide the future of transnational studies. What is significant in their array of examples is that they start with an analytical understanding of transnationalism as a concept that once again begins with a set of issues that cross national borders. The spatial understanding of the transnational as a concept that begins with an analysis of processes that transcend smaller spheres at the local and national level (even if they interact with these other levels of analysis) is left intact. The problem at hand is not, of course, that these specific issues are not of critical significance but that the skewing of the empirical sites embedded in this interdisciplinary directive produces a biased understanding of the contexts and countries that supply this analysis. The gaps in knowledge that are produced by this form of transnational feminist scholarship that focuses purely on such zones of activity are significant. The drive of transnational feminist research becomes oriented toward identifying new sites of cross-border phenomena when in fact critical factors that affect women's lives may be shaped by actors and agendas that are not solely or primarily driven by global processes.

Consider the ways in which such an approach can provide a skewed understanding of the relationship between gender, globalization, and the state. The current preoccupation with outsourcing is generating a new interest in the gendered and class-based politics of outsourcing in countries like India. Feminist studies of the call center industry in India have provided valuable analyses of the intersections of gender and class.[23] Indeed, the large concentration of women workers within the industry has marked it as a site that signifies the gendered nature of globalization in ways that parallel the focus on women workers in export-oriented zones and other gender-specific economic sites. However, when the study of gender, class, and labor restricts its analytical focus to such sites, it provides a distorted understanding of gender and political economy in India. This kind of distortion occurs in a number of ways. First, such a focus tends to reduce the study of political economy to specific zones of economy that are governed in some way by transnational companies. The result is the creation of systemic gaps in the research and analysis associated with transnational feminism. Despite the liberalization of India's economy since the 1990s, economic activity is not reducible to such zones. This kind of transnational frame of political economy thus misses both the sizable role of both domestic Indian companies and the state (both in shaping economic policies and in state-owned public sector industries that are still important economic forces). Such arenas have unsurprisingly also been marked by inequalities of gender and class. A dominant transnational framing of gender and globalization thus ignores the complex interaction between the state, Indian capital, and domestic markets that are as important as the global-oriented growth associated with "neoliberalism." This transnational frame paradoxically provides this model of neoliberal growth with an over-determined agency.

The second set of biases associated with a narrowly defined transnational analytical frame is linked more specifically to the kinds of conclusions and explanations that are derived from research on the transnational sites themselves. Feminist analyses of labor that take call centers or export-processing zones as the sole or foundational site of analysis miss the ways in which outsourcing is an extension of earlier gendered processes of labor market restructuring that have been undertaken by both Indian and global companies as a consequence of state and elite-driven policies of economic liberalization. On one level, these approaches may either conceal the role of state agendas in driving such policies or misidentify causal processes when identifying the factors that lead to the reproduction of intersecting inequalities (by presuming that the entry of foreign capital is the primary factor shaping or producing inequalities of class and gender). On another level, the focus on self-evident neoliberal economic zones of employment may overemphasize the gendered effects of these zones by presuming that these are the most significant places where women workers are employed. In practice, the implications of such transnational zones of economic activity vary widely depending on the specificities of national political economies. For instance, smaller countries with histories of colonialism may have relatively undifferentiated economies that have made them highly dependent on specific kinds of export-oriented sectors. Thus, for instance, transnational feminist research on the political economy of Caribbean societies has rightly emphasized these transnational zones because of their outsized economic role in these national economies.[24] Similarly, the strong history of international aid agencies intervening in a country like Bangladesh and the long, complex history (and tension) between international organizations, NGOs, and the state make it relevant to emphasize the ways in which transnational aid regimes shape local and national economies and rework class, gender, and sexuality.[25] However, the impact of both transnational economic forces and aid regimes plays out very differently in diversified economies in countries such as Brazil and China. Furthermore, differing state policies on social welfare and public sector employment mean that transnational economic regimes must be contextualized in very different ways. Some states may publicly embrace a transnational "neoliberal" regime, but popular political pressure may mean that national budgets may reflect a more complex set of economic priorities. Furthermore, the state's approach to this neoliberal regime may vary widely and may have as much to do with specific regional formations (such as the European Union or the regional trends in Latin America) than with a generic form of transnationalism.

Consider another example that points to the limits of this kind of transnational framing of contemporary issues. Contemporary feminist scholarship on globalization has produced a vast and expanding literature on gender, class, and consumption. Such scholarship once again focuses on the visible sites associated with globalization, such as shopping malls, advertising images, and varied social practices associated with emerging lifestyle cultures sparked by globalization in various nations. As with the examples of call centers and women working in export-processing zones, such research often rests on a methodological approach that identifies new cultural spaces such as consumption practices and media technologies that transform or transcend older locales or spaces of activity and subject formation.[26] The methodological tendency evident in this approach is to first begin by identifying sites and spaces that are signifiers of border-crossing sociocultural processes and then to extrapolate and analyze the local and national contexts that surround these sites. In the process, dislocated studies of non-Western consumer subjectivities can often provide empirically flawed studies that overestimate the nature and reach of changing consumption and lifestyle practices. Such studies have led to erroneous depictions of non-Western middle-class consumers as homogeneous transnational elites or global flexible citizens.[27] The result is that transnational feminist research has often missed the political significance of internal socioeconomic differentiation within non-Western contexts. Thus, despite the vast feminist literature that has sought to move away from stereotypical views of non-Western women, transnational feminist research on class, gender, and globalization has tended to reproduce a binary of subaltern laboring women and consuming elites.

I have been using these examples of gender, class, and globalization as illustrative points to draw some broad strokes of recent trends in transnational feminist research. My objective, as I have noted, is not to imply that all transnational feminist research fits this model or that such work has not yielded valuable insights and findings through the individual studies that have come to constitute this paradigm. Rather, I have been suggesting that these dominant trends have begun to discipline feminist knowledge about the world in ways that produce significant gaps, biases, and misunderstandings. However, my objective in engaging in this analysis is not simply to point out these limits but to use this discussion to move to a broader consideration of the politics of knowledge production and to provide constructive ways of thinking about producing knowledge about the world.

I have noted in my discussion of the examples of globalization that orienting narratives of transnational feminist research have been shaped by particular kinds of methodological practices. I have suggested that the concept of transnationalism inadvertently sets in motion a series of methodological biases through the analytical frames it has brought to feminist scholarship. The concept of "the transnational" methodologically orients feminist research toward sites that are visibly identifiable as border-crossing spaces. In this process, transnationalism in effect becomes a territorially bound definition—it is defined by the border-crossing dimension of the particular phenomenon under analysis. Thus, new generations of interdisciplinary scholars seeking to conduct innovative work on gender are drawn to search for and investigate sites of movement, visibility, and newness. At the most basic level, this has to do with simple methodological choices—for instance, how one chooses one's sites of analyses. The practice of choosing one's sites, analytical lens, and research questions based on the imperatives of visible border-crossing issues thus transforms transnational feminism into a historically specific product of the processes of globalization that such research paradoxically wants to interrogate. However, the limits of dominant trends in transnational feminism do not arise simply because of a "presentist," ahistorical emphasis on contemporary issues or current events. Certainly, historicizing transnational feminism can unsettle some of its disciplinary orientation both by calling attention to different spatial-temporal ways of organizing social, cultural, and political life and by compelling us to immerse ourselves in historical worlds in comparative contexts that do not fit the historically specific commonsense webs of meaning of our own locations. A historical perspective can also dislodge assumptions that transnational or cross-border flows are new or unique to the current moment or that they are uniquely defined by U.S.-centric diasporas. However, the limitations of dominant understandings of transnational feminism are not reducible to the problem of historicization.

The methodological limits I have pointed to arise in the study of contemporary issues and practices that transnational approaches strive to understand. Thus, the methodological problem at hand is not one of simply noting that a transnational perspective is adequate only for understanding the current global processes. It is a broader problem of the limitations in how global processes are understood as well.

In order to rethink the paradigm of transnational feminism, I engage in a discussion of methodological practices that incorporate three dimensions of knowledge production: the epistemological, the ontological, and the ethical. By addressing this question in terms of methodology, I seek to talk about knowledge as a set of practices that are deconstructive (interrogating the epistemological assumptions of our categories), constructive (engaged in an attempt to produce and represent particular places and worlds), and accountable (responsible for the effects that our knowledge has in shaping the worlds we write about and inhabit).

Worlds of Representation

Most transnational feminist debates on knowledge production have tended to focus on the epistemological realm—that is, they have focused on questions of how we know. One of the dominant trends in this epistemological understanding of transnational feminist knowledge production has been the feminist concern with strategies of representation and the dominant categories of thought in order to consider the power effects of knowledge. More specifically, such work has focused on the structures of inequality between the First World and the Third World that have historically shaped projects of transnational feminism. Such work has a long and rich intellectual history. Chandra Mohanty's essay "Under Western Eyes" pointed to the ways in which feminist research that depicted Third World women as a homogenized group of victims devoid of agency and subjectivity inadvertently ended up engaging in a kind of discursive recolonization of the women being represented in such research.[28] Meanwhile, Gayatri Spivak challenged the epistemological innocence of work that sought to depict subaltern voices and histories.[29] These classic texts sparked a new generation of scholarship that highlighted the problems inherent in attempting to represent non-Western women in transnational research. Consequently, a wide range of feminist research has attempted to respond to the power dynamics of knowledge practices by engaging in self-reflexive ethnographies, including women's voices, emphasizing women's agencies and subjectivities and producing what Donna Haraway has called "situated knowledges."[30]

Consider, for instance, Kamala Visweswaran's dramatization of a series of interviews with women participants in the Indian nationalist movement.[31] In this drama, she portrays the ways in which one woman betrays her friend by revealing to Visweswaran personal information about her friend's private life that the friend had been keeping hidden. Visweswaran's quest for information about these women's lives becomes the basis for the staging of this betrayal of confidence. Visweswaran insightfully points to the ways in which the feminist quest for knowledge in this case rests not on an uncomplicated form of sisterhood but on the power relations and pain of betrayal. Her depiction is illustrative in two ways. First, she depicts this set of events as driven by a predetermined relationship between power and knowledge. As she puts it, "An inquisition had been set in motion and I was its naïve if unwilling architect."[32] Visweswaran, while acknowledging her own agency and accountability, notes further that the issue moves beyond her own agency and culpability: "It has to do with the very organization of knowledge and structure of inquiry."[33] Visweswaran's response to this slippage between inquiry and inquisition turns to the deployment of particular strategies of representation. Thus, by presenting her ethnographic encounters in fictionalized form, she attempts to blunt the colonizing power of ethnographic claims to an objective or pure form of truth.

The deployment of textual strategies of representation in response to feminist discussions of the power-laden nature of knowledge production is in fact one of the central set of practices that feminist scholars use when attempting to navigate between national and global relationships of power. This emphasis on strategies of representation is an important dimension in navigating transnational inequalities of power that shape the production, circulation, and consumption of knowledge. For instance, as I have argued in chapter 3, paying attention to the form of representation (ethnography, film autobiography) and the strategies of representation are all necessary components for developing forms of knowledge that do not recolonize women in ways that Mohanty and others have long cautioned against. In that sense, Visweswaran attempts to strategically rework the form of her representation by blurring the boundaries between ethnography and fictional drama and by engaging in self-reflexive strategies that call attention to the relationships of power embedded in the process of fieldwork.

This attention to the politics of representation and to the epistemological dimension of knowledge production has been an important means of illustrating how our creations have material effects. Feminist scholars have transformed the study of subaltern groups by confronting the ways in which constructions of categories such as "woman" and "gender" can themselves be fraught with the potential to produce exclusions and inequalities.[34] In many ways, this epistemological project has become one of the central foundations of interdisciplinary feminist scholarship. While this epistemological turn of feminist scholarship has been an important and necessary one, it is also ultimately an insufficient response to the challenges of producing transnational feminist research within the complex power relations of a highly globalized world.

The emphasis on discursive textual representations ultimately restricts feminist responses to the epistemological realm in ways that reproduce a divide between epistemology and ontology. What this means in more simple, practical terms is that simply worrying about the textual strategies we use to depict our research restricts our responses to the politics of transnational knowledge production to a series of discursive practices that become disconnected from the very locations and sites that our research seeks to address. In effect, deeper questions regarding the relationship between power and knowledge become reduced to visible textual strategies of representation—a process that mirrors the regime of visibility that I have suggested has shaped the substantive orientation of transnational feminist research.

In my analysis of cultural forms such as the films *Bandit Queen* and *Slumdog Millionaire*, I have discussed the implications that arise from the fact that both the form and the strategies of representation are also contingent on the context, location, and audience of these representations. This discussion of context and my earlier discussion of the structured circulation of cultural products point to the limits of purely epistemological understandings of knowledge production. Economies of representation are also an aspect of the ontological dimensions of the knowledge we produce. While an epistemological response to the relationship between power and knowledge might focus on the tactics of representation, taking ontology seriously compels us to recognize that real material and discursive structures and formations shape the effects of these representations. Thus, in the discussion of the films in chapter 3, my juxtaposition of the differing implications of such cultural forms in different national contexts in effect rests on an acknowledgment that the nation continues to operate as an ontological form that both shapes and is shaped by various forms of knowledge. Or return, for instance, to the example of Visweswaran's dramatic form. Visweswaran's choice to present her research on women in the nationalist movement as a fictionalized narrative represents an epistemological project that simultaneously disrupts the Western desire for "real subaltern women" and an Indian nationalist frame of historical construction. Yet if, as we have seen, fictionalized films have uneven implications in varying local, national, and transnational spaces, fictionalized academic representations cannot escape such uneven representations either. The subversive dimensions of Visweswaran's work potentially disrupt particular relationships of power. Yet the evasion of the task of historical construction that is implicit in Visweswaran's normative response to the problems of representation reproduces a divide between reality and representation that misses what Barad had described as the entangled nature of epistemology and ontology. As Barad has well illustrated, both poststructuralist and social constructivist approaches, on the one hand, and positivist approaches, on the other, in fact rest on a shared dualistic view of reality and representation. The desire to escape from this entanglement stems from a fear of the power-laden dimensions of knowledge production. Such attempted evasion does not lead to a transcendent space of innocence. Consider the fictionalized style that Visweswaran uses. Her approach evades particular power dynamics that stem from the consumption of ethnographic materials. However, given that such work circulates in contexts where the ontology of the nation continues to exist as a material-discursive formation and given that the materiality of historical narratives *matters*, it produces other forms of material-discursive erasures. For instance, through its refusal to address still sizable gaps in the writing of histories that center women's participation in the nationalist movement in ways that call attention to the intersections of caste, class, and gender, it contributes to a continued marginalization of women from historical narratives on the nationalist movement.

Ontological "Areas," Empirical Reality and Knowledge about the Transnational

An understanding of knowledge production as a set of practices that is co-constituted by the material realities of the world unsettles current understandings of the "transnational." Take, for example, the ways in which the regime of visibility that underlies U.S. transnational feminism is linked both to the question of how we come to know the world and to the question of how the world we seek to know shapes our knowledge practices. The tendency to mark the "transnational" through particular visible border-crossing sites such as call centers has more to do with a U.S.-based conception of globalization as outsourcing than it does with a transnational understanding of the political economy of class and gender. Thus, the ontology of the U.S. nation-state continually marks and is shaped by such knowledge practices regardless of whether a particular text uses epistemological strategies of rhetoric and representation to move beyond the nation-state. This means that transnational feminist scholars must confront the ways in which epistemological claims that a transnational perspective transcends older analytical forms such as the nation-state are claims that are materialized in part by a framing that stems from the ontology (material structure) of the U.S. nation-state. Furthermore, such claims, in turn, materially shape the world through the epistemological privileges that stem from this material political location. In other words, epistemological projects that claim to be purely deconstructive and thus beyond the traps of older positivist approaches are never transcendent spaces. Such epistemological projects are materialized in part by the very structures that they claim to have moved beyond.

This materialist, practice-centered approach to knowledge production builds on Karen Barad's theory of agential realism.[35] In discussing agential realism as an approach that integrates ontology, epistemology, and ethical practice Barad notes that realism "is not about representations of an independent reality but about the real consequences, interventions, creative possibilities, and responsibilities of intra-acting within and as part of the world."[36] Drawing on her disciplinary expertise in quantum physics and on Niels Bohr in particular, she argues that knowledge practices are ontological in the sense that they produce material marks on and in the world. Thus, she argues, "The line between subject and object is not fixed, but once a cut is made (i.e., a particular practice is being enacted), the identification is not arbitrary but in fact materially specified and determinate for a given practice."[37] Barad's theory elaborates on complex historical processes that postcolonial scholars have analyzed in an endeavor to illustrate how knowledge practices have materialized the world in which we live.[38] Take Timothy Mitchell's powerful analysis of the modern historical production of "the economy." His work represents a groundbreaking intervention in postcolonial theory that is invaluable for feminist understandings of transnationalism and materiality. Mitchell demonstrates that our contemporary understanding of "the economy" as an autonomous realm that stands apart from society and culture and that can be associated with objective, uniform measurements is a relatively recent phenomenon. Consider, for instance, Mitchell's discussion of British attempts to produce cadastral maps that could systematically represent landownership to facilitate colonial administration and taxation. In keeping with colonial practices in comparative contexts, mapmaking drew on empirical, local knowledge of villages and communities but reorganized this knowledge in ways that materially reshaped these communities and places. As Mitchell illustrates:

> Political power now had a new form: the knowledge and command of space. The old cadastre was assembled from a knowledge of households and villages. Land claims and tax liabilities were the claims and liabilities of communities of persons, and expressed the relations of those communities both to the land and to those in power. Movements of information, revenue and control flowed through these relations. Under the new system, the list of persons was merely "complementary" to the map. . . .Power over persons was to be reorganized as a power over space and persons were merely the units arrayed and enumerated within that space. The spatial order of knowledge was reflected in the method of mapmaking.[39]

This set of knowledge practices that produce a uniform spatialized order, as Mitchell goes on to argue, becomes the emerging space of the Egyptian nation. Mitchell in effect produces a powerful example—one that is replicated in various colonial contexts—of the way in which this particular epistemological cut between people and land through the cadastral survey in effect becomes one of the central means for materializing new power relations that subsequently form the spatial-material structure of the nation-state. As he notes, this particular practice is simply the precursor for the way in which "the economy" itself is materially and discursively marked as an autonomous, abstracted realm that stands apart from and above the people just as the survey transforms land into a spatialized map that stands over the lists of persons and households that live on this land.[40] Once these knowledge formations are created, they become real, material formations. This process of materialization that Mitchell eloquently analyzes is different from a more basic claim that the economy is socially constructed. What is central to Mitchell's analysis is that knowledge practices are material-discursive agencies that make the world in particular, historically contingent ways, and a simplistic rejection of the methods of classification that have made this economy cannot unmake it. Thus, when Mitchell turns to an analysis of economic inequality and structural adjustment in the postcolonial period, he reverts to using both quantitative data and ethnographic observations to show how the economy now both produces and exacerbates inequalities. The economy thus has an ontological existence that has material effects. A complex set of historical, social, and technological processes may have produced this object called the economy by materially marking a realm that did not exist, yet the agential cut of this realm is now a material, ontological part of the world in which live.

Consider what this "ontology of knowing" means for the terms of transnational feminism. Transnational feminist research from such a perspective is not merely representing another part of the world but is engaged in a set of knowledge practices that materially mark this other part of the world as they make it intelligible to an academic audience. From such a perspective, the stakes of transnational feminist research become much higher, since knowledge does not simply represent reality, it also makes reality; in other words, knowledge literally matters. It is this ontology of knowledge that illustrates how and why particular narratives of oppressed Third World women or the need to rescue veiled women from some essentialized cultural oppression could so easily be harnessed in the post-9/11 U.S.-led wars against Iraq and Afghanistan. As I have illustrated in chapter 2, from a feminist ontological perspective, this state-led appropriation of the language of women's rights is more than an example of successful state ideological manipulation. It reveals that such narratives, many of which have originated within certain feminist paradigms, show us how our knowledge practices, the agencies through which we know our world, literally produce marked bodies, in this case as marked targets of war and occupation.

Consider, for instance, the unsettling points of connection between my earlier discussion of the regime of visibility that orients transnational feminist research and the regime of visibility that governs this imperial project of war and empire. Both approaches track power by the border-crossing processes associated with global power relations. In both cases, nations and states become the secondary locus in this equation; sites of interest are determined by measures of visibility and relevance—whether in relation to the global circuits of capital or the movement of militaries. While the normative agendas of transnational feminism and empire could not be more opposed to each other, such a coincidence should at least give us pause to consider the materiality of our knowledge practices. "Transnational" comes dangerously close to a vision that sees like the state and at the very least must remind us that transnationalism is not a neutral epistemological term but a specific conception of feminism that is produced within a particular context that is partly defined by the ontology of the U.S. nation-state. "Transnationalism" in this sense is a territorially bound concept that interacts with and marks the world in particular ways. Seen in this light, the transnational imperative of moving beyond the limits of the nation must be contextualized in relation to the U.S. foreign policy imperatives that have sought to delegitimize claims of sovereignty of specific nation-states. The border-crossing imperative of transnational feminism is of course very different from the border-crossing interventions of the U.S. state. Nevertheless, the U.S. state's border-crossing imperative provides one central set of historical conditions under which transnationalism has emerged as a central paradigm in the United States. The project of transnational feminism—of seeking to know, represent, or engage with another part of the world—thus remains a necessary endeavor but one that is marked by risk and the need for accountability. Furthermore, if knowledge is ontological, a mere refusal of representation cannot suffice. Models of scholarship that seek refuge in refusing to engage with subaltern speech or fictionalizing ethnography end up trying to develop purely discursive, representational strategies to a process of knowledge production that is not just discursive but also material and ethical.

How, then, can interdisciplinary transnational feminist scholarship address this complex configuration of ontology, epistemology, and ethical accountability? The search for responses does not require the invention of a new or overarching formula. In many ways, such responses involve simple steps and a reconsideration of existing knowledge practices. Such responses involve finding constructive practices that can address otherwise paralyzing discussions of power and knowledge. At one level, this can be as simple as a return to an ontological concern with the locations that transnational feminism wants to speak about and the contexts from which transnational feminists speak. For example, I would argue that within the United States, transnational feminism would benefit from a return to aspects of the interdisciplinary approach that has characterized "area studies" research. In this way, the questions that transnational feminist research chooses to highlight would then not be purely determined by what are visible border-crossing issues but would arise from within the histories, contexts, and preoccupations of the specific locations being studied. This project is as much an empirical project as it is theoretical.

There is, of course, now a well-established criticism of area studies programs in the United States. Critics have shown how these programs emerged in the historical context of the U.S. Cold War foreign policy in the 1950s and that both the definition of distinct geographic "areas" and often the intellectual orientation of such programs were shaped by U.S. state interests and ideological conceptions. In that sense the emergence of these interdisciplinary programs of study is a classic example of the ways in which knowledge of the world is shaped and produced by the historical and political specificities of the U.S. nation-state. In more recent years the nature and orientation of such programs have changed significantly. On the one hand, some of the most significant critical discussions of U.S. policy in the Middle East, for instance, have emerged from Middle Eastern studies scholars, and the notion of distinct "areas" has itself been challenged by transnational and diasporic approaches. Border-crossing in this sense has had a productive set of effects by unsettling the idea that the world is divided into a set of static areas that emerged from an American Cold War imagination. Nevertheless, despite both these limits and reorientations, one of the underlying intellectual foundations of area-based programs has been the emphasis on very specific and basic kinds of knowledge—of language and history, for instance—that contribute to a broader ontological understanding of place, nation, and region.

Taking ontology seriously means taking aspects of positivist approaches to empirical research seriously. This would require that we ask whether particular texts or frames of analysis that are being produced or disseminated within interdisciplinary women's studies are empirically accurate representations of the places that they represent. The dominance of postpositivist thought in interdisciplinary research has meant that questions about empirical research have increasingly been sidelined. Certainly the methodological restrictions of heavily positivist disciplines such as political science, economics, and to a lesser extent sociology have made interdisciplinary scholars nervous about questions of methodological rigor and empirical accuracy. Feminists in particular have had cause for wariness given that so much of feminist writing has had to call attention to hidden forms of power or practices that shape everyday life but that have not been discernible by the dominant positivist eye of social science research.

However, without attention to questions of the empirical, interdisciplinary fields that seek to know about the world risk producing an insidious form of orientalism. Edward Said, in his theory of the rise of orientalist knowledge, illustrated the ways in which the European production of knowledge of "other" places and cultures had more to do with European self-images and fantasies about the Other than with the realities of life in these places.⁴¹ These images circulated through a kind of politics of citationality in which novels, travel accounts, and academic writings produced a construction of the Orient that had little to do with the complex civilizations and polities they claimed to represent. The practice of citationality rested on the ways in which writers and thinkers in disparate fields would build on and cite metaphors, narratives, and stereotypes in recurring narratives. While much postcolonial theory has built on and extended Said's arguments to illustrate the colonial relations of ruling that extended from and used these knowledge practices, it is also useful to remember that within their own societies, these scholars and thinkers were not necessarily politically conservative or self-conscious apologists of empire.⁴²

The contemporary historical context of knowledge production is of course marked by both continuities and discontinuities from colonial times. Certainly, as I have shown in earlier chapters, orientalist constructions continue to circulate within public spheres. What is distinctive about the contemporary organization of knowledge in the United States of course is the growth of organized interdisciplinary fields that have specifically sought to address, understand, and negotiate these histories of power and knowledge. However, the danger of an uninterrogated postpositivist foundation for interdisciplinary approaches such as transnational feminism is that it risks producing knowledge that replicates this politics of citationality. The unspoken ground of this new form of citationality is a self-referential world of interdisciplinary theory and research that builds on and cites visible texts, theories, and issues that have gained currency and attention within the dominant paradigms of the field.⁴³ The world that is materialized through such citational dynamics is divorced from ontological reality in ways that parallel the making of the "Orient" in colonial times.

Such a call for a return to a systematic discussion of empirical research does not lead to a reinscription of a disjuncture between representation/epistemology and ontology/reality. There is too often in current dominant models of interdisciplinary research a confusion between empirical and empiricist research (the latter conforming to models of positivist research that presume an objective transcendent investigator). Certainly, as I have been arguing throughout this chapter, feminist theoretical conceptions of "strong objectivity" and "agential realism" remind us of the significance of addressing the empirical world. However, such a call asks us to think about the interactions between methods, empirical worlds, and epistemological questions in more complex ways.⁴⁴

Consider two of the examples that I have already discussed in this chapter. I have noted that interdisciplinary research on consumption has often overestimated the impact of changing consumption practices and the emergence of new lifestyles. Such work, preoccupied with the visibility of changes in late-industrializing countries and with the theoretical power of extrapolating from new languages and cultural expressions, has often overestimated the impact of such changes. The methodological responses to such inaccuracies are fairly simple ones. For instance, if a scholar were to systematically analyze data on consumption before she framed her research questions, she would bring a more precise analytical lens to her research. In this case, empirical research on consumption patterns is necessary to define an adequate research agenda. Questions of how to develop concepts to understand changes that have occurred (academic discourse production that stems from epistemological concerns) then arise out of this systematic empirical analysis.

On the other hand, consider the comparative example of dowry deaths in India and domestic violence in the United States that Uma Narayan insightfully juxtaposes.[45] In Narayan's hypothetical empirical estimations, the numbers of incidents of domestic violence in the two countries are comparable. The explanation for the fact that the Indian example is constructed as an essentialized "death by culture," in contrast to the U.S. example, requires an epistemological project that examines how we come to know and understand such empirical facts. In this instance, an epistemological project precedes a clear understanding of these two patterns of violence against women.

I juxtapose these brief examples to illustrate how the interrelationship and tensions between methods of research, empirical approximations of ontological realities, and epistemological interrogations of categories and concepts can productively enrich transnational feminist research in practical and sometimes fairly simple ways. However, as I will argue in the next chapter, institutional practices, cultures, and attitudes have begun to structure interdisciplinary feminist research in ways that have made it particularly challenging to systematically address such issues in ways that can enrich programs of cross-national and transnational research and teaching. Moreover, this task also requires bringing back a form of epistemological humility within interdisciplinary feminist spaces so that transnational feminist research does not simply become reduced to the discursive production of new paradigms and remains open to the realization that when ontology matters, a range of methods, epistemologies, and paradigms become necessary to know and materialize the world in transformative ways. The commitment to the transformative possibilities of knowledge that undergird much of feminist writing brings us, then, to the centrality of the question of ethics and ethical action in any discussion of knowledge as practice.

Accountable Knowledge and the Risk of Ethics

Much of the existing scholarship on transnational feminism has focused on knowledge production and the reproduction of relationships of power. The realm of ethics and ethical action is often left implicit within such discussions—it surfaces instead through discussions of the politics of fieldwork, the need to avoid the reproduction of colonial discourses in representations of "the other," and the attempts to connect transnational activism with research and writing.[46] Making this focus on ethics explicit opens up two central areas of concern for transnational feminism. First, it enables a practice-oriented conception of knowledge that breaks from existing preoccupations with visibility; such a conception of knowledge production as ethical practice becomes particularly significant given the ways in which knowledge itself participates in the materialization of the world, as I have argued in this chapter. The question of linking ethics and knowledge is not a new project—nor is it an idyllic or self-evident space that is free of power relations. The second area of concern for transnational feminist perspectives thus has to do with the ways in which the realm of ethics is itself shaped by place, history, and culture. Ethics is often a fraught terrain, and leaving the realm of the ethical unmarked may itself lead to the imposition of particular social, political, and cultural norms.

Feminists have long grappled with ethical issues in their discussions of fieldwork, activism, and knowledge production: questions of how one gains access to information and to individuals; deliberations on what kinds of questions can and should be asked; reflections on what kind of information the researcher should ethically provide to the subjects of one's research; considerations of how one uses the information one obtains not just in one's writing but in the context where one is researching. The list could, of course, go on. And such issues do not even begin to touch on the daily ethical questions that come up in individual interactions as researchers negotiate with the subjects of their study. Feminist ethnographers have spent much time considering such ethical considerations.[47] Such ethical questions have often been more openly discussed by feminist ethnographers because of the immediacy and intimacy of interaction between the ethnographic researcher and her subjects. For instance, ethnographers have addressed these questions in terms of power relationships between researcher and subject—relationships based on identities of race, nation, gender, sexuality, and class, to name the most visibly debated ones. Or they are cast in terms of the inherent power dynamics in the process of research and the power relationships between the researcher (the knower), on the one hand and the subject (the known), on the other hand.

Modes of self-reflexivity often sought to call attention to and to disrupt these power dynamics and in many ways were an implicit attempt to develop an ethical discursive response to knowledge production. As many critics have noted, however, self-reflexivity too often becomes reduced to static conceptions of social locations or unduly elaborate representations of the researcher/writer's own self in relation to the subjects of study. These modes of self-reflexivity implicitly return to a dualistic understanding of reality and representation. The first assumes that material social location determines the effects of representation; the second resorts to representational/discursive strategies to address material/ontological inequalities between researchers and their subjects of study. Both approaches rest on a split between ontology and representational practice (even as they try to bridge the split).

Other scholars have sought to disrupt the mechanistic or static dimensions of self-reflexivity by invoking and practicing a form of witnessing. The knowledge producer, in this context, is not concerned with self-reflexive reflections on her social location but is an engaged witness, shaping and being shaped by the world she writes about. Donna Haraway has proposed the possibility of feminist writer as a "modest witness" who observes, participates in, and shapes the world she writes about.[48] Haraway's modest witness is an ironic-political subversion of Robert Boyle's gendered conception of experimental scientific practice.[49] As Haraway notes, this gendered conception of the modest witness turned on a particular dynamic of visibility and invisibility—"only those who could disappear 'modestly' could really witness with authority rather than gawk curiously."[50] Thus, only white men, the embodiment of the dominant unmarked social category, could be appropriate invisible observers. The underpinnings of this modest witness, as Haraway puts it, rested on "disciplined ethical restraint."[51] Haraway endeavors to refigure this modest witness, in a search for "figures who can give credibility to matters of fact."[52] Her modest witness clearly differs from the objective observer/scholar who strives for detached invisibility. Perhaps more significantly, however, Haraway also refuses a purely epistemological response that is inherent in the self-reflexive turn to purely linguistic and representational strategies. As she puts it, "Critical reflexivity, or strong objectivity, does not dodge the world-making practices of forging knowledges with different chances of life and death built into them."[53] The ethical imperatives of Haraway's modest witness are those of an inescapable and accountable engagement regardless of the style of representational practices.

Haraway's discussion of witnessing implicitly draws on long intellectual and activist traditions that have centered on the ethical responsibility that the witness bears to the situation being witnessed. These include the practice of witnessing social injustice and oppression such as the use of testimonials (for example, *testimonio* in Latin American cultures), the practice of witnessing in Quaker traditions that draw on biblical traditions of bearing witness, as well as the work of a long history of secular social activists who have written not as objective, detached scholars but as engaged thinkers speaking out about and against the injustices they observe.[54] Such approaches have sought to turn the knowledge of oppression into a transformative act by practicing a kind of witnessing that breaks through the traditional hierarchies and relationships of power that govern how we see.

In such traditions, several key elements can shape the role of the witness. First, the witness becomes implicated in the situation or form of oppression being observed; that is, the presence of the witness changes the dynamics of the situation at hand as the witness is not simply an external observer. Second, the act of witnessing represents a learning process for the witness. The subjects being witnessed, in effect, represent the teachers in this situation; knowledge is given to the witness. This is a departure from traditional views of the intellectual as the sole individual who knows and educates others. For instance, Shoshana Felman and Dori Laub have insightfully described the way that the "narrator (a "historian," witness of the other witnesses), *learns something* from the witnessing and from the telling."[55] Writing in a very different context, Jeannie Ludlow presents a powerful account of her work in a U.S. abortion clinic in terms of both the limits and the imperatives of her own witnessing of her patients' experiences.[56] Ludlow analyzes the risks of discussing her patients' experiences in terms of the practice of witnessing; questions of her patients' confidentiality and trust, the political risks of the misappropriation of their experiences, and the political dangers of equating abortion with trauma compel Ludlow to discuss witnessing as a perilous practice. This practice of witnessing may do little to help her patients heal and potentially may hold the danger of wounding them or others in their position. Yet Ludlow is also compelled to speak about and around her witnessing in order to disrupt the dominant social narratives that serve as coercive frames for the women whom Ludlow serves in her clinic. Ludlow thus must write "in the gap between witness and testimony, 'between the seen and the told' (Bernard-Donels and Glejzer, 2000, 5), at the site of the 'things we cannot say.'"[57] Drawing on the work of Irene Kacandes, Ludlow argues for a practice of "cowitnessing" with the reader.[58] Thus, for Ludlow, witnessing cannot change her patients' experience of their abortions; the success of her work rests on the question of whether, as she puts it, "my reader-cowitnesses receive my narratives, and in turn, witness to others about the 'things we cannot say' (paraphrasing Kacandes, 2001, 140)," and in turn produce real political changes in the ways in which abortion politics play out in the United States.[59] Ludlow's account points to the ethical accountability of both the witness and the reader-cowitness in the materialization of the political world that will shape future stories and experiences of women.

Given that the witness is implicated in the situation being observed and obligated to the subjects of study, the act of witnessing brings with it a very deep form of ethical responsibility. The conception of witnessing moves beyond traditional modes of self-reflexivity by moving across traditional divides between ontology and epistemology. The stakes of thinking about knowledge practices as ethical action become much higher in this context, since such practices contribute to the making of the world. As Barad puts it, "Ethics is about mattering, about taking account of the entangled materializations of which we are a part, including new configurations, new subjectivities, new possibilities—even the smallest cuts matter."[60] The question, then, is what does this question of ethical knowledge practice—and the entangled relationship between the ontological/epistemological/ethical realm—mean for transnational feminist thought? Opening a discussion about a transnational perspective on ethics and knowledge raises complex questions of place, context, perspective, and power. From a transnational perspective, ethical action is not a self-evident or innocent realm. Barad, for instance, speaks of ethics in terms of accountability and responsibility as self-evident (and implicitly normatively positive) terms. She concludes her elaboration of a theory of an agential realist approach to knowledge production: "Ethics is therefore not about right response to a radically exterior/ized other, but about responsibility and accountability for the lived relationalities of becoming of which we are a part."[61] This concept of ethics is perhaps the least theorized aspect of Barad's discussion of knowledge. While Barad presents elaborate discussions of the materiality of knowledge production and the complex mutually embedded relationship between the material/representational and ontological/epistemological realms, she leaves the realm of ethics unexamined and untheorized. For Barad, ethics is the imperative of a responsible, accountable response to the fact that knowledge literally matters. From a transnational perspective that takes seriously the unavoidable relationalities that we are located in, responsibility and accountability cannot remain self-evident or innocent terms. At one level, to take a simple example, imperial powers have often claimed a set of ethical principles as an underlying rationale for intervention in other worlds. At another level, different places, contexts, and worlds contain within them varying conceptions of what it means to live an ethical life. From a transnational perspective, then, ethics is a necessary aspect of any discussion of knowledge production. However, ethics cannot serve as a placeless, untheorized space.

Consider, for instance, Sharon Welch's insightful discussion of both the possibilities and the limits of feminist ethics. Welch contrasts two forms of ethical action that she calls an "ethics of control" and an "ethics of risk."[62] Noting that "any ethical system can become coercive and self-deluding,"[63] she argues that dominant U.S.-based conceptions of justice are based on an ethic of control and "the assumption that effective action is unambiguous, unilateral and decisive."[64] Welch specifically links this ethic of control to U.S. militarism and the ways in which U.S. concerns with humanitarianism become bound up with militaristic and interventionist responses. She argues instead that "within an ethic of risk, actions begin with the recognition that far too much has been lost and there are no clear means of restitution. The fundamental risk constitutive of this ethic is the decision to care and to act although there are no guarantees of success."[65]

In the concluding discussion of this section, I want to consider how Welch's discussion of these contrasting approaches to ethics can inform transnational feminist knowledge. In many ways, earlier forms of feminist knowledge that colonized Third World women are emblematic of this ethic of control. Such forms of knowledge were based on the certainty of knowing that women are victims of their oppressive cultures and the unambiguous belief that a decisive response designed to save such women is normatively good. Seen from this ethical perspective, the deployment of ideologies of saving Third World women (see chapter 2) in the context of the U.S. "war on terror" also rests implicitly on this underlying ethic of control. Certain modes of activism can also rest on this ethic of control when this activism does not emerge out of a careful, engaged relationship with the communities involved.[66]

How, then, could an ethic of risk inform and unsettle our engagements with the world? Recent scholarship has sought to practice such an ethic of risk through new forms of engaged knowledge practices that give up a degree of control over research goals and agendas. Scholars conducting activist research from diverse disciplinary and interdisciplinary perspectives have begun to address knowledge production as a set of practices that are political, material, and ethical in complex and often contradictory ways.[67] Work on transnational feminist praxis has, for instance, sought to expand this ceding of control beyond simply sharing and getting feedback on the written results of research and beyond simply resorting to representational strategies that reflect on power relations.[68] Such work has sought to disrupt an ethics of control implicit in knowledge production by engaging in various forms of collaboration that disrupt the idea of an individual knowledge creator in the academy, for instance, by sharing authorship and developing and rethinking research goals and agendas through collaborations with grassroots organizations.[69] Collaborative work, of course, does not transcend ethical problems. As Laura Pulido has eloquently noted in her discussion of her own ethical dilemmas in her activist research in the United States, individuals within grassroots movements may have internal conflicts so that a representation of activist research is not a self-evident process but one that is fraught with ethical-political decisions.[70]

The ethical impetus that is implicit in such collaborative activist-research endeavors provides a powerful example of the potential of knowledge practices that break from an ethic of control. However, they cannot provide a formulaic solution to the broader problem of elaborating on what Jacqui Alexander and Chandra Mohanty have described as the need for "a sharper focus on the ethics of the cross-cultural production of knowledge."[71] In many ways, activist research still fits within long-standing feminist conceptions of justice and social change even as it disrupts the methods, practices, and impact of this engagement. Yet consider a different kind of challenge to an ethics of control—one that challenges the philosophical conception of ethics itself and consequently the very nature of what ethical engagement with the world looks like.

Consider Saba Mahmood's ethnography of the grassroots women's piety movement in Egypt.[72] Mahmood presents an intricate ethnographic analysis of women's subjectivities, bodily practices, and ethical world-views of both women religious teachers and the female participants in mosques that serve a range of women in lower-middle-class, working-class, and upper-middle-class neighborhoods in Cairo. Mahmood argues that women's participation in this movement cannot be understood through a conventional logic of repression and resistance. For Mahmood, women's agency in the mosques cannot be measured against a presumed norm of secular liberal conceptions of freedom, agency, or individual rights (for instance, as a regressive "fundamentalist" movement). The movement also cannot be understood as a simple form of resistance to such secular-liberal ideals. Rather, Mahmood compels the reader to suspend her own presumed ethical-political judgments and to immerse herself in the ethical worldviews and self-conceptions of the mosque participants. Participants in the movement are, for instance, concerned with practicing norms of modesty and submission in order to fully live a religious life and "to secure God's approval and pleasure" rather than to fulfill the potential of "the rhetoric of liberal citizenship" or to claim access to and control over economic resources or political space.[73] Mahmood's purpose is not to present a relativist worldview in which the subjects of her study are beyond critique. Indeed, one could interrogate the way in which national religious discourses and political agendas shape the modes of religious behavior that women in the movement idealize or point to the fact that Mahmood does not address the implication for the lives of women who do not adopt these normative ethical regimes. Nevertheless, Mahmood presents a powerful critique of the ethical certainties that implicitly or explicitly shape feminist analysis—including feminist analysis that addresses cultural contexts and seeks to move away from unitary models of feminist agency and subjectivity. As Mahmood puts it:

> Rather, my suggestion is that we leave open the possibility that our political and analytical certainties might be transformed in the process of exploring nonliberal movements of the kind I studied, that the lives of the women with whom I worked might have something to teach us beyond what we can learn from the circumscribed social scientific exercise of "understanding and translation." In this sense, one can say that the tension between the prescriptive and analytical aspects of the feminist project can be left productively open—that it should not be prematurely foreclosed for the sake of "political clarity."[74]

The "ethics of cross-cultural knowledge" that is embedded in Mahmood's argument is one that calls into question the certainty of the normative political objectives and norms of feminist thought. In many ways the risk that this ethical call demands of feminist thought is greater than that of redefining knowledge practices through transnational activist research. The collaborative political agendas of activist research still rest on a level of comfort within existing feminist frames. If transnational activist research raises complex and uncomfortable issues of power and commodification, it does so within an ethical framework in women's studies that has an established and recognizable, if contested, space.

An ethics of risk demands a more comprehensive and less certain approach to knowledge production, especially when addressing questions from a transnational, cross-cultural, global, or international perspective. For instance, transnational activist research may (potentially) contribute to struggles of subaltern groups to get access to resources or to political and civil rights. However, if the interdisciplinary study of women/gender across cultures, contexts, and nations solely or predominantly orients itself around such research, the knowledge field produced will result in a skewed set of representations and understandings with unanticipated or long-term political effects on the very places and groups being helped. Such knowledge practices circulate through different mechanisms of power that weave through audiences that consume this knowledge and the intricate relationships between such audiences and their states. Or the implicit instrumentality in normatively driven knowledge with the most careful and well-thought-through modes of practice may simply reproduce an ethical worldview that does not recognize that there are different ethical conceptions of the world that may have different understandings of how life is lived well. In effect, we can never fully know the implications of our knowledge practices. An ethics of risk in effect demands that we continually challenge the assumptions that we bring to the process of knowledge production, even as we continue to risk the task.

Conclusion

The challenge of confronting the ethical core of knowledge production lends a sense of uncertainty to our attempts to understand and engage with the world. A conception of an ethic of risk, in particular, asks us to reflect on the invisible dimensions that shape our practices of knowledge and unsettle the comfort that may arise from a preoccupation with visible issues or markers of what we might consider successful knowledge practices. This necessitates a break with the regime of visibility that I have discussed—an imperative of visibility is in a deeper sense more compatible with the desire for visible results that drives an ethic of control. Thinking of knowledge practices in terms of an ethic of risk has to do with an array of practices, actions, and agencies in the villages, cities, and nations in which we conduct research, the institutional sites where we disseminate knowledge, and finally our own sense of internal lived accountability to the world. My discussion in this chapter has laid out a set of questions that require reflection in the context of knowledge production of the "transnational." I elaborate on these issues in subsequent chapters. Thus, in the next chapter I turn to the role of institutional practice in shaping the questions of epistemology, ontology, and ethical action—acting, knowing, and making the world—that I have discussed here.

5

Institutional Practice and
the Field of Women's Studies

IN 2001, I was asked to co-convene a session at a national conference that brought together representatives of institutions that had launched autonomous PhD programs in the field of women's studies. In my remarks at that session, I suggested that if women's studies departments were planning to train students doing graduate-level work on international questions, these departments needed to think more systematically about the kind of preparation that students would receive. In particular, I suggested that women's studies departments may want to consider ways to ensure that students received training (in coursework and research) on questions that were not focused purely on gender or women so that they had some depth of context—of place, history, culture—with which to frame research questions and intellectual agendas. To my surprise, this suggestion produced a significant negative response from several individuals in the audience. One senior feminist scholar grumbled that this amounted to a call to turn women's studies into international studies. Such resistance stems from a presumption that a field of study designed to study women and gender in comparative or international contexts does not require a discussion of how to provide students with a broader empirical understanding of the places they would focus on. Exposure to the world may be provided through random course offerings but not as a systematic institutional organization of the field of women's studies. More than ten years later, while calls and claims of global and transnational perspectives on gender proliferate and critiques of Western feminism abound through curricular and citational practices, women's studies as an *institutionalized* field of study has not systematically changed the way in which the study of the world is organized through now-established PhD programs and through the organization of curricula practices for undergraduate majors.

Women's studies of course has a well-developed tradition of scholarship that has interrogated the relationship between power and knowledge. In fact, the preoccupation with this relationship and with the study of epistemology is one of the central emphases in women's studies research and teaching. Moreover, one of the unique strengths of women's studies as a field has been the way in which it has allowed for the intellectual space to engage in internal criticisms of its own constitution even as it has posed challenges to the limits of conventional forms of disciplinary knowledge. In many ways, the institutionalization of the field of women's studies within the U.S. academy has been continually defined by the unsettling of its foundation. Just as women's studies programs were gaining ground as a formal institutional presence, feminist scholarship was engaged in a passionate debate on the limits of the category of "woman." The field of women's studies thus emerged through a set of institutional and intellectual practices that sought to simultaneously assert its legitimacy in the face of resistant or skeptical university administrations, on the one hand, while engaging in internal debates on the question of its subject, on the other hand. Many of the major debates that emerged solely out of the formation of the field of women's studies (as opposed to those that emerged through feminist conversations and clashes with the disciplines) were focused specifically on the need to address exclusions based on race, nation, and culture that were being produced by this institutionalization of women's studies as a formalized field of knowledge.[1]

As a result, the field of women's studies has made significant inroads in its attempts to deepen its emphasis on international and transnational perspectives on women, gender, and sexuality. These trends have been evident in job searches, the content and marketability of scholarly books, the efforts of journals to focus on international issues through special issues, and individual submissions and citational practices in individual scholarly works and course curricula. These trends occur in a context in which women's studies has increasingly become an institutionalized field through the rise of formal programs of study, the departmentalization of the field, and the expansion of autonomous women's studies PhD programs. According to the National Women's Studies Association, there are currently 652 women's and gender studies programs in the United States (across the spectrum of community colleges, colleges, and universities).[2] Meanwhile, numerous universities and some colleges have begun to offer graduate degrees in the field. The scope and depth of such programs of course vary widely and are often contingent on external factors such as access to funding, teaching staff and tenure-track faculty positions, and the political climate of the institutions in which such programs are located. The measures of success of such programs may also vary according to the kind of institution in question. Emily Tai, for instance, has argued that in the context of her community college, the decision to integrate women's studies courses within existing disciplines rather than form an autonomous women's studies concentration was an effective strategy given the structure of the institution and the needs of the students at the college.[3] Catherine Orr and Diane Lichenstein argue further that debates on institutionalization are often limited to discussions of larger institutions, thus neglecting the experiences—and the successes—of programs at smaller liberal arts colleges.[4] Thus, they argue that even particular challenges and crises in the history of their institution were transformed into opportunities. These examples of the specificities of particular institutions are a useful reminder of both the variation in women's studies programs and the fact that such variation is in many ways a marker of the success of the field. Despite the importance of particular variations in individual programs, the growing institutionalization of the field means that it is both possible and useful to analyze systemic patterns that shape the organization of the field. The discursive practices that interdisciplinary scholars conventionally analyze in contemporary discussions of power and knowledge operate within the structured institutional practices of academic institutions and departments.

My analysis rests on a multilayered understanding of institutional practice. At the broadest level, women's studies programs and departments now serve as small nodes in a complex web of institutional networks that mediate the relationship between state and civil society in the United States. A recognition of the fact that interdisciplinary scholarship is located within institutional networks that are indirectly or directly (in the case, for instance, of state-funded institutions) connected to the state is important given that scholarship within such fields often (though not always) conceives of itself in discursive opposition to structures of power. In practice, academic institutions (and the intellectual fields located within these institutions) occupy a contradictory space that illustrates the hazy, shifting lines between state and civil society. Academic institutions within the United States in many ways are exemplary illustrations of a Gramscian understanding of the "trenches of civil society" through which state power is exercised in liberal democratic societies.[5] These "trenches" are the organizations and institutions within civil society that underpin the specific hegemonic structures and pacts that allow the state to exercise power. Yet, at the same time, these very trenches also hold the potential for alternative alliances and counterhegemonic movements. Such counterhegemonic formations can challenge state power and change the structures of both state and civil society.

This multilayered conception of institutional practice compels us to move away from romanticized assumptions that interdisciplinary fields such as women's studies are automatically spaces of political and intellectual subversion. Conceiving of academic feminist knowledge as institutional practice means that such knowledge holds the potential of both reproducing and subverting dominant relationships of power. More significantly, a conception of institutions as the trenches that weave together particular kinds of state–civil society relationships must also compel us to examine the relationship between the fields of knowledge we institutionalize and the workings of state power. To pose this question is not to begin with a presumption that the geopolitical location and power of the United States predetermine the nature of such knowledge in any simplistic way. Nor is such a question based on the assumption that U.S. academic feminism is trapped within some homogeneous model of Western or American feminism. Rather, my interest in this chapter is not to replay such critiques (which have already surfaced many times in earlier scholarship) and simply conclude with a condemnation of institutionalized feminist knowledge within the academy. Rather, a discussion of institutional practices serves as a starting point to begin conversations about how to deepen the international, global, transnational, and comparative analyses and perspectives of the world within the academy precisely because feminist knowledge within the academy matters. In the absence of such a conversation, any disciplinary or interdisciplinary unit risks the possibility that the knowledge regimes it produces serve as an accidental lens of the state. I therefore begin the chapter by addressing the broader macropolitical and institutional constraints that structure the knowledge marketplace within the United States and the implications that such constraints hold for women's studies.

The second layer of institutional structures that shape knowledge regimes consists of the microlevel institutional practices in individual departments and the particular college and university contexts in which they are located. At one level, interdisciplinary fields such as women's studies must operate within the parameters of the institutional regulations, norms, and practices of the universities and colleges in which they are located. Such norms and practices range from the microinstitutional practices that shape academic curricula to systemic practices of hiring and tenure and the provision of resources to the ideological norms and cultural practices of institutions that may open or foreclose intellectual space in subtle ways.[6] At another level, women's studies departments are institutional sites with their own institutional patterns and practices. Here, I focus in particular on a range of issues, including (1) the effects of the expansion of women's studies graduate programs, (2) the organization of global and transnational perspectives through curricular practices, and (3) the possibilities and limits of pedagogical practice within the classroom. The objective of this chapter is not to provide a comprehensive survey of existing programs and departments but to point to both systematic patterns and specific examples of institutional practice that can open up conversations about knowledge formation within women's studies, particularly as it relates to international perspectives.

There have already been long-standing debates over the institutionalization of women's studies. These debates have focused on the politics of institutionalization and the potential risks of depoliticizing the activist orientation of the women's movements that were often linked to the emerging field of women's studies. My concern in this chapter is not to rehearse these debates on institutionalization or to bemoan the negative effects of such institutionalization.[7] Rather, my objective is to analyze how institutional practices shape the production, circulation, and consumption of knowledge about international, transnational, and comparative/national issues in women's studies and to consider possibilities for deepening the way in which such knowledge is disseminated. In this endeavor, I do not treat discursive knowledge practices (that include teaching, syllabi, and a range of other practices within the academy) as mere effects of institutional structures. Such discursive knowledge practices are not simply effects of but are constitutive of these expansive networks of power and institutional contexts. In my analysis, I therefore conceive of the various practices that shape the organization and dissemination of knowledge (such as pedagogical, textual, and everyday social practices) as part of the networks of institutional practice that I analyze.

The internal dynamic of intellectual self-interrogation has allowed women's studies to serve as a rich terrain for interdisciplinary work. In contrast to interdisciplinary work that has emerged from the conventional disciplines, the continual unsettling of the subject of feminism has served as a central force that worked against the disciplinary impetus that inevitably accompanies the process of institutionalization.[8] With the expansion of women's studies programs and departments, curricula, and publishing markets, this institutionalization calls for further self-interrogation in the spirit of this history of unsettled interdisciplinarity. Such an interrogation requires more than the deconstruction of the dominant discursive narratives that shape the field (which I have discussed in the previous chapter).

It also requires an analysis of the institutional practices that structure knowledge in systematic ways.

Between State and Civil Society: Institutional Patterns, the Knowledge Marketplace, and the Risks of the Accidental State

Within the academy, the explicit links between knowledge production and U.S. state interests circulate in ways that are both instrumentalist and accidental. In an instrumentalist sense, particular intellectual agendas are often explicitly shaped by state objectives (for instance, in terms of the ways that the state and private foundations may fund research that falls in line with particular policy areas). In an accidental sense, the shaping of audience interests within the United States may indirectly track knowledge production in ways that center around state policy objectives. The substantive areas and questions that draw attention within transnational and international studies may inadvertently center on state-driven questions because of the consumption-driven marketplace structure of knowledge within the United States. Conflicts and political crises that are directly related to U.S. national interests generate intensified public interest that, in turn, generates student interest in learning about the particular places and issues concerned.

For instance, in the post-9/11 period, public interest in the Middle East and in Islam has grown exponentially. The convergence of state and public interest within civil society translates into academic interest in several ways. State interests in grasping the cultural and political complexities of the region are mirrored in the structures that shape the generation and dissemination of research. Avenues for research funding and fellowships, academic speaker series and intellectual events, and curriculum offerings and publication avenues also expand. This expansion is further boosted by the generation of student interest in such topics as students try to make sense of the events through which they are living. This convergence between state and civil public interest does not mean that intellectual fields within universities are automatically driven by governmental agendas. On the contrary, university sites often serve as vital spaces for contestation, and the expansion of intellectual agendas can be oriented as much toward criticisms of dominant political trends and state agendas as toward a simplistic mirroring of governmental policies. This has certainly been true of interdisciplinary fields such as women's studies (and related fields such as ethnic studies, postcolonial studies, and area studies) that have provided the intellectual and political space for critiques of U.S. state policy.[9]

The challenge that fields such as women's studies face in developing their international and transnational dimensions is thus not a simple ideological task of questioning U.S. state politics. Rather, the task is a more difficult one of circumventing the reproduction of a U.S.-centric conception of the world. For instance, paradoxically, even ideological critiques of U.S. state policies and politics may recenter an American national conception of global and transnational issues if such critiques are presented as the sole lens through which students think about the world outside of the United States. For instance, feminist research that seeks to challenge Western approaches through analyses of colonialism and Western categories of thought may inadvertently reproduce such national conceptions of the world by continually recentering the United States/West. These orienting discourses need not reflect state agendas (such as foreign policy or national security) and can occur even within the most nuanced critical perspectives. For instance, the age-old problem of the representation of non-Western women as victims of cultural oppression circulates in popular culture and media representations in ways that are autonomous of state agendas. These representations then circulate and are deconstructed within women's studies classrooms. Yet even the process of deconstruction compels a set of pedagogical practices that are oriented toward these national public narratives. It should not be surprising, then, as I have argued in chapter 2, that a series of events such as the Bush administration's post-9/11 "war on terror" enables the state to seize on and deploy these existing narratives in support of its state agendas. This process is precisely what it means to speak of the trenches in civil society through which state power is exercised. What is of particular significance here is that this convergence between state and civil society does not have to presume a predetermined form of ideological manipulation. Rather, the power of civil society as a sphere that facilitates state power lies with the fact that civil society can present itself as an autonomous sphere of institutional networks, associational life, and discursive narratives, in contrast to authoritarian states that must rely on the explicit control and censorship of educational institutions.

This process is, of course, not unique to women's studies or feminist academic knowledge production. Indeed, educational institutions in the United States have long struggled with the relationship between the state and the study of international issues. In the mid-twentieth century, it is now commonly accepted that the institutionalization of interdisciplinary international scholarship through the establishment of area studies programs was explicitly linked to the Cold War political interests of the U.S. state. In the post-9/11 period, various disciplines have had intense debates on the question of how to engage with the institution of the military in the context of the U.S. wars in Afghanistan and Iraq. In the case of anthropology, the use by the U.S. military of anthropologists sparked a furious debate about the politics and ethics of the discipline.[10] Meanwhile, one of the major journals affiliated with the national organization of political scientists, the American Political Science Association, recently hosted a forum that debated whether and how the discipline could adopt a more productive engagement with the military. In the context of this debate, Craig Calhoun, president of the Social Science Research Council (one of the leading foundations that funds social science research), attempted to walk a fine line between the autonomy of intellectual and academic life and the need to engage productively with the U.S. military.[11] Writing about strained relations between civilian academics and the U.S. military that stem from "a charged history in which civilian research—and the trust of those being studied—has been abused," Calhoun argues:

> At the same time, there are many reasons to bemoan the current relationship of suspicion and distance. Perhaps most importantly, a military that operates in seclusion from civilian concerns is antithetical to democracy. Academic social science is not as large or as basic a part of American society as the military—for better or worse—but if social science knowledge does not inform military operations and strategy, or offer fully informed criticism of it, democracy suffers, not just the military. Social scientists who live in a society with a large and active military should not proceed with their work as though it didn't exist. They can honorably proceed in pacifist opposition or in opposition to specific policies—whether strategic (like waging extensive wars in Muslim societies while trying to win Muslim allies) or operational (like discrimination against homosexuals). But they cannot so honorably simply turn the other way.[12]

Such examples do not suggest that academic knowledge production is subordinated in a simplistic manner to military objectives. Feminist scholar Cynthia Enloe, for instance, was one of the participants in the American Political Science Association debate who strongly challenged the entire process of militarization that has increasingly permeated U.S. society. Meanwhile, Calhoun makes a distinction between the U.S. military's uses of academic knowledge for strategic as opposed to tactical operations.[13] He notes that the military's Human Terrain System program that sought to recruit anthropologists and social scientists to work with combat troops placed academics within the military command structure (by tactically deploying teams in actual combat zones), in addition to using academic knowledge to understand the culture and social organizations of the populations in which the military was intervening. The Minerva Initiative, on the other hand, sought to use Department of Defense funding to promote academic research that would inform the military's strategic thinking.

Calhoun's discussion points to the complex—and varied—ways in which institutional networks link the academy, the military, and state structures within the United States. His reminder of the contrast in scale between the social sciences (and one could add the humanities) and the military is also a useful reminder of the fact that the military may have a much wider impact than academic research within civil society. State structures are in effect embedded within society through a range of military-civilian linkages. One the one hand, this means that academic institutions may be much less influential in shaping the substantive content of state–civil society linkages in the United States. Popular dismissals of the academy as an ivory tower (that come from both right-wing attacks on "liberal elites" and left-oriented debates on theory versus practice) often neglect the broader institutional (and state) structures that make academic research more marginal in public life in the United States. On the other hand, the deep embeddedness of the state within civil society through processes such as militarization means that academic knowledge production is implicitly or explicitly mediated through complex institutional and ideational linkages and dissonances.

One of the objectives of transnational perspectives has been to dislodge a state-driven approach to the world—for instance, by disrupting the Cold War institutionalized construction of arbitrary distinctions between specific "areas" of the world.[14] The substantive direction of such area-based programs has never ultimately been simplistically determined by state agendas. It is of course most telling that attempts to censor university intellectual life in the post-9/11 period focused precisely on area-based programs such as Middle Eastern studies programs.[15] Nevertheless, this history is a useful reminder of the ways in which the interdisciplinary study of international issues has always been fraught with such tensions about state–civil society relations. While such questions are not unique to any particular field of study, the implications of such institutional forces are particularly important for women's studies and feminist scholars to consider precisely because women's studies has historically rested on a self-image as an oppositional space. This sense of oppositional identity is linked both to the historical evolution of women's studies out of movement-oriented politics that confronted the state and opposed dominant exclusionary structures and to recent trends in feminist theory that have identified the interdisciplinary project as a space of philosophical and political critique.[16] As Robyn Wiegman has noted, "It is not possible to assume, then, that academic feminism can have a relation to the political that comes before the institution or that can remain institutionally innocent."[17] Yet Wiegman also too easily assumes an unspecified teleological move from the national to the transnational—a move that rests on an empirical and theoretical failure to conceptualize the linkages between institutions and the nation-state. She asserts, "It is thus the transformation of the U.S. university from a nationalist function to a transnational one that challenges Women's Studies to reconsider its own relation to knowledge production."[18] Wiegman's claim replicates some of the surface presumptions of the shift from the national to the transnational that stem from the paradigm of postnationalism that I have discussed in earlier chapters—one that misses the empirical fact that the very institutional practices that she discusses are connected to and in some cases embedded within the institutional networks that constitute state structures. This empirical fallacy forecloses a deeper discussion of the ways in which conceptions of the transnational are themselves embedded within structures of the nation-state. It is this embeddedness that challenges women's studies to reconsider its relation to knowledge production in ways that do not reproduce a facile juxtaposition between the national and transnational realms.

For example, there are several overarching patterns of national cultural and state institutional practices that impinge on the microlevel institutional practices of women's studies programs. The subtle national narratives that produce the knowledge marketplace, the historical role of the state in organizing the study of areas of the world, and the impact of the distribution of resources through both public and state sources are just a few of the factors that shape these patterns. The question that arises, then, is whether women's studies is able to effectively institutionalize knowledge practices that move beyond these constraints of the nation-state. Certainly, the relationship between women's studies and the state is far more complex than some of the more explicit questions that anthropologists and political scientists, among others, have had to grapple with. Women's studies as a field is certainly more tangential when it comes to the geopolitical struggles between the state and the academy, and the field in general has tended to be associated with criticisms of the U.S. state and its foreign policy. The question for women's studies is how its institutional practices may inadvertently allow it to serve as an accidental state structure—by replicating the lens of the state in the way it organizes and deploys its fields of study.

Canonical Knowledge and Institutional Practices within Women's Studies: The Case of the Women's Studies PhD

Two central trends have affected the institutional practices of the field of women's studies in recent years. The first is that many women's studies programs have moved toward autonomous departmental status and have been able to hire full-time faculty without needing to define these faculty in terms of a related discipline. Second, numerous women's studies departments have launched graduate programs that offer MA or PhD degrees; currently, around thirteen universities have programs that grant an autonomous PhD (without any joint affiliation with another field of study), and three institutions provide for a joint PhD with women's studies and other fields of study. In addition, dozens of women's studies programs offer terminal MA degrees in women's studies. This growing autonomy of the field has meant that it is no longer defined solely in opposition to the traditional disciplines (for example, as with early generations of scholarship that sought to change the exclusion of women and gender from disciplinary perspectives). This growth in autonomy does not mean that there is a consensus on the nature of interdisciplinarity or on the parameters of a new interdisciplinary women's studies canon. Competing models of interdisciplinarity continue to coexist both within and across departments and programs, and disciplinary orientations often continue to shape models that make radical claims of transdisciplinarity. However, the establishment of autonomous graduate programs, particularly at the PhD level, has meant that departments with these programs have had to address the problem of identifying a canon or set of (inter)disciplinary practices that can be used to train graduate students.

Consider the way in which the emergence and expansion of PhD-granting programs in women's and gender studies have shaped curricular practices. The establishment of the women's studies PhD has meant that the field now claims (whether implicitly or explicitly) the means to delineate its intellectual boundaries. Underlying this delineation of boundaries is a dynamic of reproduction. That is to say, training PhD students is qualitatively different from teaching undergraduate-level or MA students precisely because the PhD is not just an intellectual endeavor but a key element of the project of institutional reproduction. In other words, PhD students in women's and gender studies are presumably being trained at least in part to reproduce the field of women's studies. The PhD in a sense designates a scholar who is able to represent the field within academic institutions and thus to reproduce the body of knowledge that he or she has been trained to associate with this now-bounded field. In this sense, the implications of the women's studies PhD are qualitatively different from those of undergraduate education in women's studies. The significance of this credentialing process is reflected in the growing number of tenure-track academic job advertisements that now specify a women's studies PhD as a preferred or required credential. The result is that the establishment of the women's studies PhD has raised the stakes of the institutionalization of feminist knowledge. This is particularly the case since programs with autonomous PhD programs have become increasingly invested in shaping and representing interdisciplinary work given their investment in the institutional reproduction of their programs. Such PhD programs increasingly claim the role of "real" or true interdisciplinary women's studies scholars in order to both recruit new PhD students and place recent graduates in a highly competitive market (and one that is currently shrinking in the context of an economic recession). This process of recruitment and placement is necessary for the new PhD programs to sustain themselves. Given the institutional obstacles that make it very difficult for women's studies PhD students to enter the market of traditional disciplines, there is thus an institutional and economic investment for new PhD-granting programs to discipline the field of interdisciplinary feminist scholarship. Meanwhile, as new women's studies PhDs enter the field, their particular location also produces new investments in the centrality and significance of the women's studies PhD.[19]

The nature of the women's studies PhD is a challenging one precisely because it pits the disruptive impetus of interdisciplinary feminist work, with its drive toward challenging norms and structures (including the very subject of feminism itself), against the disciplining and homogenizing tendencies that stem from this institutionalized imperative to reproduce. If women's studies PhD programs must now claim a degree of expertise that other feminist scholars do not have if they work on gender and women within the traditional disciplines, they must rest this claim on some systematic canon of knowledge. It is this set of contradictions that Wendy Brown despairs of in her well-publicized critique, "The Impossibility of Women's Studies." Thus, she questions:

> In what should the graduate student in women's studies be trained? What bodies of knowledge must a women's studies doctoral candidate have mastered and why? Which women should she know about and what should she know about them? Which techniques of analyzing gender should she command and why? Ethnography or oral history? Lacanian psychoanalysis? Quantitative sociological analysis? Object relations theory? Literary theory? Postcolonial criticism? Neo-Marxist theories of labor and political economy? Social history? Critical science studies? There is a further question: who are we to teach these things simply because we are interested in feminism and feminist analysis from our own scholarly perspectives?[20]

This string of questions (posed rhetorically because Brown's response in her essay is that women's studies cannot as a field provide answers) speaks directly to the anxiety about how to both fix (specify the bodies of knowledge) and reproduce (allow doctoral candidates to master these fields in order to reproduce) the boundaries of the field.

There are, of course, numerous problems with Brown's assertions that these questions make the field of women's studies unsustainable. The questions of choosing appropriate methods (Lacanian psychoanalysis or ethnography) are not unique to women's studies. Cross-disciplinary fertilization has also occurred in the traditional disciplines, and conventional disciplines also struggle over and in some instances are steeped in long-standing wars over appropriate methods training. Furthermore, Brown's proposed solution that women's studies courses be collapsed and integrated within the existing disciplines misses the fact that there are independent intellectual genealogies associated with interdisciplinary women's studies scholarship that cannot be simply collapsed into other disciplines.[21] The unevenness of training and conflicts over curricular matters that Brown identifies as unique to women's studies are also issues that the major disciplinary-based departments may deal with (and these issues vary based on the type of institution, the resources of the institution, and the politics of how institutions distribute these resources to various departments and programs; such a consideration of this institutional variation is completely absent from Brown's arguments). Moreover, as Vivian May has argued:

> Perceptual screens of impossibility are not simply pesky misinterpretations, but signs of open resistance akin to what Judith Butler describes as a frame of unthinkability (1993). This refusal or, at the very least, befuddlement from within Women's Studies about the purpose of a freestanding interdisciplinary women's studies PhD seems particularly ironic in that Women's Studies has spent the last 25 years arguing *for* interdisciplinarity, for the necessity of a socially-conscious education, and for education as a liberatory endeavor. Women's Studies asserts its inherent centrality to the contemporary university, but then chooses marginality therein, signifying a sense of ambivalence, embarrassment, or apology about its own purpose and methods.[22]

May makes a cogent argument for many of the potential contributions of the women's studies PhD, including a self-questioning form of interdisciplinarity and feminist theory, practices of self-reflexive knowledge, and methods of intersectional analysis. In a cogent response to critics of the women's studies PhD, May rightly argues that the degree is often judged by imperializing disciplinary norms and is often targeted as being ideological while the ideological norms of the traditional disciplines remain unexamined.

One of the most significant shortcomings of such debates about the institutionalization and graduate education, however, is a lack of systemic discussion of how international or transnational approaches are being addressed by newly formed PhD programs. The question of institutionalization within the national space of the United States in effect becomes a nation-centered debate. While methods of intersectionality and the contributions of feminist theory are key aspects of approaches to comparative or international approaches, they do not provide sufficient answers to the question of whether a field that claims transnationalism as a central paradigm is adequately training students to research and have expertise on gender/sexuality/women in places outside of the United States. On the one hand, if women's studies as an emerging doctoral field is not systematically training students to research and teach on formations of gender and sexuality outside of the United States, this raises serious questions about a field whose PhD programs may be producing new generations of U.S.-centric conceptions of feminist thought and practice. On the other hand, the creation of PhD programs raises questions of how "place"—and the question of transnational, comparative and non-U.S. contexts—are being incorporated within these new interdisciplinary graduate programs.

Despite the many challenges that can be raised in response to Brown's arguments,[23] her intellectual critiques hit on one of the crucial underlying problems in this institutional disciplining of the field of women's studies— the difficulty of providing what Brown calls "the appropriate antecedents and cognates" for the topics in which students are trained, or, as she puts it, "for example, the emergence of the struggle for women's emancipation in the context of democratic and socialist revolutions in the West, or the relevance of Rousseau, Marx, Freud, and more recent philosophical and literary thinkers to feminist thought and practice."[24] As a feminist political theorist, Brown is concerned that students are not sufficiently trained with the intellectual histories and contexts out of which feminist and other related interdisciplinary theories emerge. Thus she goes on to note, "What a difference it would make to develop those background knowledges as part of students' work in philosophy, cultural studies, literature, anthropology or critical theory so that they would actually be armed to engage and contest the arguments they encounter in feminist theory and in postcolonial, queer and critical race theories as well."[25] The historical and intellectual context that Brown speaks of in relation to theory is precisely the kind of depth, background, and context that is needed for students who want to learn about gender, women, and feminism outside of the United States. If, as Brown accurately notes, knowledge about democratic and socialist revolutions in the West is necessary for an adequate comprehension of the genealogies of (Western) feminist theory, it is precisely this kind of knowledge about specific places and contexts that students need to acquire *before* they can learn about, let alone theorize about, women or feminism in contexts that they are unfamiliar with.

Yet it is precisely this discussion or even a recognition of the problems of training students to gain an ontological understanding of the world outside the United States that is absent not simply in Brown's essay but in many broader interdisciplinary women's studies conversations in the U.S. academy. For instance, Brown argues that these background knowledges about the context of Western history and theory are necessary to engage with postcolonial theory. However, "the postcolonial" is not simply an intellectual field associated with particular scholars—it marks a particular historical period of particular places. Postcolonial theory is a particular paradigm that has emerged from the study of particular regions of the world that experienced histories of colonialism. In other words, gaining expertise in postcolonial theory is not the same as gaining systemic historical, cultural, economic, and political knowledge about the world. It is notable that the only other time that Brown comes close to addressing the question of empirical knowledge is through a cursory dismissal of the "methodism" implicit in women's studies PhD course sequences that separate "theory" and "methods" into separate courses.[26] Yet, as I have argued in chapter 4, the empirical cannot be conflated with atheoretical or reductive understandings of empiricism (or methodism).

This is the question with which I began this chapter. If women's studies is serious about moving beyond U.S.-centric understandings of feminism and is committed to global and transnational perspectives on women, gender, and sexuality, then in what ways can its institutional practices provide sufficient depth and—to use a politically incorrect word—a foundation in its graduate training? Women's studies increasingly claims to have a global and transnational focus (often in keeping with and sometimes shaped by broader institutional drives within the U.S. academy to speak as sites with a global reach). Given such claims and objectives, could PhD programs begin to discuss integrating expectations that students would need to be trained in non-gender-specific areas (including language skills) if departments granting these degrees market themselves as holding expertise in global or transnational perspectives? The limits of resources (such as numbers of teaching faculty) and curricular offerings may often mean that the integration of international and transnational perspectives currently occurs in a sporadic and somewhat haphazard manner. Moreover, faculty who work on places outside of the United States are often expected to teach broad "global" courses rather than in-depth classes on particular places. The result is that students' ability to learn about the varied and complex histories of particular places may be severely limited or dependent on their accidental consumer choices. Students come away with a fractured understanding of the world, with fragments of knowledge about various places.

Within the U.S. academy, students' knowledge of places outside of the United States is highly varied. PhD-granting departments contain a mix of students, some of whom may have been immersed in learning about particular places for many years. For example, some international students as well as U.S.-trained students who come to graduate work with a long history of intellectual and/or activist work in a specific location may have in-depth knowledge about particular contexts. However, other students may have little or no exposure to or interest in feminist questions outside of the United States. Finally, some students may have a very strong interest in transnational or non-U.S. gender issues but may not have any systematic knowledge about women's and gender issues outside of the United States. The variation, of course, rests on a number of factors. These include the complexities of individual students' life histories, as well as the type of interdisciplinary or disciplinary training students have received prior to graduate work (given that women's studies PhDs may have various undergraduate majors). Finally, they also include the question of what kind of training and knowledge students have gained about the world both in college and in their high school preparation.

While these factors may seem simple or mundane, they are crucial elements that often get lost in transcendent visions of interdisciplinarity or transdisciplinarity. For instance, at both the undergraduate and the graduate level, students often lack basic geographic or empirical knowledge about various places, nations, and regions of the world. They are then exposed to sophisticated theories of transnationalism and postcoloniality that have emerged in specific conversations with and against work on particular places. Yet students are asked to learn how these new paradigms have moved beyond older approaches without any consideration of the extent of their knowledge about the places from and about which such theory is being generated. By "place" here, I do not mean simply geographic coordinates but the complex historical, political, economic, and cultural processes that are co-constituted by location, space, and territory.[27] When this sense of place is not present in any systematic and institutionalized pedagogical manner (through the organization of curricula and courses), the foundation of knowledge is, not surprisingly, replaced by an attachment to the dynamic of movement—that is, the movement beyond paradigms, beyond national boundaries, beyond categorical and linguistic precedents. This sense of movement in effect becomes the canonical knowledge that marks interdisciplinary women's studies and that women's studies PhD-granting programs can use as a basis for reproduction and to differentiate themselves from the fixed, bounded territories of conventional disciplines. In other words, the reification of rigid canons and disciplinary foundations is replaced by an equally rigid attachment to a desire to break from past paradigms. The presumed dynamism that is usually associated with moving beyond the past thus ironically becomes an anchoring, disciplinary trend.

The intellectual drive to "move beyond" older knowledge forms and practices marks the production of interdisciplinary knowledge with a colonizing impulse—one that risks mirroring the colonizing impulse that much of interdisciplinary feminist research and theory has interrogated and sought to avoid. This impulse is of course not unique to interdisciplinary or feminist scholarship. As I have noted earlier, the political economy of knowledge production is such that the market–based approach to knowledge drives us to claims of newness and moving beyond older models of scholarship. This is a process of branding that echoes the intensified dynamics of economic globalization in which academic labor is located. However, the drive toward (and the overstating of) claims about moving beyond existing forms of knowledge becomes intensified when interdisciplinary feminist knowledge becomes institutionalized through the PhD program. In contrast to graduate training in the conventional disciplines that have hegemonic (if contested) intellectual foundations, graduate training in women's studies clearly does not have a predetermined set of foundations or canons. In fact, the very project of the field of women's studies usually rests on a rejection of the norms of traditional disciplines and in some cases a rejection of any foundational approach to knowledge production (that is to say, the rejection of any attempt to produce a canon of knowledge for women's studies). Thus, it is a stylized approach to knowledge production that becomes the center (if not foundation) of what is considered interdisciplinary women's studies research. By stylized, I mean that it is the appearance of moving beyond past paradigms through linguistic innovation and categorical discontinuities that becomes the foundation of interdisciplinary knowledge. This does not mean that such work is devoid of content (including new empirical research and theoretical insights). However, the valuation of such knowledge risks becoming contingent on stylized practice—that is, a kind of performative interdisciplinarity. Thus, somewhat ironically, the framing practices that discipline this emerging corpus of knowledge rest on the claim of discontinuity. Interdisciplinary work thus runs the risk of becoming disciplined by the repetition of discontinuity (or claims of discontinuity).

It is in this context of institutionalized interdisciplinarity that transnationalism becomes an easy stand-in for this moving beyond (with its implied sense of discontinuity) existing national, comparative, and international frames of analysis. The result is the production of some of the limited discursive patterns that I have analyzed in chapter 4. When students do not have the requisite background knowledges about specific places and countries, they turn instead to spatial sites that move beyond these locations. It is precisely due to this lack of context and background that "transnationalism" becomes the kind of shorthand framing device that targets visible border-crossing issues that I have analyzed. Thus, while individual texts that focus on such issues may provide rich and nuanced analyses, when such texts become disciplined markers that are solidified by systematic institutional practices, they inadvertently intensify the exclusionary U.S.-centric risks of a border-crossing-oriented approach to transnational knowledge.

Just as the genealogy of feminist theory rests on a history of conversations and critical engagements with prior bodies of knowledge, the paradigm of transnationalism was based on a set of critical engagements with existing institutionalized forms of knowledge. As I have discussed in previous chapters, transnational analysis sought to decenter a rigid nation-centered approach through which both disciplinary and interdisciplinary area studies approaches had been organized. The nation-centered post–Cold War historical context of the organization of international and area-based knowledge was shaped by the rise of nationalist movements and the emergence of newly independent nation-states in what was called the "developing world" or "Third World." These historical processes shaped the organization of international knowledge, and the exclusive focus on nation-centered analysis often missed the salience of global and transnational forces. At a normative level, transnational (and postcolonial) research and theory have rested on a critique of the repressive, exclusionary, power-laden, and often violent practices of the modern nation-state.[28] This normative project of transnational feminist research, as well as related interdisciplinary work such as postcolonial theory,[29] has sought to find ways of moving beyond the nation-state and the particular modern technologies of power that it uses to reproduce itself.[30] However, the institutionalization of these paradigms has meant that such fields now reproduce limited empirical understandings of these places; the territorialized nation-state is simply replaced by the territorialized spaces that transcend the nation.[31]

In effect, the normative resistance to nationalism and the nation-state becomes conflated with and now increasingly drives the analytical lens used to study the world. When such discursive and intellectual practices become institutionalized within the academy, they become complicit in producing at best skewed and at worst inaccurate understandings of the places they seek to represent. This disjuncture is produced by transnational and postcolonial scholarship that tries to produce new categories of thought that can move beyond the nation-state and beyond earlier positivist approaches to the study of particular areas of the world; it stems from the fact that such interdisciplinary approaches have failed to consider the implications of their own institutionalization and growing hegemonic status within the academy. This failure to interrogate the limits of the presumed transcendence of this approach has rested on a paradoxical situation where such work has explicitly criticized the dominance of institutionalized knowledges that have naturalized the nation-state while not considering how the same project of institutionalization has now been naturalizing and therefore fixing categories such as transnationalism and postcoloniality.

Consider how these paradoxical trends play out in the project of training doctoral students in women's studies. In practical institutional terms, this translates into a set of everyday cultural and attitudinal norms that orient women's studies PhD students toward a belief that their work moves beyond the old, outdated norms of traditional disciplines. The center that holds the women's studies PhD programs together thus risks creating its foundation not on substantive questions ("Is woman a useful analytical category?") but on a set of teleological attitudinal beliefs that women studies always exceeds and perpetually must move beyond what has come before. While there is much debate on what should constitute a core for women's studies graduate training, and scholars working in such fields work from widely differing intellectual perspectives, I am arguing that the intellectual core of the interdisciplinary PhD is often defined more by a set of cultural norms *about* knowledge. The knowledge practices that I am discussing in this chapter have to do with the kind of performative and iterative practices that Judith Butler has argued produce normative categories (such as the normative heterosexual construction of the category of gender).[32] Thus, there are practices within women's studies institutional sites in which a particular mode of interdisciplinarity is performed. PhD students in women's studies are trained to continually enact and reenact this performance of discontinuous knowledge that I have been analyzing. The serious risk for interdisciplinary scholars to consider is that it is precisely this turn to citational practices (that then become disciplinary discursive mechanisms) that Edward Said asked us to understand as the practices that produced a history of orientalist thought that became a discursive-material entity with critical implications but had little correspondence to the ontological worlds it claimed to represent.[33]

These dynamics are certainly not unique to women's studies. However, they are intensified when a field like women's studies is institutionalized through modes of credentialing such as the PhD because of the conjunction of three distinct systemic factors that I have been discussing. First, as I have noted, the economic organization of the U.S. academy is such that the production of knowledge is geared toward branding and the marketing of newness. In this sense, academic knowledge production is unexceptional and is like any other industry that is operating under the particular historical conditions of a globalized capitalist economy. Second, the struggle that women's studies programs and departments have in gaining institutional resources when compared with disciplinary-based departments means that women's studies often does not have sufficient resources to provide the depth and breadth of knowledge required to handle broad-ranging international, transnational, and comparative understandings of the world. Finally, as I have argued, the absence of an agreed-on foundation or canon, either due to a philosophical attachment to a particular model of interdisciplinarity or due to a more benign inability to produce a consensual agreement on such a canon, means that the brand-oriented approach to knowledge becomes the de facto foundation of interdisciplinary knowledge. This is particularly the case when graduate students are thrown into rigorous graduate programs with peers from varying backgrounds and faculty trained in wide-ranging areas. The brand becomes contingent on the structure of the institutional cultural context at hand. Criteria such as the valorization of particular modes of inquiry and the creation of student cults that may develop around particular paradigms and thinkers are always an unspoken feature of the intellectual training of PhD students. In a degree-granting field that rests on the rejection of any foundational knowledge, such cultural practices run the risk of becoming a central disciplinary feature of the field. This kind of disciplinary dynamic holds significant implications not just for the production and dissemination of knowledge about the world but also potentially for the kind of relationship that students establish with the places they write about.[34]

An alternative to the branding cultural model of knowledge requires a deeper challenge to some of the dominant models of interdisciplinary feminist scholarship that have become mainstreamed within the academy. Such models are implicitly defined by ideologies of newness that presuppose that intellectual innovation rests on critical ruptures from past ways of knowing. This of course is not unique to feminist scholarship as the commercial organization of intellectual life commodifies knowledge so that the substantive nature of intellectual contributions is increasingly measured by the newness (and therefore the marketability) of the product. However, within interdisciplinary fields such as feminist scholarship this has also been accentuated by the teleological conception of time embodied in postmodernist approaches. The very term "post" in itself suggests moving beyond and past older forms of thought (somewhat paradoxically, since postmodernist thought itself has interrogated teleological approaches to history). The result is that there is a strong impetus within interdisciplinary feminist scholarship to emphasize the creation of concepts or linguistic expressions that can capture this sense of newness and rupture.

Genealogies of Feminist Thought and the Wave Model of U.S. Feminism

The challenges of adequately moving women's studies curricular practices outside of a U.S.-centric model of the world require a deeper reconsideration of the genealogies of feminist thought that continue to frame the field. The intellectual drive to move beyond earlier approaches is built into the broader historical construction of feminism and feminist thought as a progressive series of discrete waves.[35] In existing framings of the field (as they are often institutionalized within feminist theory courses and within many areas of feminist scholarship), transnational feminism (along with postcolonial feminist theory) in the United States is generally placed within the "third wave" of the genealogy of U.S. feminism. The framing of transnational feminism as part of the "third wave" stems from particular debates around questions of difference—including race, sexuality, and nation—and the drive to challenge the exclusionary constructions of the category of "woman." The body of scholarship associated with "third wave" feminism has had a transformative impact on contemporary feminist intellectual agendas. Such work spans a vast set of writings that have addressed the ways in which multiple forms of inequality have shaped women's subjectivities, lives, and modes of resistance. In the language of one of the classic texts that marked the emergence of this challenge, *This Bridge Called My Back*, U.S. feminists of color sought both to decenter conceptions of feminism based narrowly on the experience of white middle-class women and to call attention to inequalities that have historically shaped relationships between women in the United States.[36] The forceful political and intellectual challenges of such writing had far-reaching implications as feminist and women's studies programs sought to redefine intellectual agendas and curricula in order to systematically address and integrate questions of difference.

While the call for feminists to address questions of difference such as race, sexuality, and class had occurred in previous decades of U.S. feminist thought and activism, the impact and breadth of this new surge of writing and activism by feminists of color led to the characterization of this work as a new wave of feminism that had moved past the exclusions of past (and in particular "second wave") feminist approaches. This classification sought to capture the significance and distinctiveness of this new flourishing field within feminist scholarship. These developments dovetailed with calls among feminists of color to engage with transnational perspectives and to break from Western-oriented feminist narratives within the United States. I address the deeper intellectual linkages and engagements on the scholarship on race and transnationalism in chapter 6. For the purposes of this discussion, I focus on the relationship between the wave model of feminism and institutional practice. I examine how the study of complex intellectual feminist histories has been institutionalized through organized curricular practices based on the wave model. The result, as I argue, is the institutionalized reproduction of a distorted and partial understanding of feminist history.

The wave model of feminism has meant that conventional curricular practices in women's studies usually expose students to feminism and gender outside of the United States as a later phase of historical intellectual development. This produces a conception of place that is marked by a delayed temporality that dislocates such places from their own historical genealogies. It has in effect produced a historical narrative that has constructed feminists outside the United States as a kind of temporal other. This framing practice stems from a broader connection between race and the construction of narrative that has permeated epistemological practices in the Western academy. Johannes Fabian, for instance, has argued that the discipline of anthropology was marked by a set of practices in which Western anthropologists constructed the subjects of non-Western cultures as located within a different temporal space. Drawing on an evolutionary conception of time, this form of narrative portrayed the Western subject as the marker of progress and development through the othering of the non-Western object.[37] The process of othering is intrinsic to the hegemonic form of temporality produced by these disciplinary practices.

When women's studies curricular practices in courses such as the required feminist theory courses that are an intrinsic part of most PhD programs introduce "the transnational" or "the postcolonial" purely through critiques of Western feminism associated with this "third wave" of feminism, feminist history is in effect flattened out into a singular model despite the fact that the objective of third wave feminism was to decenter and deconstruct this very model. At one level, what is missing is a more systematic integration of nuanced, complex historical narratives in which the originary moment of feminism does not stem from a first or second wave of U.S. feminism. This is in part an effect of what Jane Newman has identified as the "presentism" in women's studies curricular practices.[38] At the level of institutional practice, for instance, the standard theory-method sequence that, as Wendy Brown accurately notes, is the conventional core of many PhD programs does not provide any space for a rehistoricization of women's movements and of feminist thought. Individual faculty members may teach specialized courses (which will usually draw students who already have a background on transnational or comparative issues) or may struggle to address such issues in the canonical theory course. However, the theory courses are already overladen with excessive expectations (as students play out complex disciplinary and ideological conflicts and divisions between theoretically oriented students and "antitheory" or antipoststructuralist sentiments in this required course). I have found in my own teaching of this kind of course over many years that it can do little more than serve as a cursory overview of a few key debates.

This missing ontology of feminist history inadvertently recasts complex international, global, and national histories into a homogenized model of U.S. history (and one that misrepresents the nuances of women's movements and feminist thought in the United States itself).[39] Moreover, these issues are not limited to graduate education. I have focused thus far on the autonomous women's studies PhD precisely because it potentially serves as a powerful disciplinary mechanism that is shaping the field in significant ways. While individual courses, projects, or texts can—and continually do—disrupt such dynamics at both the undergraduate and the graduate level, the question that remains open is how systematic institutional practices can more effectively consider the relationship between women's studies and the worlds the field seeks to represent. In many ways, given practical constraints of resources and faculty expertise, a reworking of institutional practices may require a turn toward more modest goals and expectations. This would include acknowledging the limits on the training that women's studies graduate programs can provide. For instance, women's studies departments can simply specify what location-bound conceptions of the global they have expertise in. More important, ambitious claims of geographic coverage—of the global and transnational—often mean that departments seek to hire an array of individuals working on various locales or transnational processes. It is highly unusual for departments to make interdisciplinary cluster hires that center on particular regions or places.

This may of course sound like a project that transforms women's studies into international or area studies, a concern expressed in the fear-laden anecdote at the beginning of this chapter. Yet consider the hypothetical project of hiring a cluster of feminist scholars working on Latin America and on cross-border, transnational processes within the Americas training graduate students with the depth and systematic analytical understanding of theoretical, literary, political-economic, and social contexts of local, national, and transnational processes in this continental space. It is not hard to imagine a national situation where various departments could hold varied forms of specializations—defined not by dated Cold War area studies definitions but by place-based connections rooted in more nuanced historical-spatial definitions—whether defined through regional, continental, or oceanic parameters. This is just one example of the ways in which teaching the "transnational" could be transformed by institutional practices of hiring and curricular organization.

The importance of rethinking the institutional practices that will contribute to the definition of women's studies through new graduate programs is not purely about the kind of academic scholarship that becomes emblematic of the field. It is also about the ways in which new disciplinary practices that reproduce the field will also shape undergraduate education. Many of the issues that arise in training graduate students hold similar implications for undergraduate students. Unlike in PhD-level work, the ability of undergraduate students to get sustained, individual advising that can shape and deepen their understanding of places they seek to know about and work in is much more restricted and may vary widely depending on the resources and structure of particular colleges and universities. However, the nature of undergraduate teaching may also provide more opportunities given that undergraduate students are less invested in the reproductive dynamics of the academy that permeate graduate education (a culture of reproduction that can be oriented around theoretical approaches, paradigms, models of inter/disciplinarity, or simply of a "brand model" of knowledge that is oriented around the celebrity of individual intellectual figures).

Undergraduate Education and Women's Studies

Over the past decades, undergraduate education in women's studies has made significant strides in the integration of transnational and non-U.S.-centric approaches to gender and women.[40] Most women's studies programs now actively seek to move beyond a U.S.-oriented focus. More significantly, the focus on differences between women and on the power dynamics inherent in studying "other" women has become a canonical part of the field. Theories that address intersectionality, the quandaries of cross-cultural analysis, and the problems of Western representations of women are now routinely incorporated into women's studies curricula. Yet there remain limitations to the way in which students are trained to approach comparative or transnational perspectives on gender. Many of the issues that arise with the organization of the graduate curriculum are mirrored in the training that undergraduate students receive. Jacqui Alexander and Chandra Mohanty signal the challenges inherent in this process of institutionalization in their interpretive survey of women's studies and sexuality studies syllabi. They note that older approaches that revert to easy forms of cultural relativism of U.S. and Eurocentric models of feminism often reappear in the guise of transnationalism.[41]

Adequate responses to the organization of syllabi and curricula raise complex questions that may belie easy normative formulations and may compel feminist scholars to consider the disjunctures between our intellectual-political desires as scholars, student consumer interests, and student needs. Alexander and Mohanty argue that the "transnational" too often ignores the United States and focuses on women located "elsewhere."[42] After their cogent critical discussion of this problem, Alexander and Mohanty turn to the example of prisons as an issue that can unsettle transnational framings of place as embedded in discrete locations "elsewhere" or in discrete national contexts. They argue that antiprison mobilizations serve as an example of a site for "radical sites of knowledge."[43] As they note, "More specifically, however, it is the incarceration of increasing numbers of impoverished women of color that enables us to track the links between neoliberal privatization, the U.S. export of prison technologies, organized militarization, dominant and subordinate patriarchies, and neocolonial ideologies."[44] Alexander and Mohanty seek to address the important point that a key problem with the framing of the transnational is that the United States is often displaced from analysis so that the transnational conceals the relationship between the United States and women's and gender issues in other places. They present the example of prisons as one way to make connections between the United States and the rest of the world through a focus on U.S. state practices (such as the export of surveillance technology and the training of police forces in other countries). Furthermore, as they go on to suggest, a focus on prisons raises questions regarding the politics of space and parallel conflicts around land control and land usage in the United States and in comparative contexts.

Alexander and Mohanty raise a critical point regarding the need to ensure that the United States is located within any conception of the transnational so that undergraduate students can reflect on their own location and relationship to local, national, and global processes. Certainly the recentering of U.S. state practices is understandable in the context of particular kinds of issues in the late twentieth-century and early twentieth-century periods. However, while this recentering may be useful as a first step in particular classes or at particular phases in the course of an undergraduate major's curriculum, it is not sufficient as a broader approach to the study of transnational or comparative understandings. Not all historical periods or local, national, regional, and transnational processes center around the role of the United States (or the negative effects of U.S. state policy). The prison industry is central to understanding the political economy of the United States and the role of the state in directing this industrial complex.[45] At a methodological and epistemological level, however, it is not apparent why a focus on prisons would serve as the self-evident analytical (or for that matter political) lens through which to understand the state or the political-economic structures of contexts outside the United States. The problem is not of course that prisons are not central to state structures in comparative contexts. However, the politicization of this issue and the economic centrality of the prison industry vary widely and are contingent on the type of political system, the regime in power, and the economic position of the country in question. More significantly, there may be important differences in the framing of political debates in cross-national contexts. For instance, the centrality of the issue of prisons in the United States is linked both to the political economy of the state and to grassroots social movements that are mobilizing against the prison system. Yet the political framing of prisons may occur differently in different contexts (for example, political prisoners may be more central in some contexts, but such issues may be framed in terms of civil war, secessionist movements, or attempts to overthrow repressive states), and most undergraduate students may simply lack the knowledge of such contexts.

Simply picking a worthy normative issue such as prisons to frame transnational debates may inadvertently consolidate a U.S.-centric model of knowledge (in this case one that stems from U.S. progressive political agendas). Moving students outside of a U.S.-centric perspective is a particularly challenging task in undergraduate women's studies teaching.

Given the problems inherent in organizing a comprehensive interdisciplinary curriculum, students become more comfortable both with cultural relativist narratives (the script that "we cannot intervene or judge other cultures") and with approaches that recenter the United States through criticisms of Western feminism. I have found, for instance, that students find it much more difficult to immerse themselves in the study and understanding of contexts or issues outside the United States in ways that do not recenter their own "self" in some way. This dynamic is not unique to women's studies, but it is intensified in women's studies courses because of the emphasis of feminist pedagogy on personal self-expression, on experience, and in many cases on confessional narratives of students. While such pedagogical practices that are often central to introductory-level women's studies courses can be very powerful tools in unpacking the study of social identities of race and gender, they become problematic when students must learn about comparative and transnational issues.[46] In the self-oriented context of women's studies, teaching students to learn about or even become interested in issues and contexts that may not be centrally defined in relation to their own location is often more challenging than trying to get them to criticize the U.S. state or Western feminist approaches. In this regard, Alexander and Mohanty are too quick to dismiss courses that focus "elsewhere."[47] In my own teaching, I have, for instance, found that students have much more difficulty in engaging with contexts that require them to leave aside their identities. I have come across these dynamics in a vivid manner in a course I developed on gender in South Asia in response to this gap in student preparation. The course is inherently "transnational" because it deals with global processes such as colonialism and economic liberalization, as well as with a comparative analysis of countries within the region. In every version of the course that I have taught, students struggle to engage with and ask questions about readings that require them to focus on historical events or issues with which they are unfamiliar. In contrast, they come alive and speak with comfort in sections of the course that deal with difficulties of cross-cultural understanding and critiques of U.S. or Western feminism.

The problem at hand is not with the implicit call that Alexander and Mohanty are making for students to locate themselves and their own relationship to the United States within the transnational. Rather, the conundrum for the field of women's studies is that the nature of feminist pedagogy and its emphasis on recentering students' self-expression and identity-based knowledge mean that the fine line between a focus on self-accountability and self-interest often gets blurred in troubling ways. Feminist pedagogy has for the most part been motivated by the objective of establishing an ethic of accountability in the classroom—urging students to come to terms with their sources of privilege and providing them with analytical tools to understand various forms of inequality. However, this ethic of self-account-ability can easily become circumscribed by self-interest if students come to believe that learning must stem from personal experience. When student interest becomes restricted to wanting to learn about issues that connect to their sense of self-identification (even if that self-identification is cast as a progressive critique of their own geographic location), interest in effect becomes a narrowly defined self-interest. If women's studies as a field is serious about moving out of a U.S.-centric approach, the terms that constitute feminist pedagogy need to be seriously rethought. Moving out of a U.S.-centric approach in fact may precisely mean developing pedagogical practices that allow students to learn about histories and civilizations that compel them to suspend their self-interest and personal experiential desires. Without this focus on places and histories that may be shaped by but are not reducible to U.S. politics and contemporary transnational forces of globalization, transnational perspectives risk becoming reduced to frames of self-interest.

This does not of course mean that there is no space for the experiential dimensions of feminist pedagogy when addressing transnational or cross-national concerns. Consider the pedagogical project that Pamela Trotman Reid and Ramaswami Mahalingam designed to further cross-cultural understanding for a group of undergraduate students.[48] Reid and Mahalingam took a group of African American women students and developed a forum for an exchange of personal stories and experiences between the students and Dalit women in India.[49] Drawing on what they call a practice of "self-storytelling," they set up a cross-cultural engagement that draws on the historically and socially situated worlds of the two groups in question. This instance provides a model of developing forms of cross-cultural engagement that rest on what Weinbaum et al. call a form of "connective comparison."[50] In contrast to consumption-oriented models of travel or generic study-abroad programs that may provide students with entry points to transnational issues, this kind of cultural exchange rests on a deeper understanding of comparative forms of intersectionality (race and gender for the African American students; caste and gender for the Dalit women) that structured the lives of these women in their respective countries. As Reid and Mahalingam note, rather than taking either group as an essential-ized, self-evident identity-based formation, they began with the belief that each participant in a dialogue must openly examine her own experiences of gender, ethnicity, and social class before moving to an analysis of the other's. For this group of African American women, this meant unpacking: (a) the issues of gender, social class, and color; (b) expectations placed on them by their families, their majority peers, other African Americans; (c) the institutional assumptions as embodied in policies and practices; and (d) the beliefs they held for themselves. The Dalit women also disclosed their experiences around the same set of issues rendered in culture-specific forms.[51]

Such an example points to the possibilities of drawing on feminist pedagogical traditions of experiential learning when such learning is carefully located within the particular social, historical, and political contexts of both the students and the groups and the places that they seek to learn about.

Typical pedagogical practices within the classroom unfortunately do not usually allow for this kind of focused and grounded cross-cultural engagement across national borders. A typical pedagogical challenge rests on what Dawn Rae Davis has described as the desire for mirroring, in which students expect to see themselves as the central subject of the course and the touristic imaginary through which they safely consume the study of other places and women.[52] As Davis argues, "The mirroring effect and the touristic imaginary represent flip sides of an epistemology organized by the primacy of the 'self' to identity and, in the relation of self-identity, to difference within the orthodoxies of imperialism and its western traditions."[53] Davis's analysis and her attempt to interrogate the presumed "primacy of the self to knowledge" call our attention to one of the most significant limitations of conventional understandings of feminist pedagogy.[54] Dominant understandings of feminist pedagogy that are often established in introductory courses frequently stress personal, experiential approaches to knowledge. Pedagogical practices—including those that challenge privileges of race and class—often stress the expression of students' personal relationships and understandings of such processes. Students thus associate the field of women's studies with experiential, identity-centered learning that stresses their personal voice in framing their relationship to knowledge. However, such an approach is at best inadequate when students must learn about worlds that they are not familiar with or are not directly connected to through structured identity-based relations. Davis provides a powerful discussion of her own endeavor to develop a kind of pedagogy of disidentification that disrupts student desires to recenter their own selves in their engagements with women from other contexts. Thus, she discusses a set of practices that provoke students to confront and rearrange their own desires in the classroom.

I would argue that if women's studies is to adequately develop comparative and transnational approaches through curricular and pedagogical practice, this interrogation of self-oriented knowledge would in fact need to be expanded. What students in women's studies often need is not a space to focus on the self and on personal experience but the ability to learn how to suspend their own selves when learning about the world. The experiential drive of feminist pedagogy has meant that student learning has become driven by issues that recenter their own lives. This is also a strong if nuanced dynamic in the activist-driven rhetoric of many women's studies courses and programs. Activism often becomes a way of recentering one's self through the desire to intervene. What feminist pedagogy needs most is an ethic of humility—one that teaches students that they in fact cannot find all the answers purely through voice and self-expression; that learning requires suspending self-centered desires and developing an interest in worlds that matter on their own terms; that personal opinion is not a sufficient basis for analyzing the different worlds that women live in unless it is informed by the patient labor of learning about aspects of the world that are not always entertaining or inspiring. Without such a break from the romance of the self that still serves as a foundational identity for pedagogy in women's studies—whether through theoretical or activist approaches to knowledge—the study of comparative, transnational, and international contexts will remain a glossy finish on a nation-centric conception of the field. The challenge for women's studies will be whether it wants to break from this model of U.S. transnational feminism.

Conclusion

Underlying this discussion of feminist pedagogy is a long-standing problem of the ways in which multicultural models of difference become institutionalized. The challenge for fields such as women's studies has long been how to institutionalize the study of difference in ways that do not reproduce formulaic or static understandings of complex identities, places, and contexts. One risk in the rise of the paradigm of transnationalism is that the transnational is often simply another racialized marker of difference and othernesss. Alexander and Mohanty, for instance, argue the following regarding undergraduate women's studies courses: "Thus, it seems that the transnational has now come to occupy the place that 'race' and women of color held in women's studies syllabi in the 1990s and earlier."[55] This conflation raises a number of risks and issues for curricular practices and the definition of the field of women's studies. At one level, the racialization of the "transnational" reflects the domestication of the world within national models of U.S. multiculturalism. The world outside of the United States in such a conception becomes a minority figure—a geopolitical form of geographic imagination that serves to recenter the U.S. as the panopticon for domesticated others. At another level, the substitution of transnationalism for race also raises dangers that global or transnational perspectives may sideline the systematic study of race within U.S. women's studies programs. Both these risks raise questions of how to effectively address the relationship between scholarship and work on race and transnationalism in relation to the United States and scholarship on transnational or comparative approaches that seek to break from U.S.-oriented approaches—questions I turn to in the following chapter. These dilemmas point to the challenges of institutionalizing the study of comparative, international, and /transnational perspectives within the parameters of women's studies programs and caution us to adopt a sense of humility about what we can claim to be training students to do and learn about in relation to the world. Focusing on curricular practices in terms of institutional practice reminds us of the ways in which we inadvertently discipline and territorialize the boundaries of interdisciplinary knowledge in ways that may reproduce rather than move beyond the U.S. nation-state.

6

Race, Transnational Feminism, and Paradigms of Difference

ONE OF THE key features of the paradigm of transnational feminism is that it has emerged within and is shaped in central ways by models of multicultural education that are specific to the context of the United States. A central underlying challenge in the institutionalization of transnational approaches within the field of women's studies thus lies with the way in which understandings of transnational feminism are disciplined by existing paradigms of difference. Dominant paradigms of multiculturalism often continue to cast transnationalism as another marker of identity so that the inclusion of transnational perspectives simply means the inclusion of one more category of the "other." Thus, it is not uncommon for core women's studies courses at both the undergraduate and the graduate level to allot one week to the inclusion of global or transnational (that is, non-U.S.) issues. The multicultural paradigm at work here is one that minoritizes the world. In other words, the world outside the United States is cast as one more minority identity to be included within the field of women's studies. This process of minoritization opens up a complex set of issues regarding the relationship between race and transnationalism within contemporary feminist thought. The transformation of the world into a minority identity category speaks to a particular kind of racialized geographic imagination that still haunts interdisciplinary feminist thought—one that conceives of the world as a minority group within its pluralistic multicultural framework. The transformation of transnational approaches into a paradigm of multicultural difference raises the question of how we should understand the relationship between race and transnationalism.[1]

The emergence of transnational feminist perspectives within the United States has been shaped in distinctive ways by the histories and intellectual interventions of feminists of color who have sought to call attention to the racialized, gendered politics of the U.S. state. Critical feminist thought on race and transnationalism has interrogated the U.S. nation-state and located the United States within a set a transnational relationships that foreground its position within structures of global capital and geopolitical frames of empire. One of the challenges for interdisciplinary women's studies scholars is to be able to provide a complex intellectual genealogy of feminist thought that addresses (1) the U.S. feminist of color interventions, (2) the distinctive feminist histories in comparative and global perspectives that have their own intellectual genealogies, and (3) the points of convergence between the first two strands that may arise at particular historical periods through particular transnational connections such as migration or diasporic politics. The ability to retain such complexities within academic programs and departments is further constrained given limits on resources and the institutionalization of models of multiculturalism that rest on simplified understandings of difference.

In this chapter, I interrogate dominant paradigms of difference that structure these complex genealogies of feminist thought. As I have noted in chapter 5, histories of feminism have often been institutionalized through a wave model of feminism. Scholars writing from a range of perspectives have at various points commented on and sought to transform the limiting vision of the wave metaphor of historical change. Aikau, Erickson, and Pierce, for instance, have sought to shift from an image of static, sequential waves to a more nuanced depiction of feminist generations.[2] Writing about the complex histories of feminist generations in the United States, Hokulani Aikau has sought to redefine the meaning of the wave metaphor. She argues that an understanding of the "materiality of waves" provides a "more complex view of the variations that exist within a single generation of feminists and begins to offer a way to trace the legacies of feminism through time and across space."[3] Nancy Hewitt has argued that despite a significant body of feminist scholarship that has complicated feminist histories that exceed and displace this metaphor, the wave model persists. Thus, she argues:

> It may be impossible to jettison the concept of feminist waves. Indeed. the Library of Congress is now introducing *first wave* and *second wave* as topical categories. Thus, it is especially important to think about other types of waves, such as radio waves, that can help us conceptualize the feminist past. Radio waves allow us to think about movements of different lengths and frequencies; movements that grow louder or fade out, that reach vast audiences across oceans or only a few listeners in a local area; movements that are marked by static interruptions or frequent changes of channels; and movements that are temporarily drowned out by another frequency but then suddenly come in loud and clear.[4]

Building on such critical interventions, this chapter deepens the interrogation of the wave model through an analysis of the construction of
"third wave" feminism. The application of this conventional form of historical periodization of distinctive waves of feminism has led to misreadings and misrepresentations of the substantive contributions of emerging
paradigms of difference within feminist scholarship. Dominant narratives
of third wave feminism tend to focus on three central paradigms—multicultural inclusion, identity politics, and the paradigm of intersectionality.
While these have certainly been key paradigms within feminist scholarship, "third wave" feminism represents a more complex and varied set of
debates and interventions. As Chela Sandoval has argued, the term "third
wave" casts this field of knowledge into a teleological historical narrative
that misses the ways in which such work has simultaneously occupied intellectual spaces of earlier feminist intellectual traditions even as it has often argued against or sought to move beyond dominant paradigms within
women's studies.[5] Drawing on Sandoval's theory of differential consciousness, the essay interrogates the institutionalization of third wave feminism
through narratives of multiculturalism and identity politics. It then moves
beyond these dominant narratives and elaborates on the points of connection and possible engagements between U.S. feminist of color thought and
comparative/transnational perspectives. I discuss the ways in which conceptions of race and transnationalism provide alternative understandings
of history that disrupt the teleological wave model of history. This alternative historical narrative can provide an opening for a rehistoricization of
feminist thought in ways that break with a U.S.-centric model of history.
Finally, I examine the ways in which the paradigm of intersectionality pio-
neered by African American feminists can provide a point of engagement
with feminist approaches in comparative contexts in ways that do not
appropriate or displace the historical and intellectual genealogies of this
paradigm.

"Third Wave" Feminism and Paradigms of Difference

The emergence of "third wave" feminism is conventionally associated
with the trend within women's studies and feminist scholarship to focus
on questions of differences with a particular emphasis on the integration
of studies of race, class, and gender within the United States.[6] One of the
underlying effects of the three wave model of feminism is the inadvertent

representation of feminist thought as a teleological historical narrative of progressive inclusion.

By framing new challenges to the existing terms of feminist thought and practice as a new "wave," such work is defined primarily as a move toward the greater inclusion of women of color within feminism. In other words, according to this historical narrative, if second wave feminism was the preserve of white, middle-class women, third wave feminism marked a new phase where feminists of color and questions of race and gender were now included. The feminist wave model implicitly rests on a narrative of multicultural inclusion.

Aspects of "third wave" feminist challenges to the existing feminist terrain certainly included political and intellectual claims for inclusion within institutional and intellectual feminist sites.[7] However, the substantive challenges of these writings also represented a deeper theoretical challenge to narratives of multicultural inclusion. Writing in the 1990s, Ella Shohat aptly cautioned against this tendency: "U.S. women of color and Third World women's struggle over the past decades cannot conform to the orthodox sequence of 'first waves' and 'second waves,' just as multicultural feminism cannot be viewed as simply a recent bandwagon phenomenon; it is a response to a five hundred-year history of gendered colonialist dispossession in the past and of massive post-colonial displacements in the present."[8] Norma Alarcon, for instance, argued that writings by feminists of color in *This Bridge Called My Back* represented a theoretical challenge to the "logic of identification" that had characterized the subject of feminism as "an autonomous, self-making, self-determining subject."[9] This project called for a rethinking of feminism that challenged languages of inclusion that sought to integrate "difference" within existing models of subjectivity. This challenge sought to create a feminism that did not presume gender as its foundational category or "common denominator."[10] As Alarcon put it:

> The female subject of *This Bridge* is highly complex. She is and has been constructed in a crisis of meaning situation which includes racial and cultural divisions and conflicts. The psychic and material violence that gives shape to that subjectivity cannot be underestimated nor passed over lightly. The fact that not all of this violence comes from men in general but also from women renders the notion of "common denominator" problematic.[11]

Such criticisms have, of course, now become well institutionalized as part of a broader series of debates on the category of "woman."[12] However,

Alarcon's argument also pointed to a deeper challenge, or what she called "a process of disidentification" from the existing subject of feminism that was inherent in writings characterized as "third wave" feminism.[13] It is precisely this politics of disidentification (a point I turn to later in the chapter) that has been rendered invisible by the wave model of feminism. Instead, the three-wave model has largely tended to highlight paradigms that fit within or represent a logical expansion of the narrative of inclusion.

Consider two of the central paradigms that dominant feminist intellectual narratives now associate with "third wave" feminism—identity politics and intersectionality. In the first case, hegemonic feminist narratives have often sought to depict the impact of "third wave" feminism through the frame of identity-based claims. At one level, this framing has often shaped attempts at integrating work associated with "third wave" feminism within existing curricular and feminist research agendas. In this narrative, "second wave" feminism is (erroneously) associated purely with the essentialized figure of the "middle-class white woman." "Third wave" feminism then becomes an expansion of this subject to include the voices and identities of women marked by a diverse set of identities. The politics of inclusion rests on the marking of identities that can subsequently be integrated within the subject of feminism. This project of inclusion in effect rests on the logic of identification that Alarcon describes.

Given that the wave model of feminism lends itself to a misclassification of the substantive contributions of this period of feminist thought through the politics of identification, it is perhaps unsurprising that critical responses to "third wave" feminism have often been founded on this depiction. Thus, in both everyday discourses in academic settings and intellectual writings, such critiques often rested on dominant narratives on the limits of "identity politics." At one level, this critique tends to cast the challenges of "third wave" feminist writing in terms of a set of static, discrete identity frames. This is perhaps best captured through Judith Butler's early critique of this serial approach to identity in which she calls attention to "an embarrassed 'etc.,'" which concludes the list of identities ("race, class, gender, sexuality etc.") often listed in feminist attempts at addressing diversity.[14] Butler was, of course, pointing to the theoretical limits of hegemonic multicultural models of identity politics that provide a surface understanding of subjectivity. However, this narrative of identity politics has often been mistakenly used to classify and then criticize "third wave" feminist writing. As Grace Hong has argued, "Women of color feminist practice emerged to name the contradictions of the racialized nation-state by deploying tactics that exceeded nationalism's scope: intersectional analysis, an attention to difference, and a critique of identification with the normative race, gender and sexual institutions of the state."[15] Butler's narrative mistakenly submerges this critical break with the nation-state through her narrative of a hegemonic national narrative of multiculturalism. The underlying assumption in this conflation between multiculturalism and "third wave" feminism is that the contributions of U.S. feminists of color are reducible to a series of political-intellectual claims for inclusion within the discursive and institutional sites associated with feminism. In this narrative, the varied intellectual contributions of U.S. feminists of color become reducible to the creation of "women of color" as a singular identity category seeking citizenship within the nation-state.[16]

The wave model representation of "third wave" feminism has thus proved problematic in a number of ways. I have been suggesting that this teleological model of feminist progression has served to reinforce a particular identity-based framing of feminist thought that reproduces hegemonic models of multiculturalism.[17] Feminist thought is presented as a series of expanding identities that need to be included within contemporary feminism. This approach has little to do with the complex, substantive contributions and challenges of writing classified as "third wave." However, the impact of this framework used to characterize contemporary U.S. feminism is not just a question of rhetoric about identity politics. The intellectual and political challenges that provide the foundation for what is now classified as "third wave" feminism unfolded in and were in effect temporally part of the same historical period as "second wave" feminism. Leading feminist thinkers such as Gloria Anzaldúa, bell hooks, Cherríe Moraga, and Audre Lorde were clearly located within the historical period associated with "second wave" feminism.

One of the distinctive features commonly associated with "third wave" feminism is the challenge to the category of "woman." It is now unremarkable in feminist discussions to speak of differences between women and the varied and complex construction of gender. However, this intellectual shift was marked by the convergence of two distinct (though sometimes overlapping) streams—U.S. feminist of color thought and poststructuralist feminism. The 1980s and 1990s witnessed the growing dominance of poststructuralist challenges to conventional categories and forms of feminist thought. Joan Scott's seminal essay on gender as a central category of historical analysis was emblematic of the use of this category to denote the process of historical and cultural construction (as opposed to essentialist understandings of "woman").[18] The assumption that such critiques of the category of woman occurred in a distinctive temporal phase after the expansion of feminist writings and activism in the 1960s and 1970s partly stems from a misunderstanding and erasure of the writings of U.S. feminists of color during this earlier period of "second wave" feminism. Many poststructuralist feminists writing in the 1980s and 1990s constructed the earlier writings and political claims of feminists of color as lodged within static identity claims (that poststructuralists depicted as another version of essentialism). For instance, feminist poststructuralist critiques of the use of "experience" as a basis for feminist knowledge were targeted as much at U.S. feminists writing about racism as they were at "second wave" middle-class feminists.[19] The deeper theoretical contributions of these earlier writings (and the complexity of simultaneously making identity-based claims while providing alternative theories of subjectivity) were not recognized within much of poststructuralist feminism as an existing theoretical approach to the construction and interrogation of categories such as difference, experience, and identity (rather than simply as an expression of difference).[20] Thus, ironically, the shift from an emphasis on equality associated with "second wave" feminism to differences between women associated with "third wave" feminism was temporally conflated with the rise of the poststructuralist feminist emphasis on difference. This conflation was also unintentionally facilitated by the ways in which new feminist discussions of race and postcoloniality began to draw on poststructuralism as tools for decentering Eurocentric conceptions of feminism.[21]

A critical reconsideration of the wave framework of feminism asks us to pause and consider some of the implications of the conception of time that is now commonly used to periodize the history of feminist thought. I argue that two key issues are at stake in this (mis)framing of feminist history. The first rests on the ways in which this periodization stems from some of the misunderstandings of the substantive contributions of feminists of color that I have been discussing. The second issue stems from the deeper links between race and conceptions of temporality. The disciplinary impetus to classify discrete waves of feminism in effect ended up drawing boundaries that displaced the substantive interventions of "second wave" feminists writing about race into a different temporal and geographic space. This displacement has had two key effects. On the one hand, it has produced a construction of "second wave" feminism as a white, middle-class movement rather than a complex and conflicted social and intellectual movement that was struggling over defining the terms of feminism. On the other hand, histories of feminism outside of the United States are located as a later development in time because such challenges are associated with critiques of U.S. and Eurocentric visions that emerged in the 1980s within the United States. The result is a racialized, nation-centered conception of time and space underlying this historical model of feminism.

This question of miscasting feminist historical narratives and the temporality of feminist thought points to a deeper question about the political and intellectual significance of historical memory. In an essay reflecting on her memories of *This Bridge Called My Back*, Jacqui Alexander writes:

> What brings us back to re-membrance is both individual and collective; both intentional and an act of surrender; both remembering desire and remembering *how* it works (Morrison, *Beloved* 20). Daring to recognize each other again and again in a context that seems bent on making strangers of us all. Can we *intentionally* remember, all the time, as a way of never forgetting, all of us, building an archaeology of living memory, which has less to do with living in the past, invoking a past, or excising it, and more to do with our relationship to time and its purpose. There is a difference between remember *when*—the nostalgic yearning for some return—and a living memory that enables us to re-member what was contained in *Bridge* and what could not be contained within it or by it.[22]

It is precisely this living memory, which embodies the original insights of work such as *This Bridge Called My Back*, that is lost within a wave model of feminism. Alexander's eloquent discussion of the transformative power of memory provides us with a deeper possibility for producing a richer and more transformative narrative that can capture the complexities of feminist intellectual and social history.

What would such a living memory of the histories of U.S. feminism look like? Such an alternative would potentially be more powerful but also more challenging. In one sense, such a living memory would enable successive generations of feminists to realize that nonlinear understandings of history (breaking from evolutionary conceptions of temporality) in fact necessitate periodic and tactical returns to earlier political and intellectual strategies and visions.

This is in effect one of the central implications of Sandoval's method of differential consciousness. A move from the wave model of feminism to a history rooted in living memory is not simply a symbolic strategy of honoring the contributions of earlier generations of feminists. Rather, it is a question of remembering that successive generations of feminism can never move beyond earlier histories through a simplistic attempt at creating a clear temporal break from the past.

Consider the example of *This Bridge Called My Home*,[23] a text published as both a commemoration of and a continuation of the intellectual work of *This Bridge Called My Back*. The volume provides an important example of Jacqui Alexander's discussion of an alternative approach to memory and history. The subject of *This Bridge Called My Home* presents both substantive continuities and critical engagements with the first *Bridge*. As with the first *Bridge*, the volume presents a series of essays that speak to the persistence of discrimination, in particular forms of racism and homophobia both within contemporary society and as persistent elements within feminist spaces. Yet several of the contributors also speak to some of the discrepancies with the first book. AnaLouise Keating, coeditor of the volume, introduces the collection with a cautionary note: "If you've opened this book expecting to find a carbon copy of *This Bridge Called My Back*, don't bother. Stop now."[24] In contrast to the first *Bridge*, this volume includes contributions by both men and white women (a decision that Keating writes produced some significant criticism as a violation of the spirit of the first *Bridge*). This question of inclusion reflects a deeper critique of identity inherent in the volume as several of the contributors provide critical theoretical and substantive alternatives to concepts such as "identity" and "authenticity."[25] Taken together, the two *Bridge* volumes provide a rich illustration of an alternative to feminism as a series of discrete waves. The second *Bridge* embodies the continued intellectual and political relevance of the first volume even as it produces new visions for social change. Helen Shulman Lorenz calls this a theory of "reframing and restoration" that was embedded in *This Bridge Called My Back*.[26] Such an approach, Lorenz argues, both continually ruptures naturalized borders and inclusions and looks for restoration in the resources of prior histories—"with one foot in older discourses and another at a growing opening edge."[27] What is lost in the wave model of feminist history is both the sense of living memory that Alexander describes and an understanding of the historical continuities and resources that are vital for feminism and feminist thought.[28]

The use of feminist waves as an epistemological device has produced gaps in our understandings of feminist scholarship. The discrete periodization of feminist waves has tended to miss both intellectual continuities and discontinuities between work that has been classified within "second" and "third wave" feminisms. The idea of feminist waves, as I have been arguing, tends to present an image of homogeneous waves of knowledge that underestimates the differences and divergences between writers located within specific waves of feminism. Let us consider this further through a central model that is now conventionally identified with "third wave" feminism—the paradigm of intersectionality. Intersectionality has become one of the most recognized paradigms associated with "third wave" feminism. The concept of intersectionality refers to a series of cross-disciplinary interventions that analyzed the ways in which the intersection between inequalities such as race, gender, and class shaped women's lives and structured the social location of specific groups of women of color in distinctive ways. For instance, Kimberlé Crenshaw's groundbreaking work analyzed the relationship between gender, race, and the law in the United States. In one of her seminal essays on violence against women, she analyzed the ways in which both the experiences of such violence and the effects of institutional and political responses were structured in distinctive ways by the intersections of race and gender.[29] Or, to take another example, Evelyn Nakano Glenn's classic essay on the stratification of reproduction illustrated the ways in which systemic historical inequalities of race and gender structured the labor market in ways that tracked specific groups of women of color into paid domestic work in different historical periods.[30] A defining element of such contributions was the reconceptualization of our understandings of the structural reproduction of inequalities and the move away from unitary understandings of social structure to what Patricia Hill Collins calls "interlocking systems." As she argues:

> Viewing relations of domination for Black women for any given socio-historical context as being structured via a system of interlocking race, class, and gender oppression expands the focus of analysis from merely describing the similarities and differences distinguishing these systems of oppression and focuses greater attention on how they interconnect. Assuming that each system needs the others in order to function creates a distinct theoretical stance that stimulates the rethinking of basic social science concepts.[31]

As these scholars have illustrated, conventional understandings of structural inequality as a series of discrete, singular, and homogenized categories failed to capture the unique structural location of African American women in the United States. However, as Collins has noted, the need for an analysis of intersecting inequalities was not purely a descriptive project for African American women but a theoretical analysis of the broader "matrix of domination" that has shaped contemporary American society.[32] The paradigm of intersectionality provided a broader theoretical reconceptualization of the systemic nature of domination and inequality in order to redress the erasure of women of color by existing concepts.

Given the focus of these approaches on structural and systemic inequality, the paradigm of intersectionality has proved particularly fruitful in shaping research agendas in the social sciences and related fields. The structural dimensions of the paradigm have allowed social scientists to operationalize the paradigm through a range of methodologically diverse empirical studies.[33] Meanwhile, within interdisciplinary feminist writing and teaching, intersectionality has now become the central paradigm associated with "third wave" feminism. Such developments have produced a rich intellectual agenda. As Bonnie Thornton Dill and Ruth Zambrana have argued, scholarship on intersectionality has produced a range of theoretical innovations that they outline as the centering of people of color's experiences, the complication of conventional understandings of identity, the analysis of power in terms of intersecting structures of inequality, and the practical promotion of social change and justice.[34]

Despite the complex empirical and theoretical contributions of the paradigm of intersectionality, the wave model of feminism has often served to institutionalize intersectionality in ways that have foreclosed a richer and broader understanding of such contributions. Intersectionality has increasingly become the paradigm that both stands in for "third wave" feminism and signifies a break from "second wave" feminism. This overlooks some of the deeper intellectual continuities between "second wave" and "third wave" feminism. At one level, for instance, Collins's rethinking of systemic inequality drew heavily on standpoint theory even as it challenged and sought to rethink the concept of "standpoint." Or, to take another example, Glenn's work represented a critical engagement with existing strands of materialist feminist research on labor. At another level, the transformation of intersectionality as a signifier of "third wave" feminism has led to homogenized understandings of both intersectionality and "third wave" feminism.[35] In its institutionalized forms within women's studies curricula and intellectual agendas in the academy, intersectionality is increasingly becoming a marker of multicultural inclusion in many of the same ways as earlier narratives of identity politics.[36] Intersectionality in this context is mistakenly transformed into a heuristic device that is used to signify a politics of inclusion rather than the transformative agenda that, as Dill and Zambrana argue, has changed inter-disciplinary feminist understandings of identity, inequality, and power.[37]

Between the Waves of Feminism: Shifting Fields of Consciousness

In *Methodology of the Oppressed*, Chela Sandoval uses a reading of works by feminists of color to challenge conventional historical accounts of femi-nist intellectual history that emerged in the 1980s.[38] Sandoval argues that these accounts presented the evolution of feminism through four phases of historical intellectual development—liberal, Marxist, radical/cultural, and socialist. Drawing on a reading of typologies by leading feminist scholars writing during this period,[39] Sandoval argues that this historical narrative corresponded to four conceptions of feminist consciousness. Liberal femi-nism rested on the notion of women's equality with men, Marxist feminism sought to focus on the primacy of class, and radical/cultural feminism fo-cused on the differences between men and women and the superiority of such feminized differences. The last phase of socialist feminism, according to Sandoval, sought to confront racial and class divisions between women. She argues that this feminist typology both subsumed critiques by U.S. feminists of color and erased the specific theoretical alternatives produced by these critiques.

Sandoval argues that writings by feminists of color in the 1970s and 1980s in fact provided the groundwork for an alternative theory and method of oppositional consciousness. U.S. Third World feminism, the concept Sandoval uses to classify this approach, represented a distinctive form of "differential mode of oppositional consciousness."[40] As Sandoval explicates:

> I think of this activity of consciousness as the "differential," insofar as it enables movement "between and among" ideological positionings (the equal rights, revolutionary, supremacist, and separatist modes of opposi-tional consciousness) considered as variables, in order to disclose the dis-tinctions among them. In this sense, the differential mode of conscious-ness functions like the clutch of an automobile, the mechanism that per-mits the driver to select, engage, and disengage gears in a system for the transmission of power. The differential represents the variant; its presence emerges out of correlations, intensities, junctures, crises.[41]

According to Sandoval's theory/method of oppositional consciousness, the writings and challenges produced by feminists of color did not represent a simplistic rejection of or progression beyond earlier modes of feminist consciousness or practice. Rather, these writings produced a distinctive form of consciousness that have simultaneously occupied, moved between, and produced new spaces and sites of thought and practice.

While Sandoval's theoretical formulation does not explicitly address the current three-wave model of feminism, it provides critical insights that can be used to think through and move beyond some of the limits of that model. The idea of "third wave" feminism, of course, has moved us beyond the four-phase model of feminism that Sandoval criticizes. "Third wave" feminism is meant to represent the body of thought that Sandoval argues was rendered invisible by earlier feminist typologies that subsumed scholarship on race and ethnicity. In that vein, the delineation of a "third wave" of feminism has represented an advance over earlier histories of feminist thought. However, the wave approach to feminism reproduces the underlying epistemological framework of these earlier typologies in ways that miss the dynamic movement of differential consciousness that Sandoval presents. What remains unchanged is a teleological approach that divides feminist thought into a series of discrete and progressive stages of evolution.

Within the wave model of feminism, intersectionality often has been erroneously depicted as a somewhat static model of identity. Karen Barad, for instance, has criticized the use of this metaphor, arguing that it reproduces a limited Euclidean geometric imaginary. Thus, Barad argues:

> The view of space as container or context for matter in motion—spatial coordinates mapped via projections along axes that set up a metric for tracking the locations of the inhabitants of the container, and time divided into evenly spaced increments marking a progression of events—pervades much of Western epistemology.[42]

This depiction in many ways captures some of the dangers in which dominant narratives now depict intersectionality as a mechanistic tool that stands in for difference and inclusion. While Barad tangentially notes that feminists of color did not use such mechanistic analyses, she does not address the ways in which this Euclidean geometric formulation within Western epistemology cannot be viewed as an accurate historical-material context for understanding intersectionality—whether in terms of paradigm, metaphor, or political practice. Drawing on an understanding of differential consciousness that operates within the historical context of U.S. feminists of color, intersectionality is a theory that is both located within Western epistemological foundations associated with earlier waves of feminism (such as standpoint theory and materialist feminism) and a move to represent social locations, subjectivities, and forms of consciousness that cannot be captured by earlier conceptions. Seen from this perspective, intersectionality is neither a static formulation nor a signifier of a homogeneous field of "third wave" feminism; intersectionality is a method/theory that expresses one aspect of the mode of differential consciousness that Sandoval speaks of. Sandoval's discussion of differential consciousness illustrates the way that the mobile and fluid nature of this form of consciousness stems precisely from the intersectional nature of the social location of women of color. As I have noted earlier, a key focus of intersectionality theory has been on the workings of intersectional structures that shape the locations of social groups. The mobility of this form of consciousness is thus tactical because of the complex material and discursive "intersectional" nature of this location. This tactical mobility is not reducible to poststructuralist understandings of the fluidity of identity and difference. This subject simultaneously occupies the contained space of a structured social group even as it moves beyond the limits of these contexts and forms of consciousness. Sandoval's concept of differential consciousness is thus not a rejection or critique of intersectionality; rather, the subject of differential consciousness provides us with an understanding of the theoretical, political, and historical context of "third wave" feminism that is not reducible to singular paradigms of difference.

This discussion of intersectionality is illustrative of the ways in which paradigms of difference within women's studies and interdisciplinary feminist thought have the unintentional effect of disciplining existing intellectual histories of feminism in ways that produce silences and erasures. Despite the richness of much of the writing on intersectionality and the growing complexity of research in this field, the mainstreaming of this paradigm has entrenched the three-wave approach to contemporary U.S. feminism in ways that marginalize alternative political and intellectual visions of the subjects of feminist history. This miscasting of history is, of course, intensified when we move beyond the borders of the United States. As I have argued in chapter 5, the wave model casts non-U.S. feminism (and non-Western feminism in particular) as a later historical stage, or "wave," of feminism. This teleological misrepresentation of feminist history is usually institutionalized within women's studies teaching. Thus, introductory courses for women's studies majors rarely present multiple histories of feminism that emerge simultaneously in comparative contexts (and that precede the colonial encounter that postcolonial feminism presumes as an originary point of history in postcolonial contexts). The paradigm of the transnational often further consolidates this ahistorical model, since transnational processes are often conflated with current processes of globalization that have accelerated particular flows of culture and capital or, at best, with colonial histories. Meanwhile, at an institutional level, the fact that transnational or comparative approaches to gender are often taught as upper-level "specialized" courses reinforces this presumption that feminism in "other" places is a later development or "wave." However, this miscasting of feminist waves is not limited to an erasure of histories of feminism and women's movements in comparative contexts. It also displaces alternative histories of trans/national spaces that have emerged from within the United States.

Race, History, and Transnational Feminism

One of the key contributions of U.S. feminist of color scholarship has been the development of specific political-theoretical conceptions of the transnational. Consider Sandoval's formulation of such contributions as a form of U.S. Third World feminism. Sandoval's categorization seeks to capture a key strand in feminist of color approaches that sought both to develop transnational conceptions of race (through a focus on migration and diaspora) and to forge political alliances between U.S. feminists of color and women outside the United States, particularly from non-Western, postcolonial contexts that also were shaped by racialized histories of colonial rule. This geographic imagination of a transnational political space did not seek to reproduce a static racialized identity; rather, it stemmed from a deeper political and theoretical attempt to decenter the hegemony of both Eurocentric worldviews of the former colonial powers and the nation-centric conception of dominant understandings of U.S. feminism. Feminist visions of U.S. women of color could only emerge in uneasy tension with and rupture from the U.S. nation-state. Such ruptures have meant that feminists of color have challenged conventional understandings of gender-based issues and responses to such issues. Thus, it is worth underlining the fact that Crenshaw developed her conception of intersectionality in relation to the racialized gendered limits of the law (and, for instance, the problems of narrow state responses to violence against women). Similar ruptures and contestations can be seen in feminist challenges to the state-driven prison economy and the racialized and gendered implications of this system.[43]

These breaks from a U.S. state-centric approach within the field of U.S. feminist of color scholarship embody a distinctive reframing of history that disrupts both national narratives and the kind of nationalist conceptions of "transnationalism" that I have interrogated in previous chapters. Writing about Chicana feminist literary traditions and *testimonio*, Sonia Saldivar-Hull, for instance, argues that

> these border feminists contextualize themselves within a global literary history. The U.S. Latinas speak of their specific histories: for the Chicana, the history of the absorption of the Mexican territories by the United States; for the Nuyorican and the Chilena, their different histories as exiles, as people forced to emigrate to the United States from homelands— one Puerto Rico, which remains a colony of the United States, and the other Chile, devastated by economic and military wars financed and led by U.S. economic interests.[44]

As Saldivar-Hull illustrates, such feminist traditions disrupt a narrower nation-centered view of U.S. history. It is this nation-centered view that underlies the wave model of history that continues to shape genealogies of feminist thought in the United States.

Consider further how a theory or method of differential consciousness necessitates a break of this nation-centric three-wave model of feminism. One of the classic works often associated with "third wave" feminism is Gloria Anzaldúa's *Borderlands*.[45] Anzaldúa's articulation of a "new mestiza" consciousness provides an important example of a text that disrupts the discrete periodization between "second" and "third wave" feminism. The new mestiza subject that Anzaldúa creates occupies spaces of opposition associated with "second wave" feminist conceptions of patriarchy and feminized spaces even as it moves and is transformed into the liminal spaces of the "borderland" that are the well-known identifiers of her work. In Anzaldúa's analysis of the gendering of culture and religion, "Culture is made by those in power—men. Males make the rules and laws; women transmit them. . . .The culture expects women to show greater acceptance of, and commitment to, the value system than men. The culture and the Church insist that women are subservient to males."[46]

Anzaldúa presents a critique of the reproduction of patriarchal culture that has long been associated with earlier waves of feminist thought. As she further notes, echoing Simone de Beauvoir, "Woman is the stranger, the other. She is man's recognized nightmarish pieces, his Shadow-Beast."[47] Anzaldúa moves in and out of this intellectual and political narrative of woman as a foundational source of otherness throughout the text. Yet this conception of women's identity is continually remade by complex processes that are constituted by religion, spirituality, race, and class. As Saldivar-Hull argues, Anzaldúa's work provides a complex historical project— "a methodology for a new consciousness based on recovering history and women's place in that history."[48] Anzaldúa's new mestiza consciousness, for instance, rests on the writing of a matrilineal history. The new mestiza subjectivity is inextricably linked to Anzaldúa's reworking of embodiments of a conception of a "divine feminine." She reclaims the goddess Cihuacoatl from early Aztec society, and it is this figure that provides the material-psychic passageway into new mestiza subjectivity. Anzaldúa describes this formation of subjectivity as a complex process that is simultaneously an engagement with a primordial sense of selfhood and bodily knowledge and an engagement with the liminal political and discursive spaces produced by intersecting identities. This "Coatlique state" of transformation for Anzaldúa "is the consuming internal whirlwind, the symbol of the underground aspects of the psyche. *Coatlique* is the mountain, the Earth Mother who conceived all celestial beings out of her cavernous womb. Goddess of birth and death, *Coatlique* gives and takes away life; she is the incarnation of cosmic processes."[49]

This process of engaging with her inner self, which Anzaldúa also depicts materially as a process that "pulsates in my body,"[50] embodies concepts of the self that are clearly at odds with later "third wave" feminist writings that have claimed a sharp break with languages that appear to echo any form of essentialism. One of the discursive effects of the wave model of feminism has been the erasure of such dimensions of Anzaldúa's thought. Scholars writing from a "third wave" perspective have sought to secularize Anzaldúa's work in order to fit it within conventional narratives that seek to represent "third wave" feminism purely in terms of secularized concepts such as intersectionality, diaspora, and hybridity. In dominant representations of "third wave" feminism, Anzaldúa's concept of borderlands is usually invoked and disciplined by such concepts.[51]

Anzaldúa's work in fact exceeds the binary opposition between "second" and "third wave" feminism. If Anzaldúa's new mestiza cannot be disciplined by the concept of intersectionality, neither can she be reduced to a return either to earlier conceptions that identified patriarchy as the foundational concept of feminism or to essentialist ideas of feminine culture. As Sandoval's theory/method of differential consciousness indicates, the new mestiza tactically occupies and moves between such defined fields that have been territorialized as "second wave" or intersectional locations. However, the nature of differential consciousness is such that the new mestiza is marked by a process of disidentification from such spaces. She argues:

> But it is not enough to stand on the opposite river bank, shouting questions, challenging patriarchal, white conventions. A counterstance locks one into a duel of oppressor and oppressed; locked in mortal combat, like the cop and criminal, both are reduced to a common denominator of violence. . . .At some point, on our way to a new consciousness, we will have to leave the opposite bank, the split between the two mortal combatants somehow healed so that we are on both shores at once, and at once, see through the serpent and eagle eyes. Or perhaps we will decide to disengage from the dominant culture, write it off altogether as a lost cause, and cross the border into a wholly new and separate territory.[52]

Anzaldúa's phrase "separate territory" is not reducible to a cultural nationalist narrative of separatism. Rather, she is speaking of a politics of disidentification that moves beyond conventional oppositional modes of thought that demarcate oppositions such as those between subject and object, male and female, and the psychic/spiritual and rational/material.[53] This disidentified subject occupies the material space defined by intersectional structures of inequality and recognizes the reality of identity categories, yet it moves us far from dominant narratives of identity politics and static understandings of intersectionality. Such a form of subjectivity cannot be contained within homogenized waves of feminism even as it represents the heart of the distinctive intellectual and political challenges associated with a nation-centered historical model of waves of feminism.

The Possibilities and Risks of Traveling Paradigms

My discussion of the wave model of feminism has underlined the dangers of adopting models of multiculturalism that rest on a flattened conception of difference that misses the epistemological differences between various strands of feminist of color thought and complex relationships and distinctions between understandings of transnational feminism that emerge from migration to and from the United States, on the one hand, and the varied histories of feminism that have emerged from places outside of the United States, on the other hand. The question that arises, then, is how conversations between U.S. feminist debates on race, migration, and transnationalism can take place productively. What is implicit in this concern is the question of how the paradigm of transnationalism travels within U.S. knowledge sites. At one level, transnational perspectives have been useful in interrogating the idea that the United States can be treated as a closed or self-contained geopolitical space. In contrast to many disciplinary practices that produce separate fields for the study of the U.S. and comparative/ international contexts,[54] transnational understandings of concepts such as race and diaspora serve to relocate the United States within a broader global understanding of the movements of people, capital, and culture. Meanwhile, as I have argued in earlier chapters, these possibilities are accompanied by the risks of reproducing U.S.-centric conceptions of transnationalism.[55] These risks may potentially be intensified if transnationalism becomes a paradigm that is reduced to migration and diasporic processes that recenter U.S.-centric experiences; in this context, transnationalism becomes a disciplinary device for understanding difference.

The possibilities and risks of such engagements on race and transnationalism are not, however, limited to the ways in which knowledge on U.S. racial politics deploys the paradigm of transnationalism. U.S. feminist of color paradigms have also traveled to the study of identity and inequality in comparative and international contexts. Writing about this possibility, Patricia Hill Collins argues, "As a Western social theory and set of practices, intersectionality contains numerous blind spots that make it less applicable to non-Western societies, but only if the specificity of the Western experience continues to stand in for everyone else."[56] Thus, for example, intersectionality may serve as a useful theoretical and methodological tool that sets up productive comparisons between race and gender inequality in the United States and specific contexts in Latin America.[57] Meanwhile, the dynamics of intersectionality that have placed women of color within particular locations of structured inequality are also relevant to comparative contexts such as India, where the intersections of caste, gender, and class have structured the lives of lower-caste, working-class women in parallel ways. However, such possibilities may be best addressed through a comparative rather than a transnational analytical lens.

If this ability of intersectionality to travel holds fruitful possibilities for interdisciplinary engagement, it also poses risks. Intersectionality has increasingly traveled to other disciplines and become mainstreamed through disciplinary practices in a range of disciplines. Much of this scholarship has made crucial contributions and has expanded the space for the study of women of color and a deepened understanding of race in ways that have enriched the conventional disciplines.[58] However, the way in which this paradigm has been absorbed within various disciplines has also had varied implications. At one level, as Collins has noted, this mainstreaming risks producing a "sanitized, depoliticized version of intersectionality." As she argues, "Unlike the invisibility that plagued the field of intersectionality at its inception, it now faces an entirely new challenge of being hypervisible within equally novel conditions of global, commodity capitalism."[59] In many cases, the attempt to mainstream intersectionality has led to an erasure of the intellectual histories and contributions of the feminists of color that produced these understandings. Writing about intersectionality and the discipline of political science, Nikol Alexander-Floyd has argued that this mainstreaming (and disciplinary intellectual and institutional practices) has served to displace such contributions in ways that appropriate the intellectual labor and distort the intellectual contributions of African American feminist scholars.[60] Alexander-Floyd argues that the attempt "to systematize intersectionality" through disciplinary mainstreaming works to "disappear Black women."[61] As she argues:

Current efforts to universalize intersectionality, to consolidate its meaning such that it is disconnected from the lived experiences of women of color and made available to larger numbers because of a focus on an academic demand for quantitative methods, can serve to colonize intersectionality and re-deploy it in ways that deplete its radical potential.[62]

Such risks that arise from the ways in which this paradigm travels are only compounded when the paradigm is applied in non-U.S. or comparative contexts. For instance, in the case of political science, comparative feminist conceptions of intersectionality are now increasingly assessed by whether the effects of intersecting inequalities can be measured by quantitative methods.[63] This kind of (mis)representation of the paradigm produces a kind of double colonial move. On the one hand, the interdisciplinary and cross-disciplinary contributions of U.S. feminists of color are measured according to a set of hegemonic methodological norms in a move that erases the *methodological* interventions of U.S. feminists of color.[64] The contributions of feminist of color thought have historically been both substantive (empirical/theoretical) and methodological precisely because (as with significant dimensions of feminist scholarship) traditional measures and conceptions of gender and race missed the interstitial experiences, lives, and agencies of women of color. On the other hand, these hegemonic norms are then held up as the standard for international scholarship on gender. Yet, as with many marginalized groups of women—particularly in non-Western contexts—macrolevel quantitative measures have often proved inadequate in addressing their lives in comparative contexts—the very social groups that are in fact comparable to women of color within the United States. The result is the risk of appropriating the insights of U.S. feminists of color and recasting them within a form of disciplinary-driven methodological imperialism that produces a factually flawed intellectual genealogy of the paradigm of intersectionality. The violence of this kind of intellectual appropriation is particularly stark given that intersectionality is one of the few paradigms that is publicly acknowledged as a groundbreaking contribution that emerged from the interdisciplinary intellectual engagements and political and social movement struggles of feminists of color in the United States.

Conclusion

Static models of multicultural difference and feminist thought such as the wave model of feminism have in many ways shortchanged our understandings of the substantive contributions of writings classified as "third wave feminism." As I have sought to illustrate, the static nature of this model has lent itself to a reduction of the rich and varied contributions of such work in terms of modular and reductive representations of paradigms such as intersectionality and identity politics. In this discussion, I have drawn on a number of scholars who in practice bridge and simultaneously occupy feminist locations associated with second, third, and fourth wave feminism. The method of oppositional consciousness that Sandoval delineates speaks precisely to this form of simultaneity. The movement between these temporal/political spaces of feminist thought represents the spirit of much of this writing. As "third wave" feminist writings become mainstreamed through these singular devices, these deeper understandings of time, politics, and subjectivity risk being written out of history. This has been intensified by some modes of disciplinary-driven appropriations of the intellectual contributions of U.S. feminists of color as paradigms travel between disciplines and places. The movement inherent in the conceptions of temporality and memory contained in the writings that I have discussed exceeds the metaphor of a series of waves crashing onto land and then receding. Feminist thought, in retrospect, requires a conception of history that can contain both insights of the past and the potential breakthroughs of the future within the messy, unresolved contestations of political and intellectual practice in the present. It is this sense of texture, depth, and challenge that can serve as a basis for productive collaborations on questions of race, transnationalism, and feminism.

7

Afterword

The Moment of Transnational Feminism
in the United States

THE ESSAYS IN this book have examined the implications that transnational perspectives have for the way in which we make sense of a complex and deeply interconnected world. The paradigm of transnational feminism provides a critical case study for such reflection both because transnational perspectives have sought to capture contemporary global phenomena that have unsettled modern nation-states and because such perspectives have been at the forefront of interdisciplinary knowledge that has grappled with the real material and political effects of our knowledge practices. Indeed, as this book has shown, transnational feminist scholarship has produced rich theoretical and empirical understandings of a wide range of sociocultural, political, and economic phenomena. However, the significance and growing dominance of this body of knowledge also challenge us to examine both the possibilities and the limits that this lens brings to the way in which we learn and teach about the world. If we take interdisciplinary understandings of the relationship between power and knowledge seriously, the stakes of this examination of transnational feminism are high. What is at stake in this consideration is the way in which our knowledge practices ultimately help make the worlds in which we live. Knowledge matters, as I have argued, because it is shaped by material conditions within the world, and it helps materialize the world in which we live.

How, then, does transnational feminism come to matter in the contemporary moment? To answer this question, I have argued for an approach that examines the material (ontological) circumstances out of which this perspective emerges. I have analyzed the ways in which the particular kind of primacy that the paradigm of the transnational holds is shaped by the specific national context of the United States. Thus, I have identified the emergence of a specific model of "U.S. transnational feminism" in the U.S. academy. Through this process, I have analyzed the national imagination of the transnational—that is, the way the field of the nation-state shapes the paradigm of transnationalism. Too often in the context of interdisciplinary studies there is a kind of temporal and spatial teleology underlying the emphasis on the transnational. Temporally it is seen as the newest organizing modality for the world. This sense of newness is conflated with the historical present in ways that reproduce a teleological juxtaposition between the fluid border-crossing of the postmodern present with a more static bounded view of the past. This teleological view of time is also spatialized in complex ways. The transnational is viewed as a geographic unit (the broadest one that impacts on or interacts with narrower units of the national and local) that encompasses a range of border-crossing activities and entities.

The rise of transnational perspectives and the growing dominance of the paradigm of transnational feminism in interdisciplinary fields like women's studies have been shaped by an attempt to grapple with these historical and geopolitical processes that have been consolidated in the late twentieth century and the first decades of the twenty-first century. Rapid technological changes that have increased the speed of flows of information, cultural ideas, and financial/economic transactions across national borders seemed to unsettle, if not displace, the nation as a central organizing political-economic unit of the world. Indeed, the scale of such global change seemed to transform Benedict Anderson's claim that "nation-ness is the most universally legitimate value in the political life of our time" into a historical artifact of the twentieth century.[1] Yet a closer examination of such processes has made proclamations of a new postnational era seem at best premature. Indeed, nuanced scholarship on transnationalism has shown that contemporary global phenomena are shaped by complex linkages between local, national, and transnational processes.

The culture of intellectual life is such that the presumed newness of such transnational spatial-temporal practices is now often conflated with the newness of interdisciplinary insights in fields such as women's studies. There is, as I have argued, a disciplinary impetus in women's studies and related fields to identify specific kinds of transnational spaces and movements as the analytical and empirical starting points that increasingly drive knowledge about the world. However, these disciplinary practices that lurk behind interdisciplinary fields often serve to consolidate a U.S.-centric world—even if in opposition to the structures of power that have produced the geopolitical dominance of the United States. I have sought to call attention to and unsettle such disciplinary mechanisms by locating the paradigm of transnational feminism within specific local and national discursive and institutional practices both within and outside the U.S. academy.

This interrogation provokes us to step back and reflect on the moment in which the transnational has become a dominant lens for grasping the world—that is, the political field in which this paradigm has emerged. In many ways, the transnational serves as an analytical mirror of the contemporary moment of globalization—the fast-paced, technologically driven world where movement and visuality seem to drive large-scale world events, the organization of economic life, and the everyday formation of cultural and political identities. The primacy of the transnational as a framing perspective for the study of the world must also be located in the current political context in which central principles of state sovereignty associated with the Westphalian system have been unsettled in the post-9/11 period. The distinctive significance of such cracks in the Westphalian system can be seen in overt or self-evident examples such as the U.S. wars and military occupations of Iraq and Afghanistan and the growing infringements of Pakistani state sovereignty. Other instances include the phenomenon of political assassinations as an accepted (or at least unpreventable) means of warfare, the expanded ability to carry out cross-border territorial attacks through technological advances (such as drones), the ability to denationalize citizens deemed suspected terrorists by denying them status as prisoners of war according to the conventional rules of war between nation-states, and the ability to use outsourced or deterritorialized systems of incarceration in ways that displace nation-state-centered legal structures (both in terms of internal legal systems of particular nations in question and in terms of global treaties signed by states).

Military intervention, war, and tactics marking unequal relationships of power have long been features of the Westphalian system. The use of both covert and overt forms of military intervention in other nations is not a new phenomenon that is unique either to the post-9/11 period or to the United States. What is distinctive in the current period is the paradoxical process in which there is a simultaneous expansion of state security apparatuses even as there is this a kind of systemic destabilization of the principles of state sovereignty. The transnational in this context is in effect a device of the security state. It is this formation of the transnational as an integral dimension of an expanding state apparatus that marks the historical moment and the political field in which our own processes of knowledge production emerge. This moment should at the very least caution us against easy attachments that produce a kind of romance around transnational perspectives even when such paradigms emerge from interdisciplinary formations that have noble normative intentions. Transnational imperatives have no more political innocence and are no less violent than the imperatives of the modern nation-state.

Transnationalism and the National Public in the United States

Let us reflect on how knowledge about the world is constituted by this political field in the public national domain in the United States. Rey Chow has argued that we have increasingly come to view the world as a target.[2] Indeed, this is self-evident in the ways in which the broader national public comes to "know" areas and places through the politics of crisis or through the lens of U.S. military intervention. This occurs in obvious ways in mainstream public discourses. Thus, when wars break out, media outlets bring out the customary maps and graphics, and cities and places that Americans have not heard of enter the public language as embodiments of war, crisis, or natural disasters. Names such as Benghazi, Baghdad, and Abbottabad circulate as symbols of current geopolitical conflicts, and interests that are dislocated from the depth of their own histories and civilizations. The public geographic imagination is driven by this targeted representation. As I have argued, such circulating discourses and images then get thickened through the market forces that drive the publishing industry, funding organizations, research agendas, and the direction of student consumption of knowledge about particular areas of the world.

Yet the "world as a target" frame does not provide a conceptual lens that can fully grasp the complexities of how knowledge about the world is framed in the current political field in the United States. Consider two contemporary moments that highlight the knowledge dynamics that surround public discourses around the U.S. war in Afghanistan. In July 2010, WikiLeaks released thousands of classified documents that provided detailed information on U.S. military failures in its war in Afghanistan. However, most mainstream print and TV news reporters produced a narrative around the documents as being irrelevant because the fact that the war was not going well was not a new finding to anyone. As a report in *Time* magazine put it:

> The trove of leaked documents affirms all these facts. And in their texture and detail—which it will take some time for other new outlets to sift in full—certainly offer a new appreciation for how difficult the war effort is. But based on their presentation by the news organizations given time by

Wikileaks to study them before their release, the documents don't seem
to reveal fundamental new truths.³

In fact, mainstream public discourses, driven by the ritual repetition
characteristic of the twenty-four-hour cable channels, focused on the reproduction of the narrative that there were no new truths in the documents. The document releases did not, however, lead to any new coverage on the details of the messiness, violence, and struggles of the war
that would mark a "new appreciation for how difficult the war is." Thus,
television reporting that often drives mainstream public attention has
been characterized by a continued absence of any depth of attention
to the war. Continued death and violence and the unpleasant details of
war have not qualified as new truths that can warrant sustained media or
public attention.

Meanwhile, on April 17, 2011, the CBS news show *60 Minutes* broke a
story that provided evidence and allegations that author Greg Mortenson's
best-selling books *Three Cups of Tea* and *Stones into Schools* had fabricated
key stories about his travels in Pakistan and about the extent of his welfare work building girls' schools in Afghanistan and Pakistan.⁴ The significance of these allegations was marked both because of the popularity of
the books in the United States and because *Three Cups of Tea* had become
part of the training materials for U.S. troops in Afghanistan (in conjunction with an attempt to link military strategy with a humanitarian "gender
and development" policy). Perhaps one of the most glaring examples of alleged fabrications is Mortenson's story of being kidnapped by the Taliban
in Pakistan's South Waziristan's tribal region. Mansur Khan Mahsud, the
research director of a well-known think tank in Pakistan, hosted Mortenson during his trip and has widely decried Mortenson's attempt to portray
him as a "kidnapper." As one detailed report revealed:

Mahsud says Mortenson was even made the guest of honor at the village's
annual soccer tournament. On one trip the villagers took Mortenson to
the Ladha Fort, a government security outpost. On his laptop computer
at his office in Islamabad, Mahsud shows a photo of Mortenson that was
taken that July. The picture shows Mortenson, smiling, standing shoulder
to shoulder with eight other men. They are all armed with AK-47s. So is
Mortenson. He too is cradling an AK-47 with a huge 75-round magazine
attached. "He claims we are all kidnappers," says Mahsud. "You can clearly
see this man is not a frightened, kidnapped man, but a very happy one.

In another picture, a smiling Mortenson is sitting on a carpet, between two other men, leaning against a wall. Mahsud says Mortenson stayed at his uncle's house and even played CDs of Pashto and Turkish music that he was carrying with him for the family's entertainment. Mahsud says Mortenson's claim that he was forced to pick up a copy of the Quran, perform ablutions, and promise to convert to Islam is false. "All the time we treated him very well according to Pashtunwali values," according to Mahsud.[5] Mahsud provided photos that were widely broadcast through various media outlets. Indeed, that such a major accusation of a criminal act could go unchecked and that a community's hospitality to an "honored guest" could so easily be transformed into kidnapping echo the processes of the foreclosure of civilian space in vast regions of the world that I have analyzed.

These two snapshots on the U.S. war and "knowledge" about Afghanistan provide deeper insights into the political context that shapes the public approach to knowledge about the world in the United States. Both moments show a distinctive kind of approach to "truth" about the world. If the Mortsenson incident reveals a careless disregard for truth or fact in the service of ideologically invested representations of a region as hostile and violent, the WikiLeaks response is marked by a sense of boredom with the truth and with factual accuracy. Reality that is not heroic or new in some way cannot attain the status of being worthy of public attention. While these moments may seem far removed from the complexity of interdisciplinary academic scholarship (particularly since such work is explicitly critical of such dynamics of knowledge production), they provide the public context and common sense that I argue leak into such fields of knowledge through the complex discourses, institutional practices, and market-driven organization of the production and consumption of knowledge. There are echoes of this boredom with reality in the search for "the new" and a casual lack of concern with empirical reality that creep into the cultural practices of interdisciplinary fields that seek to produce knowledge about the world. The drive for the next new paradigm, the next wave, the new approach, the new stylistic or linguistic turn of phrase that can move beyond older concepts echoes this fascination and desire for the new and the heroic.

This public, material context that shapes the emergence of intellectual paradigms compels us to consider the risks of our knowledge practices and challenges us to move away from easy assumptions that any space of intellectual work can occupy a transcendent or innocent understanding of the world. Yet, as I have argued in chapter 4, an ethical approach to knowledge production can treat risk as a possibility rather than an insurmountable obstacle. Intellectual paradigms, as Pierre Bourdieu has shown us, are always complex products of particular fields (sociocultural, economic, geopolitical) in which they arise.[6] This does not mean that intellectual work is determined in a simplistic or reductive way by such factors. As I have shown in chapter 3, the relationship between cultural texts and contexts is a complex one that is shaped by structural factors but always marked by contingencies of form and interpretive context. Approaching knowledge production through an ethics of risk opens up the space to continue to take on the challenges of refusing the illusory safety of a purely deconstructive approach. An ethics of risk compels us to take on the challenges of creating knowledge that dares to engage with the messiness of real, material worlds.

Risks and Possibilities: The Stakes of Transnational Feminism

In the face of such risks and challenges, interdisciplinary feminist scholarship remains a critical force for making sense of the world. Gendered ideologies continue to permeate key aspects of sociocultural, political, and economic life in specific places and also continue to serve as a key ideological device that states use both as national boundary markers and as rhetorical justifications for military intervention that violates state sovereignty. Meanwhile, women in cross-national contexts create innovative responses and survival strategies in order to withstand varying forms of economic inequality, violence, and injustice that are often extreme in nature. Transnational feminist perspectives provide an invaluable means for both understanding and responding to these conditions. For scholars who develop such perspectives within the United States, the stakes of transnational feminism are high given that the United States continues to play a role in shaping both global structures and institutions, as well as in shaping many local contexts through political alliances, economic aid, and other foreign policy means (that may be linked to but are not reducible to overt military action).

The challenges for transnational feminist knowledge production in the United States are thus steep because they require simultaneously calling attention to the way in which the position of the U.S. nation-state shapes the consumption of knowledge about women/gender and displacing a preoccupation with U.S. (or Western) genealogies and representations in order to understand complex worlds that are not reducible to relations with the United States or the West. These challenges, as I have argued, are even more complex when they unfold in the classroom, where students may need certain modes of learning that do not conform either to their consumption-based desires or to the intellectual imperatives of interdisciplinary paradigms such as transnational feminism. Yet such challenges are accompanied by the space that interdisciplinary fields such as women's studies open up for self-criticism and innovation. Unlike conventional disciplines that are weighed down by their histories of self-regulation, the nature of interdisciplinarity is such that it contains the possibility of interrogating its own limits. Interdisciplinary fields thus have the potential to interrogate and disrupt the creeping disciplinarity that inevitably accompanies institutionalization and the consolidation of its perspectives within the academy. It is in this spirit that I have risked provoking scholars to critically examine the paradigm of transnational feminism.

Transnational feminism is a rich body of knowledge that holds real possibilities and serious risks in the way it helps us understand and shape the world. The political context in which we are located shapes our relationship to the world in unseen and often inadvertent ways. The point is, of course, not to condemn interdisciplinary knowledge or paradigms such as transnational feminism or to equate them with the state ideologies with which it is often in contention. The most profound potential of interdisciplinary feminist scholarship has been its ability to interrogate its own complicities in the structures of power it has sought to change. Thus, the purpose of focusing on such moments—and the purpose of these essays—has been to provoke a discussion of the distinctive political and ethical challenges that emerge as we try to create knowledge about the world in this historical moment. It is this risky acceptance of the messiness of our own creations and the unintended consequences they have in and for the world that these essays have tried to infuse into our attempts to understand interdisciplinary models of the world that are being produced within and outside the academy.

Notes

Notes to Chapter 1

1. E-mail communication from *Ms.* executive director, Feminist Majority organization, September 8, 2011.

2. For a mainstream feminist version of this symbol, see, for instance, the film *Thelma and Louise* (1991).

3. These area studies programs carved up the study of international politics through a series of distinct area-based programs such as Latin American, Middle East, and South Asian studies. The links between such programs and the Cold War orientation of U.S. foreign policy have been well debated among scholars of international studies. See, e.g., Miyoshi and Harootunian, *Learning Places*, 2002; Szanton, *Politics of Knowledge*, 2004; Waters, *Beyond the Area Studies Wars*, 2000.

4. This is evident in the rise of global studies programs, new paradigms such as transnationalism that have sought to move beyond the nation-state, and a widespread rhetorical use of the lens of "the global."

5. Some of the key texts that first defined this field include Appadurai, *Modernity at Large*, 1996; Bhabha, *Location of Culture*, 1994; Brah, *Cartographies of Diaspora*, 1996; Chow, *Writing Diaspora*, 1993; Gilroy, *Black Atlantic*, 1993; Ōmae, *End of the Nation-State*, 1995; Ong, *Flexible Citizenship*, 1999; Shohat, *Taboo Memories, Diasporic Voices*, 2006.

6. This has included work on transnational social movements (Keck and Sikkink, *Activists beyond Borders*, 1998; Tarrow, *New Transnational Activism*, 2005); transnational religious formations (Rudolph and Piscatori, *Transnational Religion*, 1996); and transnational feminism (Basu, *Women's Movements*, 2010; Ferree and Tripp, *Global Feminism*, 2006; Grewal and Kaplan, *Scattered Hegemonies*, 1994).

7. This belief in the decline of the nation-state was particularly characteristic of early cultural studies scholarship on globalization. More recent work has sought to bring back the state in studies of globalization. See, e.g., Sassen, *Territory, Authority, Rights*, 2006.

8. Such movements have included opposition to cuts in state welfare provisions in Europe and the United States, anger at state financial support for banks and corporations (through bailouts and tax breaks), and conservative opposition in the United States to state intervention in the economy.

9. On cultural globalization and deterritorialized identities, see Appadurai, *Modernity at Large*, 1996. On the emergence of long-distance nationalism, see Anderson, *Imagined Communities*, 1983.

10. There is a rich and varied scholarship on cosmopolitanism. Scholars working in this field have sought to find ways of developing alternative modes of identification and citizenship that can transcend the exclusionary dimensions of nationalism and

to navigate between universalistic and culturally specific identities and categories of thought. See, e.g., Appiah, *Cosmopolitanism*, 2007; Cheah and Robbins, *Cosmopolitics*, 1998; Nussbaum, "Patriotism and Cosmopolitanism," 1994; Reilly, "Cosmopolitanism, Feminism, and Human Rights," 2007. For a critique of cosmopolitanism, see Tarrow, *New Transnational Activism*, 2005. Tarrow argues that such forms of cosmopolitanism are "rooted" within state structures. For a critique of feminist forms of cosmopolitanism that reproduce transnational relations of power, see Kaplan, "Hillary Rodham Clinton's Orient," 2001.

11. Appiah, *Cosmopolitanism*, 2007; Bhabha, *Location of Culture*, 2004; Brah, *Cartographies of Diaspora*, 1996; Gilroy, *Black Atlantic*, 1993.

12. Shohat, *Taboo Memories, Diasporic Voices*, 2006, 7.

13. Chuh, *Imagine Otherwise*, 2003.

14. Ibid., 10.

15. The nationalist construction of the "global" is not unique to the United States. See, e.g., Fernandes, "Nationalizing 'the Global,'" 2000.

16. See, e.g., Sugata Bose's important work using oceanic rather than territorialized borders as a conceptual device for reframing areas studies in *A Hundred Horizons*, 2009.

17. Chatterjee, *Nation and Its Fragments*, 1993.

18. Appadurai, *Modernity at Large*, 1996.

19. Ibid., 38.

20. Ibid., 159.

21. Ibid., 173.

22. Ibid.

23. See Lipset, *American Exceptionalism*, 1997.

24. For works that have sought to critically engage with the formation of interdisciplinary fields, see Miyoshi and Harootunian, *Learning Places*, 2002; Nelson and Gaonkar, *Disciplinarity and Dissent*, 1996; Scott, *Women's Studies*, 2008; Wiegman, "Academic Feminism," 2002.

25. Appadurai and Breckenridge, "Public Modernity in India," 1995.

26. Grewal and Kaplan, "Global Identities," 2001, 664.

27. Basu, "Globalization of the Local," 2000; Naples and Desai, *Women's Activism and Globalization*, 2002; Peterson, *Critical Rewriting*, 2003; Shohat, *Taboo Memories, Diasporic Voices*, 2006; Spivak, *Other Asias*, 2008; Swarr and Nagar, *Critical Transnational Feminist Praxis*, 2010.

28. Such a critical lens has tended to focus predominantly on area studies but not on later interdisciplinary fields such as women's studies, postcolonial studies, or cultural studies.

29. For work that has called attention to such inequalities, see,, e.g., Enloe, *Maneuvers*, 2000; Mohanty, *Feminism without Borders*, 2003.

30. Mohanty, "Under Western Eyes," 1988.

31. For an example of this kind of approach, see Morgan, *Sisterhood Is Global*, 1996.

32. Mohanty, "Under Western Eyes," 1988.

33. On colonial processes and gender, see, e.g., Ahmed, *Women and Gender in Islam*, 1993; Burton, *Burdens of History*, 1994; Stoler, *Carnal Knowledge*, 2002.

34. See Fernández-Kelly, *For We Are Sold*, 1984; the classic film that she coproduced, *The Global Assembly Line*; Ong, *Spirits of Resistance*, 2010; Mies, *Patriarchy and Accumulation*, 1999, among many others.

35. Alexander, "Not Just Any(Body) Can Be a Citizen," 1994.

36. Ibid., 6.

37. Mohanty, *Feminism without Borders*, 2003.

38. See, e.g., McClintock, *Imperial Leather*, 1995; McClintock, Mufti, and Shohat, *Dangerous Liaisons*, 1997; Yuval-Davis, *Gender and Nation*, 1997.

39. Studies on globalization and migration include Alvarez, "Translating the Global," 2000; Cantú and Naples, *Sexuality of Migration*, 2009; Davis, *Making of Our Bodies*, 2007; Gopinath, *Impossible Desires*, 2005; Naples and Desai, *Women's Activism and Globalization*, 2002; Parreñas, *Servants of Globalization*, 2001. More theoretically inclined works include Grewal and Kaplan, *Scattered Hegemonies*, 1994; Spivak, *Critique of Postcolonial Reason*, 1999. For a rich discussion of feminist activism, see Swarr and Nagar, *Critical Transnational Feminist Praxis*, 2010.

40. Grewal and Kaplan, in "Global Identities," 2001, make the point that transnational work often does not focus on the United States, producing an intellectual division between U.S. ethnic studies programs and postcolonial/transnational studies. Exceptions to this include work on U.S. diasporic communities that have linked U.S. immigrant communities with their countries of origin.

41. In my own experience of teaching women's studies, undergraduate students are most interested in discussing such cultural issues and in grappling over whether they have the right to judge other cultures. Whether they embrace or reject cultural relativism, they are drawn to such visible signifiers of difference. On such dynamics within feminist organizations and activist sites, see Alvarez, "Translating the Global," 2000; Basu, "Globalization of the Local," 2000.

42. On pedagogy, see hooks, *Teaching Community*, 2003; Keating, *Teaching Transformation*, 2007; Spivak, *Other Asias*, 2008.

43. Scott, *Women's Studies*, 2008.

44. Ibid., 6.

45. Ibid., 8.

46. Ibid., 9–11.

47. See, e.g., the exchange between Brown, "Impossibility of Women's Studies," 2008, and Wiegman, "Feminism, Institutionalism, and the Idiom of Failure," 2008, on the impossibility and possibilities of women's studies that opens the Scott volume.

48. Scott, *Women's Studies*, 2008, 8.

49. Najmabadi, "Unavailable Intersections," 2008.

50. Mahmood, "Feminism, Democracy and Empire," 2008.

51. For a useful exposition of this debate, see the Brown-Wiegman exchange in Scott, *Women's Studies*, 2008.

52. On European feminism and colonialism, see Ahmed, *Women and Gender in Islam*, 1993; Burton, *Burdens of History*, 1994. For useful discussions of the complexities involved in transnational advocacy and representation, see the volumes by Ferree and Tripp, *Global Feminism*, 2006; and Hesford and Kozol, *Just Advocacy?*, 2005.

53. Tripp, "Challenges in Transnational Feminist Mobilization," 2006, 297.

54. http://www.avaaz.org/en/stop_stoning.

55. See, e.g., Abu-Lughod, "Do Muslim Women Really Need Saving?," 2002; Fadlalla, "State of Vulnerability," 2011; Nnaemeka, *Female Circumcision*, 2005; Razack, "Geopolitics," 2005.

56. See, e.g., Barad, *Meeting the Universe Halfway*, 2007.

57. For a defense of the focus on identity, see Alcoff, *Visible Identities*, 2005.

58. For an example of a sociological study of contrasting views on intellectualism among upper-middle-class men, see Lamont, *Money*, 1994. Examples of the trends I am describing can be seen in sites such as popular cultural representations in film and television and in political debates. Consider, for example, the ways in which anti-intellectual presidential candidates are usually portrayed as being in touch with the real America.

59. For useful work on activism and knowledge production, see Hale, *Engaging Contradictions*, 2008; Swarr and Nagar, *Critical Transnational Feminist Praxis*, 2010.

60. Gramsci, *Prison Notebooks*, 1971.

61. See, e.g., Fernandes, *India's New Middle Class*, 2006.

62. This question was one of the organizing thematic issues for the National Women's Studies Association's 2009 conference.

63. Shohat and Stam, *Multiculturalism*, 2003.

64. Shohat, "Introduction," in Shohat, *Talking Visions*, 2001.

65. See, e.g., Appadurai, *Modernity at Large*, 1996; Featherstone, *Global Culture*, 1990.

66. See, e.g., Abu-Lughod, *Dramas of Nationhood*, 2004; Mankekar, *Screening Culture*, 1999; Rajagopal, *Politics after Television*, 2001.

67. Abu-Lughod, *Dramas of Nationhood*, 2004.

68. Fernandes, *India's New Middle Class*, 2006.

69. Kozol, "Domesticating NATO's War," 2004.

70. See, e.g., Hesford, *Spectacular Rhetorics*, 2011; Hesford and Kozol, *Just Advocacy?*, 2005, Tapia, *American Pietàs*, 2011.

71. Ahmed, *Cultural Politics*, 2004.

72. See, e.g., Trinh, *Woman, Native, Other*, 1989; Narayan, *Dislocating Cultures*, 1997; Mohanty, *Feminism without Borders*, 2003.

73. Barad, *Meeting the Universe Halfway*, 2007.

74. I am using Bourdieu's concept of a field as an intellectual terrain that represents a structured and confined terrain but that does not predetermine or preclude the direction or insights of individual authors or texts. See, e.g., Bourdieu, *Pascalian Meditations*, 2000, 151.

75. My thinking on this point was sparked by the conference on waves of feminism organized by Nancy Hewitt. See Hewitt, *No Permanent Waves*, 2010, for a comprehensive rethinking and critique of the wave model of U.S. feminism.

76. Works on transnational issues that have explicitly addressed ethical questions are Cornell, *At the Heart of Freedom*, 1998; Fernandes, *Transforming Feminist Practice*, 2003.

77. For a useful discussion of Foucault's own conceptions of ethics, see Huffer, *Mad for Foucault*, 2009.

78. Behar and Gordon, *Women Writing Culture*, 1996; Clifford, *Predicament of Culture*, 1988; Spivak, "Can the Subaltern Speak?," 1988.

Notes to Chapter 2

1. Acid attacks are a form of violence against women that have taken place in Pakistan and other countries within South Asia. Nitric acid and hydrochloric acid are used for agriculture and are thus relatively easily available. The attacks are usually linked to familiar patterns of violence against women in comparative contexts that involve marital conflicts (such as divorce) or money and property disputes. The questioning was reported in http://www.nytimes.com/2009/01/13/us/politics/13text-clinton.html?pagewanted=26.

2. This was echoed throughout Obama's initial speeches, as well as Clinton's speeches during the first weeks of the administration, and signaled this shift to a foreign policy that emphasized diplomacy and rested on what Clinton termed "smart power"—an approach combining military, development, and human rights issues. The Obama administration has dropped much of the Bush era public rhetoric on terror/terrorism while continuing aggressive military policies in Afghanistan and Pakistan.

3. See, e.g., Abu-Lughod, "Do Muslim Women Really Need Saving?," 2002; Ahmed, *Women and Gender in Islam*, 1993; Fadlalla, "State of Vulnerability," 2011; Mani, *Contentious Traditions*, 1998.

4. Bunch, "Transforming Human Rights," 1995; MacKinnon, *Are Women Human?*, 2006.

5. Alvarez, "Translating the Global," 2000; Basu, "Globalization of the Local," 2000.

6. Grewal, "'Women's Rights as Human Rights,'" 1999, 344. Proponents of the human rights framework have argued in return that such criticisms miss the practical constraints on activists and also the ways in which human rights provides an effective strategy regardless of the theoretical critiques of rights-based frameworks. They also note that the language of rights can be deployed and contextualized within local and national contexts in more nuanced ways than critics such as Grewal have recognized.

7. Basu, "Globalization of the Local," 2000, 81.

8. See Reilly, "Cosmopolitanism, Feminism, and Human Rights," 2007, for an example of theoretical work that seeks to mediate between universalistic conceptions of rights and questions of difference.

9. Schaffer and Smith, *Human Rights and Narrated Lives*, 2004, 7. For an example of an organization that has focused on challenging and changing the conception of human rights by drawing on the lives of economically underprivileged women, see the Programme on Women's Economic, Social and Cultural Rights (PWESCR). For a report on this work, see Phillips, *Dignity and Human Rights*, 2011.

10. Visweswaran, "Gendered States," 2004, 51.

11. For analyses of the ways in which U.S. state representational practices have been constituted by race and sexuality, see Puar, *Terrorist Assemblages*, 2007; Butler, *Frames of War*, 2010.

12. This is in line with a strong stream in American political science that has asserted that the United States has typically been characterized by a weak state.

13. I would argue that a large part of this problem is due to the resistance of interdisciplinary approaches to the disciplinary knowledge of social science research in political science and sociology. I address these problems in greater depth in chapter 4.

14. Puar, *Terrorist Assemblages*, 2007.

15. For work that focuses primarily on visual practices, see Hesford, *Spectacular*

Rhetorics, 2011; Hesford and Kozol, *Just Advocacy?*, 2005; Puar, *Terrorist Assemblages*, 2007.

16. There is a vast body of work on gender and nationalism. See, e.g., Alexander, *Pedagogies of Crossing*, 2005; McClintock, *Imperial Leather*, 1995; Ranchod-Nilsson and Tetreault, *Women, States, and Nationalism*, 2000; Yuval-Davis, *Gender and Nation*, 1997.

17. Yuval-Davis, *Gender and Nation*, 1997, 47.

18. See Said, *Orientalism*, 1979.

19. Such discourses also exist, as they always have, with long histories of women's activism in a variety of forms ranging from women's resistances to Taliban rule in Afghanistan that long predated the current U.S. military campaign, to local women's peace campaigns that provide nonviolent alternatives to social change in a range of regional and national contexts.

20. Migdal, *State in Society*, 2001.

21. Mitchell, "Limits of the State," 1991.

22. Ibid., 90.

23. There are, of course, both historical continuities with earlier forms of U.S. state formation and shifts in the post-9/11 period, which are my main focus of analysis. For a useful discussion of such continuities and discontinuities, see Steinmetz, "State of Emergency," 2003.

24. Jessica Lynch served in the army during the 2003 invasion of Iraq. She was wounded and captured by Iraqi forces. She became a national media icon when Special Operations Forces were reported to have rescued her in a heroic operation. However, investigative reporting revealed that she was in fact being cared for in an Iraqi hospital and that there had been arrangements made by the Iraqis to hand her over to the United States. For useful analyses of such practices, see Hunt and Rygiel, *(En)gendering the War*, 2007; Oliver, *Women as Weapons of War*, 2007.

25. See Grewal, "Women's Rights as 'Human Rights,'" 1999; Visweswaran, "Gendered States," 2004.

26. On feminist activism and the United States, see Riley, Mohanty, and Pratt, *Feminism and War*, 2008.

27. See, e.g., Campbell, *Writing Security*, 1998.

28. For instance, the association between World War II and the more recent intervention in the Balkans. See Fitzpatrick, "Enduring Right," 2002.

29. Ibid., 118.

30. The Iraq War was actively opposed by most liberals in the United States. Since then, NATO's military intervention in Libya has been constructed by many U.S. liberals as the right kind of military intervention on behalf of human rights. This construction does not contest the idea of war being waged for human rights but rests instead on a binary opposition of good versus bad wars.

31. Bush, "Address to the United Nations," 2003, 2.

32. See, e.g., Steinmetz, "State of Emergency," 2003; Ferguson, "Hegemony or Empire?," 2003; Gonzalez et al., *Labor versus Empire*, 2004. For the purposes of this essay, I will focus more on questions of state power rather than engaging with this debate on the nature of hegemony and empire.

33. On the Middle East, see Abu-Lughod, "Do Muslim Women Really Need Saving?,"

2002; Ahmed, *Women and Gender in Islam*, 1993; Mahmood, *Politics of Piety*, 2005. On sati in India, see Mani, *Contentious Traditions*, 1998.

34. See, e.g., Cohn, "Sex and Death," 1987; Elshtain, *Women and War*, 1987; Enloe, *Maneuvers*, 2000.

35. Kinsella, *Image before the Weapon*, 2011, 26.

36. Ibid., 27.

37. Ibid.

38. Wilcox, "Gendering the Cult of the Offensive," 2009, 236.

39. The actual extent of such nation-building is, of course, debatable given the relative lack of resources the United States has actually invested in reconstruction in Afghanistan and Iraq. See Ignatieff, "Nation-Building Lite," 2002.

40. This is also central element of the official U.S. definition of terrorism. In my own view, violence of any form that deliberately targets civilian spaces does begin to provide a useful working basis for a construction of terrorism, and al-Qaeda's targeting of civilians is a self-evident example of this form of violence.

41. Herold, "Dossier on Civilian Victims," 2001.

42. See i.casualities.org.

43. Butler, *Frames of War*, 2010.

44. Herold, "Dossier on Civilian Victims," 2001.

45. See, e.g., Greenwald, "Human Toll," 2011.

46. See, e.g., *Dodge City Daily Globe*, "U.S. Troops Smash into Homes," 2003.

47. Kinsella, *Image before the Weapon*, 2011.

48. Ibid., 10.

49. See Bradley and Petro, *Truth Claims*, 2002, for a discussion of other cases in which states have appropriated the language of human rights.

50. Jabri, "Shock and Awe," 2006, 830.

51. MSNBC, "We Have Ways," 2003.

52. Migdal, *State in Society*, 2001, 38.

53. MacKinnon, *Are Women Human?*, 2006, 259.

54. Ibid., 261.

55. Ibid., 276.

56. Ibid., 270–271.

57. Ibid., 277.

58. Davis, *Are Prisons Obsolete?*, 2003; Gilmore, *Golden Gulag*, 2007.

59. Human Rights Watch, *Presumption of Guilt*, 2002.

60. Ibid., 9.

61. Ibid., 3. The number is an estimate in the report, as there are no official or public data on the number of detentions, arrests, and interrogations. The report is based on extensive interviews with current and former detainees and their lawyers.

62. Glenn, *Unequal Freedom*, 2004, 2.

63. Human Rights Watch, *Presumption of Guilt*, 2002, 12.

64. For a discussion of the role of bodies in the realm of state security and international relations and the possibilities for bodily resistance, see Shinko, "Ethics after Liberalism," 2010.

65. Gilmore, *Golden Gulag*, 2007.

66. Caruso, "Anti-terror Laws," 2003.

67. Human Rights Watch, *Presumption of Guilt*, 2002, 84.

68. Note that a U.S. Department of Justice report, issued by the Office of the Inspector General, has confirmed abuse of 9/11 detainees and the findings of the Human Rights Watch report *Presumption of Guilt*, 2002.

69. These issues were addressed in a nuanced and careful analysis by Saadia Toor in "Between Neoliberal Globalization," 2009.

70. See, e.g., the killing of Al-Awlaki (a suspected al-Qaeda member on the U.S. state's global terrorist list who was living in Yemen but was also a U.S. citizen) and his sixteen-year-old son. For a discussion of the lack of mainstream criticism of such acts, see Greenwald, "Killing of Awlaki's 16-Year-Old Son," 2011.

71. Cole, "The Great Pakistani Deluge," 2010.

72. I explore some of the regional dimensions of contemporary empire in Fernandes, "Class, Space and the State," 2004.

73. See, e.g., Fadllalla's discussion of the case of Sudan in "State of Vulnerability," 2011.

74. See by Basu et al., "Introduction," 2002.

Notes to Chapter 3

1. On national programming, see Abu-Lughod, *Dramas of Nationhood*, 2004; Rajagopal, *Politics after Television*, 2001; Shohat, *Israeli Cinema*, 1989; Shohat, *Taboo Memories, Diasporic Voices*, 2006. On transnational media, see Shohat and Stam, *Multiculturalism*, 2003.

2. See, e.g., Thussu, *Media on the Move*, 2006; Zayani, *Al-Jazeera Phenomenon*, 2005.

3. See Desai, *Beyond Bollywood*, 2003; Gopinath, *Impossible Desires*, 2005.

4. Appadurai, *Modernity at Large*, 1996; Gopinath, *Impossible Desires*, 2005.

5. See Alarcon, "Theoretical Subject," 1990; Zinn et al., "Costs of Exclusionary Practices," 1990.

6. Spivak, "Can the Subaltern Speak?," 1988, 294.

7. For her later views, see Spivak, *Critique of Postcolonial Reason*, 1999.

8. This dovetailed with the simultaneous rise of poststructuralist feminism. For an overview of these debates, see Flax, *Thinking Fragments*, 1990. In response to Spivak's criticisms, feminist scholars have attempted to devise particular types of textual strategies that could subvert the power dynamics inherent in textual representations of subalternity. Feminist ethnographers in particular have sought to deal with this problem of representation and the question of including and representing women's voices. Behar, *Translated Woman*, 1993; Visweswaran, *Fictions*, 1994.

9. Gopinath, *Impossible Desires*, 2005, 128.

10. Mahmood, "Feminism, Democracy and Empire," 2008.

11. See, e.g., Ahmed, *Cultural Politics*, 2004; Berlant, *Compassion*, 2004; Gregg and Seigworth, *The Affect Theory Reader*, 2010.

12. Ahmed, *Cultural Politics*, 2004, 8.

13. Ibid., 45.

14. Ibid.

15. Ibid.

16. See, e.g., Ahmed, *Promise of Happiness*, 2010; Gregg and Seigworth, *Affect Theory Reader*, 2010.

17. Eng, *Feeling of Kinship*, 2006.

18. Ibid., 57.

19. Grewal and Kaplan, *Scattered Hegemonies*, 1994.

20. Gramsci, *Prison Notebooks*, 1971.

21. See McCall, "Complexity of Intersectionality," 2005.

22. See discussions of a parallel process within area studies in Miyoshi and Harootunian, *Learning Places*, 2002.

23. Gramsci, *Prison Notebooks*, 1971, 235

24. Shinko, "Ethics after Liberalism," 2010, 739.

25. Kapur, *Bandit Queen*, 1994; Phoolan Devi, *I, Phoolan Devi*, 1996.

26. Boyle, *Slumdog Millionaire*, 2008; Swarup, *Q & A*, 2005.

27. See Jameson, "Third-World Literature," 1986; and Ahmad, "Jameson's Rhetoric," 1987, for an exchange regarding the ways in which Western scholarship recasts Third World literature within allegories of the nation.

28. See Trinh, *Woman, Native, Other*, 1989, for discussion of how difference is deployed in ways that reproduce hierarchies of power.

29. See Appadurai, "Putting Hierarchy," 1988, for a discussion of the ways in which caste has been constructed as an essentialized marker of social organization and hierarchy in India.

30. See Chow, "Violence," 1991.

31. Ibid., 84

32. Ibid., 83.

33. See Rony, *Third Eye*, 1996. Such questions regarding cinematic form have also been addressed in relation to the category of gender. See Kaplan, *Women and Film*, 1983. This raises important questions for future research regarding the parallels and intersections among the spectacle of race, the spectacle of woman, and "woman of color."

34. Such categories thus continue to have salience in cultural analysis (even while we deconstruct them) not merely as analytical tools but because they are reproduced through practices of cultural production.

35. Such processes are not of course linked only to the Third World. For instance, consider the racialized, gendered politics of images of black men and the politics of lynching in the United States. See Hall, "Mind That Burns," 1983.

36. Shohat, *Taboo Memories, Diasporic Voices*, 2006, 17.

37. Ibid., 39.

38. For a historical discussion of such colonial ideologies of masculinity, see Stoler, "Carnal Knowledge," 1991.

39. The film is a British venture by well-known director Danny Boyle but was shot in India with an Indian "codirector."

40. Also, of course, with China and fear of Chinese economic growth and control of U.S. debt.

41. Bolter and Grusin, *Remediation*, 2000, 84.

42. Ibid., 70.

43. Ayush Mahesh Khedekar, Azharuddin Mohammed Ismail, and Rubina Ali, who

played the three central characters of the film: Jamal, Jamal's brother (Salim), and Jamal's love (Latika).

44. Nelson and Henderson, "Slumdog Child Stars Miss Out," 2009 (emphasis added).

45. Ibid

46. Marxian cultural analysis has all but disappeared from interdisciplinary paradigms within women's studies. Meanwhile, earlier studies that foregrounded First World–Third World relationships of economic extraction are now largely viewed as defunct, deterministic views.

47. Roy, "Great Indian Rape Trick," 1994.

48. Fernandes, *India's New Middle Class*, 2006.

49. Popular films do not generally depict nudity and until recently did not show explicit sexual intimacy, including kissing.

50. Such reports were often tinged with particular class narratives and the deployment of stereotypes of "uncivilized" working-class men, who cheered at such violence.

51. Such special screenings are not new or unique to *Bandit Queen* and can be traced back to the early twentieth century. See Vasudevan, "Film Studies," 1995.

52. All references to Kapur's perspective are based on a televised interview, which was aired on the interview program *In Focus*, Home TV channel, India, June 10, 1996.

53. Kumar, *History of Doing*, 1993.

54. Note that the film also presents a gendered reworking of a significant genre of popular commercial Hindi films that depict the male outlaw figure: for instance, through representations of male dacoits or the male working-class hero who transgresses the law.

55. For strong critical reviews, see Kishwar, "Bandit Queen," 1994; Roy, "Great Indian Rape Trick," 1994.

56. Vasudevan, "Film Studies," 1995, 2809.

57. Niranjana, "Integrating Whose Nation?," 1994, 79.

58. Ibid.

59. Fernandes, *India's New Middle Class*, 2006.

60. Vasudevan, "Film Studies," 1995, 2813.

61. Ghosh, "Deviant Pleasures," 1996.

62. Fernandes, "Politics of Forgetting," 2004.

63. The films were *Deewar* (1975), *Satya* (1998), and *Black Friday* (2004). See Kumar, "Slumdog Millionaire's Bollywood Ancestors," 2008.

64. Phoolan Devi, *I, Phoolan Devi*, 1996.

65. See, e.g., Gilmore, *Limits of Autobiography*, 2001; Smith and Watson, "Introduction," 1992; Smith and Watson, *Women, Autobiography, Theory*, 1998.

66. Smith and Watson, "Introduction," 1992, xix.

67. Contrast this to the careful strategies of representation in Ruth Behar's *Translated Woman*, 1993, particularly in relation to the ways in which Behar makes explicit her role as a (privileged) witness.

68. On commodification, see Carr, "Crossing the First World/Third World Divides," 1994. On the transgressive potential, see Beverly, *Against Literature*, 1993.

69. Beverly, *Against Literature*, 83.

70. Schaffer and Smith, *Human Rights and Narrated Lives*, 2004, 30.

71. Ibid.

72. Phoolan Devi, *I, Phoolan Devi*, 1996, 11

73. Ibid., 65.

74. Ibid., 73.

75. Ibid., 12.

76. Ibid., 51.

77. Ibid., 58.

78. Ghosh, "Deviant Pleasures," 1996, 159.

79. Ibid. For an interesting interrogation of the notion "to speak is to become a subject," see Pathak and Rajan, "Shahbano," 1992, 26.

80. Kaplan, "Resisting Autobiography," 1992, 134.

81. Phoolan Devi, *I, Phoolan Devi*, 1996, 450.

82. Ibid., 464.

83. Swarup, *Q & A*, 2005, 28.

84. Ibid., 47.

85. Ibid., 49.

86. Gopinath, *Impossible Desires*, 2005.

87. This naming device—linking Muslim, Christian, and Hindu names in the figure of a hero—is a long-standing technique in Indian popular culture to depict an idealized vision of state secularism. See, for instance, the well-known Hindi film *Amar Akbar Anthony*.

88. Swarup, *Q & A*, 2005, 258.

89. Fernandes, *India's New Middle Class*, 2006.

90. Swarup, *Q & A*, 2005, 316.

91. Ibid.

92. For a discussion of Third World feminist cinematic traditions, see Shohat, *Taboo Memories, Diasporic Voices*, 2006, 290.

93. Lewis, *Boomerang*, 2011.

94. See, e.g., Bardan, "Enter Freely," 2007; Marciniak, Imre, and O'Healey, *Transnational Feminism in Film*, 2007. Note, however, that this does not detract from the discussion of historical and contemporary forms of colonialism. Consider, for instance, both the ways in which the legacies of Soviet colonialism in Afghanistan prefigure and shape American strategies in the area and the ways in which U.S. foreign policy has used strategic alliances with some Eastern European nations in its war on terrorism. This has ranged from placing prisoners in "black sites" in the area to using support from Eastern European allies to play down opposition to the Iraq War from countries such as France and Germany.

Notes to Chapter 4

1. Anderson, *Imagined Communities*, 1983.

2. See, e.g., Naples and Desai, *Women's Activism and Globalization*, 2002; Peterson, *Critical Rewriting*, 2003; Swarr and Nagar, *Critical Transnational Feminist Praxis*, 2010.

3. In interdisciplinary sites in the U.S. academy, "transnationalism" has become a colloquial term that now commonly serves as a descriptive signifier of work that moves

outside of a U.S.-centric focus. Such research encompasses a wide range of approaches that focus on women and gender issues in comparative, international, and global perspective and that draw on varied disciplinary and interdisciplinary frameworks. These approaches can range from the study of transnational women's movements, to ethnographic studies of women and labor, to the literary analysis of women's novels. My concern in this chapter is not with this vast body of work but more specifically with the intellectual paradigm of transnational feminism.

4. See, e.g., Davis, *Making of Our Bodies*, 2007; Thayer, *Making Transnational Feminism*, 2010.

5. Pratt, "Seeing beyond the State," 2010, 84.

6. Massey, "Geographies of Responsibility," 2004.

7. See, e.g., the long tradition of feminist and postcolonial scholarship on questions of knowledge production.

8. It is often forgotten that Anderson's key project was to explain why it was that Marxists had failed to understand the power of nationalism and the nation-state. See Anderson, *Imagined Communities*, 1983.

9. See, e.g., Chakrabarty, *Provincializing Europe*, 2000.

10. I point to Marx as an example here because the history of European political thought that has become dominant common sense in U.S. feminist scholarship often mistakenly assumes that discussions of knowledge and power were initiated only with poststructuralist thought.

11. Marx and Engels, *German Ideology*, 1998.

12. Anzaldúa, *Borderlands*, 1987, 26.

13. Barad, *Meeting the Universe Halfway*, 2007.

14. Ibid., 54.

15. Ibid., 91.

16. These examples also caution us against assuming that identifying these three sets of practices provides an easy response to the challenges we face when producing knowledge that attempts to moves beyond relationships of power. In that sense, such examples remind us of the wisdom of the poststructuralist impetus to continually interrogate the effects of our knowledge formations.

17. See, e.g., Bishop and Robinson, *Night Market*, 1998; Chang, *Disposable Domestics*, 2000; Ong, *Spirits of Resistance*, 2010; Parreñas, *Servants of Globalization*, 2001.

18. Ong, *Spirits of Resistance*, 2010; see also Fernández-Kelly, *For We Are Sold*, 1984; Freeman, *High Tech and High Heels*, 2000; Hewamanne, *Stitching Identities*, 2010; Muñoz, *Transnational Tortillas*, 2008; Ward, *Women Workers*, 1990; Wright, *Disposable Women*, 2006.

19. Parreñas, *Servants of Globalization*, 2001; see also Hochschild, "Love and Gold," 2003.

20. Narayan, *Dislocating Cultures*, 1997.

21. Ibid., 84.

22. Grewal and Kaplan, "Global Identities," 2001.

23. See, e.g., Poster, "Who's on the Line?," 2007.

24. Freeman, *High Tech and High Heels*, 2000.

25. Karim, *Microfinance*, 2011; Shehabuddin, *Reshaping the Holy*, 2008.

26. Grewal, *Transnational America*, 2005; Sen and Stivens, *Gender and Power*, 1998.

27. See, e.g., Ong, *Flexible Citizenship*, 1999.

28. Mohanty, "Under Western Eyes," 1988.

29. Spivak, "Can the Subaltern Speak?," 1988.

30. Haraway, "Manifesto for Cyborgs," 1989.

31. Visweswaran, *Fictions*, 1994.

32. Ibid., 47.

33. Ibid.

34. See, e.g., Alarcon, "Theoretical Subject," 1990.

35. Barad, *Meeting the Universe Halfway*, 2007.

36. Ibid., 37.

37. Ibid., 155.

38. See, e.g., Oldenburg, *Dowry Murder*, 2002; Mitchell, *Rule of Experts*, 2002; Said, *Orientalism*, 1979.

39. Mitchell, *Rule of Experts*, 2002.

40. Ibid., 91.

41. Said, *Orientalism*, 1979.

42. On the relationship between colonialism, orientalism, and feminism, see, e.g., Ahmed, *Women and Gender in Islam*, 1993; Burton, *Burdens of History*, 1994.

43. The critique of visibility should not be conflated with a critique of visual evidence or visual culture, which is a key dimension of transnational processes, as I have argued in chapter 3.

44. On strong objectivity, see Harding, *Science Question*, 1986; on agential realism, see Barad, *Meeting the Universe Halfway*, 2007.

45. Narayan, *Dislocating Cultures*, 1997.

46. Feminist ethics has long been an important subfield within feminist theory. My goal in discussing the ethical component is not to engage in a comprehensive theoretical discussion of this field but to step back and consider how thinking about ethics as a methodological practice could contribute to existing work on transnational feminism. Transnational feminism, like all feminist research, with its normative project of addressing inequality and exclusion, has an ethical component built into it. See, e.g., Chatterjee, "Imperial Pedagogies," 2009; Cornell, *At the Heart of Freedom*, 1998; Swarr and Nagar, *Critical Transnational Feminist Practice*, 2010.

47. See, e.g., Abu-Lughod, "Do Muslim Women Really Need Saving?," 2002; Behar and Gordon, *Women Writing Culture*, 1996; Wolf, *Feminist Dilemmas*, 1996.

48. Haraway, *Modest_Witness*, 1997. See also Ruth Behar's conception of the witness as that of a "vulnerable observer" in *Vulnerable Observer*, 1996.

49. Haraway borrows the terms from Shapin and Schaffer, *Leviathan*, 1985.

50. Ibid., 25.

51. Ibid., 31.

52. Ibid., 35.

53. Ibid., 37.

54. See, e.g., biblical traditions of witnessing and liberation theology in Latin America.

55. Felman and Laub, *Testimony*, 1991, 110.

56. Ludlow, "Things We Cannot Say," 2008.

57. Ibid., 31.

58. Kacandes, "Testimony," 2001.

59. Ludlow, "Things We Cannot Say," 2008, 40.

60. Barad, *Meeting the Universe Halfway*, 2007, 384.

61. Ibid., 393.

62. Welch, *A Feminist Ethic of Risk*, 1990.

63. Ibid., 18.

64. Ibid., 25.

65. Ibid., 68.

66. However, as many scholars working from such perspectives have long known and argued, activism itself is not an innocent or power-free zone. See also Swarr and Nagar, *Critical Transnational Feminist Practice*, 2010. On ethics and activism see Pulido, "Frequently (Un)asked Questions," 2008.

67. Hale, *Engaging Contradictions*, 2008.

68. Sudbury and Okazawa-Rey, *Activist Scholarship*, 2009; Swarr and Nagar, *Critical Transnational Feminist Praxis*, 2010.

69. See, e.g., Sangtin Writers and Nagar, *Playing with Fire*, 2006.

70. Pulido, "Frequently (Un)asked Questions," 2008, 357.

71. Alexander and Mohanty, "Cartographies of Knowledge," 2010, 42. Note also that scholars such as Laura Pulido precisely argue against turning activist research into a self-evident formulaic response. "Frequently (Un)asked Questions," 2008.

72. Mahmood, *Politics of Piety*, 2005.

73. Ibid., 132.

74. Ibid., 39.

Notes to Chapter 5

1. See, e.g., Alarcon, "Theoretical Subject," 1990.

2. Mapping Women's and Gender Studies Data Collection, http://72.32.34.202/projects/mapping.php.

3. Tai, "Women's Work," 2005.

4. Orr and Lichtenstein, "Politics of Feminist Locations," 2004.

5. Gramsci, *Prison Notebooks*, 1971.

6. See, e.g., Burghardt and Colbeck, "Women's Studies Faculty," 2005; Safarik, "Feminist Transformation," 2003.

7. For examples of these debates, see Brown, "Impossibility of Women's Studies," 2008; Wiegman, "Feminism, Institutionalism, and the Idiom of Failure," 2008.

8. Feminist responses to this contradictory position of women's studies have varied. Some responses have pointed to the impossibility of the project of women's studies; others have viewed the internal criticisms as an unproductive destabilization of the feminist subject.

9. For critiques of U.S. post-9/11 policy, see, e.g., Alexander et al., *Sing, Whisper*, 2003; Hunt and Rygiel, *(En)gendering the War on Terror*, 2007; Oliver, *Women as Weapons of War*, 2007. In recent years, the significance of such contestation was self-evident in the

aftermath of 9/11. Media coverage, for instance, was rife with stories and accusations of anti-American sentiments. While such stories were commonplace on cable channels such as Fox, other media writings specifically attacked postcolonial perspectives and public figures such as Edward Said. See, e.g., Bawer, "Edward W. Said, Intellectual," 2002, 620, and a column condemning postcolonial writings as anti-Western ideologies potentially complicit with terrorist threats (Rothstein, "Attacks," 2001) published less than two weeks after the 9/11 attacks. Meanwhile, Daniel Pipes founded Campus Watch to monitor activities in Middle East studies programs and has engaged in activities such as listing professors considered anti-Israel or anti-American; http://www.campus-watch.org.

10. Commission on Anthropology's Engagement with the Security and Intelligence Communities, *Final Report*, 2009; Eskander, "Minerva Research Initiative," 2008.

11. Calhoun, "Social Science Research," 2010, 1105.

12. Ibid.

13. Ibid., 1102.

14. This relationship between state and scholarship has also, of course, been true of many academic disciplines. See Mitchell, "Limits of the State," 1991.

15. http://www.campus-watch.org.

16. Scott, *Women's Studies*, 2008.

17. Wiegman, "Academic Feminism" 2002, 23.

18. Ibid., 22.

19. For a useful discussion, see May, "Disciplinary Desires," 2002.

20. Brown, "Impossibility of Women's Studies," 2008, 22.

21. E.g., Wendy Brown reduces her discussion of scholarship on women of color and race to a discussion of emotions in ibid.

22. May, "Disciplinary Desires," 2002, 143.

23. See Wiegman, "Feminism, Institutionalism, and the Idiom of Failure," 2008, for a different response to Wendy Brown.

24. Brown, "Impossibility of Women's Studies," 2008, 35.

25. Ibid.

26. Ibid., 18.

27. Massey, *Space, Place and Gender*, 1994; Harvey, *Spaces of Capital*, 2001.

28. On feminist research on the gendered and sexual politics of nationalism, see McClintock, Mufti, and Shohat, *Dangerous Liaisons*, 1997; Yuval-Davis, *Gender and Nation*, 1997.

29. E.g., work associated with the subaltern school. See Chatterjee, *Nation and Its Fragments*, 1993; Chakrabarty, *Provincializing Europe*, 2000.

30. See, e.g., Appadurai, *Modernity at Large*, 1996, for the clearest elaboration of the postnational thesis.

31. The significance of this analytical decentering, as I have noted in earlier chapters, is heightened because our contemporary historical moment of globalization has intensified the salience and visibility of movement across nations and generated discussions of the weakening of the nation-state. The transnational emphasis of contemporary interdisciplinary scholarship has been shaped in part by globalization (and the emergence of new classes such as diasporic elites and middle classes) and an interventionist U.S. state conception of a world where national sovereignty has been subordinated to the

United States' pursuit of foreign policy goals (whether these have been militaristic or humanitarian).

32. Butler, *Gender Trouble*, 1990.

33. Said, *Orientalism*, 1979.

34. Similar dynamics occur in theory/practice debates. Yet what requires more systematic conversation in debates on interdisciplinarity is not simply how curricular practices can enable students to more successfully bridge or jettison the divide between theory and practice but what kind of relationship to place is formulated through curricular practices. The theory/practice debate is often produced or intensified by the institutional structures that shape graduate education. The emergence of the autonomous women's studies PhD has often produced new kinds of fissures and tensions between interdisciplinary PhD knowledge practices and the interdisciplinary training of MA and undergraduate students. The scope, focus, and expectations of MA programs in women's studies vary widely. Like many MA programs (across disciplinary and interdisciplinary fields), the quality and organizations of such programs is uneven, with MA students placed in courses with PhD students who are located within a different institutional framework and who may enter their courses with a different set of expectations than students seeking a terminal MA degree. Such tensions are not unique to women's studies and have more to do with the devaluation of the MA degree in most nonprofessional schools (that is, unlike degrees such as the MBA or some degrees in public policy that may confer legitimacy and entry into high-paying occupations). New interdisciplinary degrees such as women's studies have thus emerged within a particular institutional and economic structure that rests on the stratification of knowledge and the social and economic capital derived from credentialing practices. The unique dynamic that these institutionalized hierarchies take on within women's studies is a projected tension between theory and activism. While there may be variation across programs and departments, in general the women's studies MA (like many terminal MA degrees) is conceived of as one that will train students for some form of practical or activist-oriented work. Women's studies MA programs often incorporate a practice-oriented component (some form of practicum or fieldwork-based project). The result is that preexisting constructions of a presumed separation between theory and practice may be reproduced and intensified through this institutional organization. In this juxtaposition, PhD work becomes identified with theory-driven scholarship and MA work with the activist dimensions of feminism.

35. Hewitt, *No Permanent Waves*, 2010.

36. Moraga and Anzaldúa, *This Bridge Called My Back*. See also Glenn, "From Servitude to Service Work," 1992.

37. Fabian, *Time and the Other*, 1983.

38. Newman, "Present and Our Past," 2002.

39. On the complexities of national histories and genealogies of feminism and their engagement with global flows, see Lal et al., "Recasting Global Feminisms," 2010, and the Global Feminisms Project at the University of Michigan, http://www.umich.edu/~glblfem/about.html.

40. My focus in this book is solely on the teaching of international and transnational work. For a general discussion of undergraduate work and a practical guide for students, see Berger and Radeloff, *Transforming Scholarship*, 2011.

41. Alexander and Mohanty, "Cartographies of Knowledge," 2010, 34.

42. Ibid.

43. Ibid., 38.

44. Ibid.

45. Gilmore, *Golden Gulag*, 2007.

46. On race and pedagogy, see hooks, *Teaching to Transgress*, 1994; hooks, *Teaching Community*, 2003; Keating, *Teaching Transformation*, 2007.

47. Alexander and Mohanty, "Cartographies of Knowledge," 2010.

48. Reid and Mahalingam, "Dialogue at the Margins," 2007, 263.

49. *Dalit* refers to the outcaste social group previously called "untouchables" (a derogatory term connoting sociocultural notions of impurity) that has experienced systematic discrimination.

50. Weinbaum et al., *Modern Girl*, 2008.

51. Reid and Mahalingam, "Dialogue at the Margins," 2007, 257–258.

52. Davis, "Unmirroring Pedagogies," 2010.

53. Ibid., 145.

54. Ibid., 149.

55. Alexander and Mohanty, "Cartographies of Knowledge," 2010, 35.

Notes to Chapter 6

1. Race may be a central factor in shaping particular transnational processes (such as colonialism) or in structuring comparative forms of inequality in comparative contexts (such as Latin America or Europe). However, other contexts may be structured by forms of inequality that have little or nothing to do with race— such as rural-urban divisions, caste inequalities, or regional disparities.

2. Aikau, Erickson, and Pierce, *Feminist Generations*, 2007.

3. Aikau, "Between Wind and Water," 2007.

4. Hewitt, *No Permanent Waves*, 2010, 8.

5. Sandoval, *Methodology of the Oppressed*, 2000.

6. "Third wave" feminism also has included work on international issues, with early seminal interventions by scholars such as Chandra Mohanty and Jacqui Alexander explicitly connecting such questions to U.S.-based debates on race and gender. See, e.g., Mohanty, "Under Western Eyes," 1988; Alexander, "Not Just Any(Body) Can Be a Citizen," 1994.

7. See, e.g., Smith, "Racism and Women's Studies," 1982; Zinn et al., "Costs of Exclusionary Practices," 1990.

8. Shohat, *Talking Visions*, 2001, 19.

9. Alarcon, "Theoretical Subject," 1990, 357.

10. Ibid., 359.

11. Ibid.

12. These challenges to the category of woman were not limited to feminists of color but also included poststructuralist critiques of essentialism and queer theorist critiques of heteronormative constructions of gender. See, e.g., Butler, *Gender Trouble*, 1990.

13. Alarcon, "Theoretical Subject," 1990, 366.

14. Butler, *Gender Trouble*, 1990, 143.

15. Hong, *Ruptures*, 2006, xix.

16. This has led to a feminist variant of the backlash against identity politics in the U.S. academy that periodically resurfaces in the everyday practices and discourses of universities. My point is not that there are no streams of thought in third wave feminism that focus on identity-based claims, but that is only one aspect of a much more diverse intellectual field.

17. Scholarship on identity of course continues to make invaluable contributions to the field (see Alcoff, *Visible Identities*, 2005, for a defense of identity politics). See also Saldivar-Hull for a discussion of misreadings of the political project of U.S. feminists of color (*Feminism on the Border*, 2000). My point is not to discount such contributions but to illustrate how other forms of analysis are ignored and miscast as essentialized understandings of identity.

18. Scott, *Gender and the Politics of History*, 1988.

19. See, e.g., Joan Scott's well-known essay "Experience," 1992.

20. Such theories by feminists of color either were not viewed as theoretically relevant or were used as empirical, embodied references. Thus,, e.g., Donna Haraway's "Manifesto for Cyborgs" did draw on Anzaldúa's conception of hybridity as an example of cyborg identity but did not include an extensive theoretical discussion of Anzaldúa's work on identity and experience. See Haraway, "Manifesto for Cyborgs," 1989.

21. Classic theorists, writing at the time from different perspectives but drawing on critical engagements with poststructuralist theory, were Gayatri Spivak and Chandra Mohanty. Scholars such as Chela Sandoval and Norma Alarcon, writing about race and gender within the United States, have also drawn on and critically engaged with poststructuralist theory.

22. Alexander, "Remembering This Bridge," 2002, 96.

23. Ibid.

24. Keating, "Charting Pathways, Marking Thresholds," 2002, 17.

25. See, e.g., Keating, "Forging El Mundo Zurdo," 2002; Cervenak, Souza, and Straub, "Imagining Differently," 2002.

26. Lorenz, "Thawing Hearts," 2002, 497.

27. Ibid., 503.

28. Thus, in the wave model that persists, it is now a common assumption that we can move past "third wave" feminism and no longer need to address older issues such as racial exclusion. Racism is thus increasingly viewed as a dated issue in women's studies that was characteristic of "third wave" feminism. The "postracial" assumptions are a somewhat ironic reflection of the "postfeminist" rhetoric in public discourses. The liminal identities associated with the borderlands (in-between cultures, U.S.-Mexico territorial borders, racial-ethnic-gender identities, and psychic-material spaces) have meant that Anzaldúa is often classified along with theorists of diaspora and hybridity.

29. Crenshaw, "Mapping the Margins," 1991.

30. Glenn, "From Servitude to Service Work," 1992. See also Glenn, "Racial Ethnic Women's Labor," 1985; and Glenn, *Unequal Freedom*, 2004.

31. Collins, *Black Feminist Thought*, 1990, 222.

32. Ibid.

33. See McCall, "Complexity of Intersectionality," 2005; for a response to McCall, see Alexander-Floyd, "Disappearing Acts," 2012.

34. Dill and Zambrana, "Critical Thinking" 2009.

35. Most recently, the 2008 Democratic primary election provided the terrain for this distorted wave model of feminism. In an online article, Linda Hirshman presented women's support for Barack Obama over Hillary Clinton as an effect of a generational shift toward a focus on intersectionality rather than gender. Hirshman reproduces the teleological approach to feminism, where she conflates differences between "second wave" and "third wave" feminism with a generational shift from gender to intersectional analyses (conflating "third wave" feminism with intersectionality). In this endeavor she essentializes and misrepresents both "second wave" and "third wave" feminism, implicitly coding "second wave" feminism as a gender-based struggle for issues raised by middle-class white women, and "third wave" feminism as shifting feminism away from women's issues. Hirshman, "When Dreams Collide," 2008, B01.

36. In this discussion I am distinguishing between the actual substantive contributions of writers associated with the paradigm and the dominant intellectual discourses and institutional sites in which the paradigm has become institutionalized. On the need to retain a focus on intersectionality, see Brah and Phoenix, "Ain't I a Woman?," 2004.

37. Dill and Zambrana, "Critical Thinking," 2009. For instance, in my own discipline, political science, intersectionality has just now emerged as a central paradigm of interest. Yet the paradigm as it is debated and deployed is usually decontextualized from the richer and more varied field of "third wave" feminist writing. The result is a mainstreaming of the paradigm in ways that have produced important research agendas but also silences and erasures as the paradigm has been "disciplined" to meet the dominant norms of political science. See Collins, *Fighting Words*, 1998, for a discussion of some of the dangers in the ways in which the concept of intersectionality has been misappropriated.

38. Sandoval, *Methodology of the Oppressed*, 2000, 43. Note that Sandoval uses the term "U.S. Third World Feminism" rather than "third wave feminism" in her classification of the writings by feminists of color that emerged in the 1970s and 1980s.

39. Sandoval argues that this historical narrative was shared by a diverse group of scholars, including Julia Kristeva, Toril Moi, Hester Eisenstein, and Allison Jaggar. Ibid., 47.

40. Ibid., 54.

41. Ibid., 57. Note that the phrase "the equal rights, revolutionary, supremacist, and separatist modes of oppositional consciousness" that Sandoval uses is her classification of paradigms inherent within the four phases of liberal, Marxist, radical/cultural, and socialist feminism.

42. Barad, *Meeting the Universe Halfway,* 2007, 223. Barad's critique of intersectionality is fully elaborated in "Re(con)figuring Space, Time, and Matter," 2001.

43. Gilmore, *Golden Gulag,* 2007.

44. Saldivar-Hull, *Feminism on the Border,* 2000, 47–48.

45. Anzaldúa, *Borderlands,* 1987.

46. Ibid., 16.

47. Ibid., 17.

48. Saldivar-Hull, *Feminism on the Border*, 2000, 63.

49. Ibid., 46.

50. Ibid., 51

51. See Keating, *Entre Mundos/Among Worlds*, 2005, on this point.

52. Anzaldúa, *Borderlands*, 78.

53. I elaborate on the question of disidentification at greater length in *Transforming Feminist Practice*, 2003.

54. See, e.g., the division between the fields of American politics and comparative politics or the splits between U.S.- and international-oriented work in sociology.

55. Ajayi-Soyanki, in "Transcending the Boundaries," 2005, draws on an analysis of Alice Walker's representation of genital mutilation in Africa to illustrate that women of color in the United States can also reproduce orientalist or ethnocentric conceptions of non-Western countries and regions.

56. Collins, "Foreword," 2009, xii.

57. On race in Latin America, see, e.g., Hanchard, *Orpheus and Power*, 1998; Winddance Twine, *Racism in a Racial Democracy*, 1997.

58. See, e.g., Cole, "Intersectionality," 2009; Jordan-Zachery, "Commentary," 2006; Moin, "Disciplinarity," 2010; Smooth, "Intersectionality," 2006.

59. Collins, "Foreword," 2009, xiii.

60. Alexander-Floyd, "Disappearing Acts," 2012.

61. Ibid., 18.

62. Ibid.

63. Weldon, "The Structure of Intersectionality," 2006.

64. See also Alexander-Floyd, "Disappearing Acts," 2012, on this point.

Notes to Chapter 7

1. Anderson, *Imagined Communities*, 1983, 12.

2. Chow, *Age of the World Target*, 2006.

3. Crowley, "What the Wikileak Means," 2010.

4. Mortenson, *Three Cups of Tea*, 2006; Mortenson, *Stones into Schools*, 2009.

5. Moreau and Yousafzai, "We Never Kidnapped Greg Mortenson," 2011.

6. Bourdieu, *Pascalian Meditations*, 2000.

Bibliography

Abu-Lughod, Lila. "Do Muslim Women Really Need Saving? Anthropological Reflections on Cultural Relativism and Its Others." *American Anthropologist* 104, no. 3 (2002): 783–790.

———. *Dramas of Nationhood: The Politics of Television in Egypt.* Chicago: University of Chicago Press, 2004.

Aftab, Tahera. "Lobbying for Transnational Feminism: Feminist Conversations Make Connections." *NWSA Journal* 14, no. 2 (2002): 153–156.

Ahmad, Aijaz. "Jameson's Rhetoric of Otherness and the 'National Allegory.'" *Social Text* 17 (1987): 3–25.

Ahmed, Leila. *Women and Gender in Islam: Historical Roots of a Modern Debate.* New Haven: Yale University Press, 1993.

Ahmed, Sara. *The Cultural Politics of Emotion.* New York: Routledge, 2004.

———. *The Promise of Happiness.* Durham, NC: Duke University Press, 2010.

Aikau, Hokulani. "Between Wind and Water: Thinking about the Third Wave as Metaphor and Materiality." In *Feminist Generations: Life Stories from the Academy,* ed. Hokulani Aiku, Karla Erickson, and Jennifer Pierce, 232–249. Minneapolis: University of Minnesota Press, 2007.

Aikau, Hokulani, Karla Erickson, and Jennifer Pierce, eds. *Feminist Generations: Life Stories from the Academy.* Minneapolis: University of Minnesota Press, 2007.

Ajayi-Soyanki, Omofolabo. "Transcending the Boundaries of Power and Imperialism: Writing Gender, Constructing Knowledge." In *Female Circumcision and the Politics of Knowledge: African Women in Imperialist Discourses,* ed. Nnaemeka, Obioma, 47–80. Westport, CT: Praeger, 2005.

Alarcon, Norma. "The Theoretical Subject of *This Bridge Called My Back* and Anglo-American Feminism." In *Making Face, Making Soul/Haciendo Caras: Creative and Critical Perspectives by Feminists of Color,* ed. Gloria Anzaldúa, 357–369. San Francisco: Aunt Lute Books, 1990.

Alcoff, Linda. *Visible Identities: Race, Gender, and the Self.* New York: Oxford University Press, 2005.

Alexander, Jacqui. "Not Just (Any)Body Can Be a Citizen: The Politics of Law, Sexuality and Postcoloniality in Trinidad and Tobago and the Bahamas." *Feminist Review* 48 (Autumn 1994): 5–23.

———. *Pedagogies of Crossing: Meditations on Feminism, Sexual Politics, Memory and the Sacred.* Durham, NC: Duke University Press, 2005.

———. "Remembering This Bridge, Remembering Ourselves: Yearning, Memory and Desire." In *This Bridge We Call Home: Radical Visions for Transformation*, ed. Gloria Anzaldúa and AnaLouise Keating, 81–103. New York: Routledge, 2002.

Alexander, Jacqui, Lisa Albrecht, Sharon Day, and Mab Segrest, eds. *Sing, Whisper, Shout, Pray! Feminist Visions for a Just World*. Fort Bragg, CA: EdgeWork Books, 2003.

Alexander, Jacqui, and Chandra Talpade Mohanty. "Cartographies of Knowledge and Power: Transnational Feminism as Radical Praxis." In *Critical Transnational Feminist Praxis*, ed. Amanda Lock Swarr and Richa Nagar, 23–45. Albany: State University of New York Press, 2010.

Alexander-Floyd, Nikol G. "Disappearing Acts: Reclaiming Intersectionality in the Social Sciences in a Post-Black Feminist Era." *Feminist Formations* 24, no. 1 (2012): 1–25.

Alvarez, Sonia. "Translating the Global: Effects of Transnational Organizing on Local Feminist Discourses and Practices in Latin America." *Meridians: Feminism, Race, Transnationalism* 1, no. 1 (2000): 29–67.

Anderson, Benedict. *Imagined Communities: Reflections on the Origin and Spread of Nationalism*. London: Verso, 1983.

Anzaldúa, Gloria. *Borderlands = La Frontera: The New Mestiza*. San Francisco: Aunt Lute Books, 1987.

Appadurai, Arjun. *Modernity at Large: Cultural Dimensions of Globalization*. Minneapolis: University of Minnesota Press, 1996.

———. "Putting Hierarchy in Its Place." *Cultural Anthropology* 3 (February 1988): 36–49.

Appadurai, Arjun, and Carol A. Breckenridge. "Public Modernity in India." In *Consuming Modernity: Public Culture in a South Asian World*, ed. Carol A. Breckenridge, 1–20. Minneapolis: University of Minnesota Press, 1995.

Appiah, Kwame Anthony. *Cosmopolitanism: Ethics in a World of Strangers*. New York: Norton, 2007.

Appiah, Kwame Anthony, and Henry Louis Gates. *Africana: The Encyclopedia of the African and African American Experience*. New York: Oxford University Press, 2005.

Associated Press. "U.S. Troops Smash into Homes, Shops in Raid; 2,500 Soldiers Hunt for Guerrillas in Turbulent City." *Telegraph-Herald*, December 18, 2003. http://www.highbeam.com/doc/1P2-11108157 (accessed November 11, 2011).

Barad, Karen. *Meeting the Universe Halfway: Quantum Physics and the Entanglement of Matter and Meaning*. Durham, NC: Duke University Press, 2007.

———. "Re(con)figuring Space, Time, and Matter." In *Feminist Locations: Global and Local, Theory and Practice*, ed. Marianne deKoven, 75–109. New Brunswick, NJ: Rutgers University Press, 2001.

Bardan, Alice Mihaela. "'Enter Freely, and of Your Own Will': Cinematic Representations of Post-socialist Transnational Journeys." In *Transnational Feminism in Film and Media*, ed. Katarzyna Marciniak, Anikó Imre, and Áine O'Healy, 93–110. New York: Palgrave, 2007.

Basu, Amrita. "Globalization of the Local/Localization of the Global: Mapping Transnational Women's Movements." *Meridians: Feminism, Race, Transnationalism* 1, no. 1 (2000): 68–84.

———. *Women's Movements in the Global Era: The Power of Local Feminisms*. Boulder, CO: Westview Press, 2010.

Basu, Amrita, Paula Giddings, Inderpal Grewal, and Kamala Visweswaran. "Introduction to Feminist Perspectives on 9/11." *Meridians: Feminism, Race, Transnationalism* 2, no. 2 (2002): 250–253.

Bawer, Bruce. "Edward W. Said, Intellectual." *Hudson Review* 54, no. 4 (2002): 620.

Behar, Ruth. *Translated Woman: Crossing the Border with Esperanza's Story.* Boston: Beacon Press, 1993.

———. *The Vulnerable Observer: Anthropology That Breaks Your Heart.* Boston: Beacon Press, 1996.

Behar, Ruth, and Deborah Gordon, eds. *Women Writing Culture.* Berkeley: University of California Press, 1996.

Berger, Michele, and Cheryl Radeloff. *Transforming Scholarship: Why Women's Studies Students Are Changing Themselves and the World.* New York: Routledge, 2011.

Berlant, Lauren. *Compassion: The Culture and Politics of an Emotion.* New York: Routledge, 2004.

Beverly, John. *Against Literature.* Minneapolis: University of Minnesota Press, 1993.

Bhabha, Homi K. *The Location of Culture.* London: Routledge, 1994.

Bishop, Ryan, and Lillian S. Robinson. *Night Market: Sexual Cultures and the Thai Economic Miracle.* New York: Routledge, 1998.

Bohlen, Anne, Mariá Patricia Fernández-Kelly, and Lorraine Gray. *The Global Assembly Line.* New York: New Day Films, 1986.

Bolter, Jay, and Richard Grusin. *Remediation: Understanding New Media.* Boston: MIT Press, 2000.

Bose, Sugata. *A Hundred Horizons: The Indian Ocean in the Age of Global Empire.* Cambridge: Harvard University Press, 2009.

Bourdieu, Pierre. *Pascalian Meditations.* Cambridge, UK: Polity Press, 2000.

Boyle, Danny. *Slumdog Millionaire.* Fox Searchlight Pictures, 2008.

Bradley, Mark, and Patrice Petro. *Truth Claims: Representation and Human Rights.* New Brunswick, NJ: Rutgers University Press, 2002.

Brah, Avtar. *Cartographies of Diaspora: Contesting Identities.* New York: Routledge, 1996.

Brah, Avtar, and Ann Phoenix. "Ain't I a Woman? Revisiting Intersectionality." *Journal of International Women's Studies* 5, no. 3 (2004): 75–86.

Brown, Wendy. "The Impossibility of Women's Studies." In *Women's Studies on the Edge,* ed. Joan Wallach Scott, 17–38. Durham, NC: Duke University Press, 2008.

Bunch, Charlotte. "Transforming Human Rights from a Feminist Perspective." In *Women's Rights, Human Rights: International Feminist Perspectives,* ed. Julia Peters and Andrea Wolper, 11–17. New York: Routledge, 1995.

Burghardt, Deborah A., and Carol L. Colbeck. "Women's Studies Faculty at the Intersection of Institutional Power and Feminist Values." *Journal of Higher Education* 76, no. 3 (2005): 301–330.

Burton, Antoinette M. *Burdens of History: British Feminists, Indian Women, and Imperial Culture, 1865–1915.* Chapel Hill: University of North Carolina Press, 1994.

Bush, George W. "Address to the United Nations." Transcript of Bush UN address. http://cnn.com/2003/US/09/23/sprj.irq.bush.transcript/index.html (accessed September 23, 2003).

Butler, Judith. *Frames of War: When Is Life Grievable.* New York: Verso, 2010.

————. *Gender Trouble: Feminism and the Subversion of Identity*. New York: Routledge, 1990.

Calhoun, Craig. "Social Science Research and Military Agendas: Safe Distance or Bridging a Troubling Divide?" *Perspectives on Politics* 8, no. 4 (2010): 1101–1106.

Campbell, David. *Writing Security: United States Foreign Policy and the Politics of Difference*. Minneapolis: University of Minnesota Press, 1998.

Campus Watch. "Monitoring Middle East Studies on Campus." http://www.campus-watch.org/.

Cantú, Lionel, and Nancy Naples. *The Sexuality of Migration: Border Crossings and Mexican Immigrant Men*. New York: NYU Press, 2009.

Carr, Robert. "Crossing the First World/Third World Divides: Testimonial, Transnational Feminisms and the Postmodern Condition." In *Scattered Hegemonies: Postmodernity and Transnational Feminist Practices*, ed. Inderpal Grewal and Caren Kaplan, 153–172. Minneapolis: University of Minnesota Press, 1994.

Caruso, David. "Anti-terror Laws Increasingly Used against Common Criminals." September 15, 2003. http://cnn.com/2003/LAW/09/14/anti.terror.laws.ap/index.html. Now available at http://www.november.org/stayinfo/breaking/Patriot.html (accessed July 11, 2012).

Cervenak, Karina Cespedes, Caridad Souza, and Andrea Straub. "Imagining Differently: The Politics of Listening in a Feminist Classroom," In *This Bridge We Call Home: Radical Visions for Transformation*, ed. Gloria Anzaldúa and AnaLouise Keating, 341–356. New York: Routledge, 2002.

Chakrabarty, Dipesh. *Provincializing Europe: Postcolonial Thought and Historical Difference*. Princeton: Princeton University Press, 2000.

Chang, Grace. *Disposable Domestics: Immigrant Workers in the Global Economy*. Cambridge, MA: South End Press, 2000.

Chatterjee, Partha. *The Nation and Its Fragments: Colonial and Postcolonial Histories*. Princeton: Princeton University Press, 1993.

Chatterjee, Piya. 2009. "Imperial Pedagogies: Imagining Internationalist/Feminist/Antiracist Literacies." In *Activist Scholarship: Antiracism, Feminism, and Social Change*, ed. Julia Sudbury and Margo Okazawa-Rey, 131–148. Boulder, CO: Paradigm, 2009.

Cheah, Pheng, and Bruce Robbins, eds. *Cosmopolitics: Thinking and Feeling beyond the Nation*. Minneapolis: University of Minnesota Press, 1998.

Chopra, Yash. *Deewar*. Performed by Shashi Kapoor, Amitabh Bachchan, Neetu Singh, Nirupa Roy, and Parveen Babi. Distributed by Gulshan RaiTrimurti Films Pvt. Ltd.; Digital Entertainment; Eros Entertainment; Polydor, 1975.

Chow, Rey. *The Age of the World Target: Self-Referentiality in War, Theory, and Comparative Work*. Durham, NC: Duke University Press, 2006.

————. "Violence in the 'Other' Country." In *Third World Women and the Politics of Feminism*, ed. Chandra Mohanty, Ann Russo, and Lourdes Torres, 81–100. Bloomington: Indiana University Press, 1991.

————. *Writing Diaspora: Tactics of Intervention in Contemporary Cultural Studies*. Bloomington: Indiana University Press, 1993.

Chuh, Kandice. *Imagine Otherwise: On Asian Americanist Critique*. Durham, NC: Duke University Press, 2003.

Clifford, James. *The Predicament of Culture: Twentieth-Century Ethnography, Literature, and Art.* Cambridge: Harvard University Press, 1988.

Cohn, Carroll. "Sex and Death in the Rational World of Defense Intellectuals." *Signs: A Journal of Women in Culture and Society* 12, no. 4 (1987): 687–718.

Cole, Elizabeth R. "Intersectionality and Research in Psychology." *American Psychologist* 64 (2009): 170–180.

Cole, Juan. "The Great Pakistani Deluge Never Happened." *Huffington Post,* September 9, 2010. http://www.huffingtonpost.com/juan-cole/the-great-pakistanidelug_b_710 613.html (accessed July 14, 2012).

Collins, Patricia Hill. *Black Feminist Thought: Knowledge, Consciousness, and the Politics of Empowerment.* Boston: Unwin Hyman, 1990.

———. *Fighting Words: Black Women and the Search for Justice.* Minneapolis: University of Minnesota Press, 1998.

———. "Foreword: Emerging Intersections- Building Knowledge and Transforming Institutions." In *Emerging Intersections: Race, Class and Gender in Theory, Politics and Practice,* ed. Bonnie Thornton Dill and Ruth Enid Zambrana, vii–xiv. New Brunswick, NJ: Rutgers University Press, 2009.

Commission on Anthropology's Engagement with the Security and Intelligence Communities (CEAUSSIC). *Final Report on the U.S. Army's Human Terrain System Proof-of-Concept Program.* Submitted to the American Anthropological Association, October 14, 2009. http://www.aaanet.org/cmtes/commissions/CEAUSSIC/upload/CEAUSSIC_HTSFinal_Report.pdf, (accessed August 11, 2011).

Cornell, Drucilla. *At the Heart of Freedom: Feminism, Sex, and Equality.* Princeton: Princeton University Press, 1998.

Crenshaw, Kimberlé. "Mapping the Margins: Intersectionality, Identity Politics, and Violence against Women of Color." *Stanford Law Review* 43, no. 6 (July 1991): 1241–1299.

Crowley, Michael. "What the Wikileak Means for the Afghanistan War." http://swampland.time.com/2010/07/25/what-the-wikileakmeans-for-the-afghanistan-war/#ixzz1LxGsHhRH, July 25, 2010 (accessed May 10, 2011).

Davis, Angela. *Are Prisons Obsolete?* New York: Seven Stories Press, 2003.

Davis, Dawn Rae. "Unmirroring Pedagogies: Teaching with Intersectional and Transnational Methods in the Women and Gender Studies Classroom." *Feminist Formations* 22, no. 1 (2010): 136–162.

Davis, Kathy. *The Making of Our Bodies, Ourselves: How Feminism Travels across Borders.* Durham, NC: Duke University Press, 2007.

Desai, Jigna. *Beyond Bollywood: The Cultural Politics of South Asian Diasporic Film.* New York: Routledge, 2003.

Desai, Manmohan. *Amar Akbar Anthony.* Performed by Amitabh Bachchan, Vinod Khanna, Rishi Kapoor, Neetu Singh, Parveen Babi, and Nirupa Roy. Distributed by Digital Entertainment; Eros Entertainment; Shemaroo Video Pvt. Ltd.; Tip Top Entertainment 1977.

Dill, Bonnie Thornton, and Ruth Enid Zambrana. "Critical Thinking and Inequality: An Emerging Lens." In *Emerging Intersections: Race, Class, and Gender in Theory, Politics, and Practice,* ed. Bonnie Thornton Dill and Ruth Enid Zambrana, 1–21. New Brunswick, NJ: Rutgers University Press, 2009.

————. eds. *Emerging Intersections: Race, Class, and Gender in Theory, Politics, and Practice*. New Brunswick, NJ: Rutgers University Press, 2009.

Dodge City Daily Globe. "U.S. Troops Smash into Homes, Shops in Raid for Guerrillas." December 18, 2003.

Elshtain, Jean. *Women and War*. New York: Basic Books, 1987.

Eng, David. *The Feeling of Kinship: Queer Liberalism and the Racialization of Intimacy*. Durham, NC: Duke University Press, 2006.

Enloe, Cynthia. *Bananas, Beaches, and Bases: Making Feminist Sense of International Politics*. Berkeley: University of California Press, 1990.

————. *Maneuvers: The International Politics of Militarizing Women's Lives*. Berkeley: University of California Press, 2000.

Eskander, Saad. "Minerva Research Initiative: Searching for the Truth or Denying Iraqis the Right to Know the Truth?" http://essays.ssrc.org/minerva/2008/10/29/eskander, October 29, 2008 (accessed August 11, 2011).

Fabian, Johannes. *Time and the Other: How Anthropology Makes Its Object*. New York: Columbia University Press, 1983.

Fadlalla, Amal. "State of Vulnerability and Humanitarian Visibility on the Verge of Sudan's Secession: Lubna's Pants and the Transnational Politics of Rights and Dissent." *Signs: A Journal of Women, Culture and Society* 37, no. 1 (2011): 159–184.

Featherstone, Michael, ed. *Global Culture: Nationalism, Globalization and Modernity*. London: Sage, 1990.

Felman, Shoshana, and Dori Laub. *Testimony: Crises of Witnessing in Literature, Psychoanalysis, and History*. New York: Routledge, 1991.

Ferguson, Niall. "Hegemony or Empire." *Foreign Affairs* 82, no. 5 (2003): 154–161.

Fernandes, Leela. "Class, Space and the State in India: The Politics of Empire in Comparative Perspective." In *Labor versus Empire: Race, Gender and Migration*, ed. Gilbert Gonzalez, Raul Fernandez, Vivian Price, David Smith, and Linda Trinh Vo, 89–104. New York: Routledge, 2004.

————. *India's New Middle Class: Democratic Politics in an Era of Economic Reform*. Minneapolis: University of Minnesota Press, 2006.

————. "Nationalizing 'the Global': Media Images, Cultural Politics, and the Middle Class in India." *Media, Culture and Society* 22, no. 5 (2000): 611–628.

————. "The Politics of Forgetting: Class Politics, State Power and the Restructuring of Urban Space in India." *Urban Studies* 41, no. 12 (2004): 2415–2430.

————. *Transforming Feminist Practice: Non-violence, Social Justice, and the Possibilities of a Spiritualized Feminism*. San Francisco: Aunt Lute Books, 2003.

Fernández-Kelly, María Patricia. *For We Are Sold, I and My People: Women and Industry in Mexico's Frontier*. Albany: State University of New York Press, 1984.

Ferree, Myra Marx, and Aili Mari Tripp, eds. *Global Feminism: Transnational Women's Activism, Organizing, and Human Rights*. New York: NYU Press, 2006.

Fitzpatrick, Peter. "Enduring Right: Law, War, and the Market." *Alternatives: Turkish Journal of International Relations* 1, no. 2 (2002): 108–124.

Flax, Jane. *Thinking Fragments: Psychoanalysis, Feminism, and Postmodernism in the Contemporary West*. Berkeley: University of California Press, 1990.

Freeman, Carla. *High Tech and High Heels in the Global Economy: Women, Work, and Pink-Collar Identities in the Caribbean.* Durham, NC: Duke University Press, 2000.

Gardiner, Judith Kegan. "Paradoxes of Empowerment: Interdisciplinary Graduate Pedagogy in Women's Studies." *Feminist Studies* 29, no. 2 (2003): 409–421.

Ghosh, Shohini. "Deviant Pleasures and Disorderly Women: The Representation of the Female Outlaw in *Bandit Queen and Anjaam.*" In *Feminist Terrains in Legal Domains: Interdisciplinary Essays on Women and Law in India,* ed. Ratna Kapur, 150–183. New Delhi: Kali for Women, 1996.

Gilmore, Leigh. *The Limits of Autobiography: Trauma and Testimony.* Ithaca: Cornell University Press, 2001.

Gilmore, Ruth Wilson. *Golden Gulag: Prisons, Surplus, Crisis, and Opposition in Globalizing California.* Berkeley: University of California Press, 2007.

Gilroy, Paul. *The Black Atlantic: Modernity and Double Consciousness.* Cambridge: Harvard University Press, 1993.

Glenn, Evelyn Nakano. "From Servitude to Service Work: Historical Continuities in the Racial Division of Paid Reproductive Labor." *Signs: A Journal of Women, Culture, and Society* 18, no. 1 (1992): 1–43.

———. "Racial Ethnic Women's Labor: The Intersection of Race, Gender, and Class Oppression." *Review of Radical Political Economics* 17, no. 3 (1985): 86–108.

———. *Unequal Freedom: How Race and Gender Shaped American Citizenship and Labor.* Cambridge: Harvard University Press, 2004.

Global Feminisms Project at the University of Michigan. http://www.umich.edu/~glblfem/about.html.

Gonzalez, Gilbert, Raul Fernandez, Vivian Price, David Smith, and Linda Trinh Vo, eds. *Labor versus Empire: Race, Gender and Migration.* New York: Routledge, 2004. Gopinath, Gayatri. *Impossible Desires: Queer Diasporas and South Asian Public Cultures.* Durham, NC: Duke University Press, 2005.

Gramsci, Antonio. *Selections from the Prison Notebooks of Antonio Gramsci.* Trans. Quintin Hoare and Geoffrey Nowell-Smith. London: Lawrence and Wishart, 1971.

Greenwald, Glenn. "The Human Toll of the U.S. Drone Campaign." *Salon.com,* November 2, 2011. http://www.salon.com/2011/11/02/the_human_toll_of_the_u_s_drone_campaign/ (accessed November 9, 2011).

———. "The Killing of Awlaki's 16-Year-Old Son." *Salon.com,* October 20, 2011. http://www.salon.com/2011/10/20/the_killing_of_awlakis_16_year_old_son/ (accessed October 20, 2011).

Gregg, Melissa, and Gregory Seigworth, eds. *The Affect Theory Reader.* Durham, NC: Duke University Press, 2010.

Grewal, Inderpal. *Transnational America: Feminisms, Diasporas, Neoliberalisms.* Durham, NC: Duke University Press, 2005.

———. "'Women's Rights as Human Rights': Feminist Practices, Global Feminism, and Human Rights Regimes in Transnationality." *Citizenship Studies* 3, no. 3 (1999): 337–354.

Grewal, Inderpal, and Caren Kaplan, "Global Identities: Theorizing Transnational Studies of Sexuality." *GLQ: A Journal of Lesbian and Gay Studies* 7, no. 4 (2001): 663–679.

———. eds. *Scattered Hegemonies: Postmodernity and Transnational Feminist Practices.* Minneapolis: University of Minnesota Press, 1994.

Hale, Charles. *Engaging Contradictions: Theory, Politics, and Methods of Activist Scholarship.* Berkeley: University of California Press, 2008.

Hall, Jacquelyn Dowd. "The Mind That Burns in Each Body." In *Powers of Desire: The Politics of Sexuality,* ed. Ann Snitow, Christine Stansell, and Sharon Thompson, 328–349. New York: Monthly Review Press, 1983.

Hall, Stuart. "The Local and the Global." In *Culture, Globalisation and the World System: Contemporary Conditions for the Representation of Identity,* ed. Anthony King, 19–39. Minneapolis: University of Minnesota Press, 1997.

Hanchard, Michael. *Orpheus and Power: The Movimento Negro of Rio de Janeiro and São Paulo, Brazil 1945–1988.* Princeton: Princeton University Press, 1998.

Haraway, Donna. "Manifesto for Cyborgs: Science, Technology, and Socialist Feminism in the 1980s." In *Feminism/Postmodernism: Thinking Gender,* ed. Linda J. Nicholson, 190–233. New York: Routledge, 1989.

———. *Modest_Witness@Second_Millennium. FemaleMan®_Meets_OncoMouse™: Feminism and Technoscience.* New York: Routledge, 1997.

Harding, Sandra. *The Science Question in Feminism.* Ithaca: Cornell University Press, 1986.

Harvey, David. *Spaces of Capital: Towards a Critical Geography.* New York: Routledge, 2001.

———. *Spaces of Global Capitalism: Towards a Theory of Uneven Geographical Development.* New York: Verso, 2006.

Herold, Marc. "A Dossier on Civilian Victims of United States's Aerial Bombing of Afghanistan: A Comprehensive Accounting." December 2001. http://www.cursor.org/stories/civilian_deaths/htm. Now available at http://pubpages.unh.edu/~mwherold/ (accessed September 15, 2003).

Hesford, Wendy S. *Spectacular Rhetorics: Human Rights Visions, Recognitions, Feminisms.* Durham, NC: Duke University Press, 2011.

Hesford, Wendy S., and Wendy Kozol. *Just Advocacy? Women's Human Rights, Transnational Feminisms, and the Politics of Representation.* New Brunswick, NJ: Rutgers University Press, 2005.

Hewamanne, Sandya. *Stitching Identities in a Free Trade Zone: Gender and Politics in Sri Lanka.* Philadelphia: University of Pennsylvania Press, 2010.

Hewitt, Nancy A., ed. *No Permanent Waves: Recasting Histories of U.S. Feminism.* New Brunswick, NJ: Rutgers University Press, 2010.

Hirshman, Linda. "When Dreams Collide: Looking to the Future, Feminism Has to Focus." *Washington Post,* June 8, 2008. http://www.highbeam.com/doc/1P2-16678963.html (accessed July 14, 2008).

Hochschild, Arlie. "Love and Gold." In *Global Woman: Nannies, Maids and Sex Workers in the New Economy,* ed. Barbara Ehrenreich and Arlie Hochschild, 15–30. London: Granta Books, 2003.

Hong, Grace Kyungwon. *The Ruptures of American Capital: Women of Color Feminism and the Culture of Immigrant Labor.* Minneapolis: University of Minnesota Press, 2006.

Hooks, Bell. *Teaching Community: A Pedagogy of Hope.* New York: Routledge, 2003.

————. *Teaching to Transgress: Education as the Practice of Freedom*. New York: Routledge, 1994.

Huffer, Lynne. *Mad for Foucault: Rethinking the Foundations of Queer Theory*. New York: Columbia University Press, 2009.

Huffington, Ariana. *Third World America: How Our Politicians Are Abandoning the Middle Class and Betraying the American Dream*. New York: Crown, 2010.

Human Rights Watch. *Presumption of Guilt: Human Rights Abuses of Post-September 11 Detainees*. Vol. 14, no. 4(G), August 2002. http://www.hrw.org/legacy/reports/2002/us911 (accessed September 15, 2003).

————. "U.S. Justice Department Report Confirms 9-11 Detainee Abuses." http://hrw.org/press/2003/03/us031203.htm. Now accessible through http://www.hrw.org/en/news/2003/06/01/us-justice-department-report-confirms-9-11-detainee-abuses (accessed November 15, 2011).

Hunt, Krista, and Kim Rygiel. *(En)gendering the War on Terror: War Stories and Camouflaged Politics*. Burlington, VT: Ashgate, 2007.

Ignatieff, Michael. "Nation-Building Lite." *New York Times Magazine*, July 28, 2002. http://www.nytimes.com/2002/07/28/magazine/nation-building lite.html?pagewanted=all&src=pm (accessed July 28, 2002).

Iraq Coalition Casualty Count. 2009. http://www.icasualties.org/.

Jabri, Vivienne. "Shock and Awe: Power and the Resistance of Arts." *Millennium: Journal of International Studies* 34, no. 3 (2006): 819–839.

Jameson, Fredric. "Third-World Literature in the Era of Multinational Capitalism." *Social Text* 15 (1986): 65–88.

Jordan-Zachery, Julia. "Commentary: The Practice and Functioning of Intersectionality and Politics." *Journal of Women, Politics and Policy* 28, no. 3 (2006): 205–212.

Kacandes, Irene. "Testimony: Talk as Witnessing." In *Talk Fiction: Literature and the Talk Explosion*, 89–149. Lincoln: University of Nebraska Press, 2001.

Kaplan, Caren. "Hillary Rodham Clinton's Orient, Cosmopolitan Travel and Global Feminist Subjects." *Meridians: Feminism, Race, Transnationalism* 2, no. 1 (2001): 219–240.

————. "Resisting Autobiography: Out-Law Genres and Transnational Feminist Subjects." In *De/Colonizing the Subject: The Politics of Gender in Women's Autobiography*, ed. Sidonie Smith and Julia Watson, 115–138. Minneapolis: University of Minnesota Press, 1992.

Kaplan, E. Ann. *Women and Film: Both Sides of the Camera*. New York: Methuen, 1983.

Kapur, Shekhar. *Bandit Queen*. Channel Four Films, 1994.

Karim, Lamia. *Microfinance and Its Discontents: Women in Debt in Bangladesh*. Minneapolis: University of Minnesota Press, 2011.

Kashyap, Anurag. *Black Friday*. Arindam MitraAdlab Films, 2004.

Keating, AnaLouise. "Charting Pathways, Marking Thresholds. . . A Warning, an Introduction." In *This Bridge We Call Home: Radical Visions for Transformation*, ed. Gloria Anzaldúa and AnaLouise, Keating, 6–20. New York: Routledge, 2002.

————. *Entre Mundos/Among Worlds: New Perspectives on Gloria E. Anzaldúa*. New York: Palgrave Macmillan, 2005.

————. "Forging El Mundo Zurdo: Changing Ourselves, Changing the World." In *This Bridge We Call Home: Radical Visions for Transformation*, ed. Gloria Anzaldúa and AnaLouise Keating, 519–529. New York: Routledge, 2002.

————. *Teaching Transformation: Transcultural Classroom Dialogues*. New York: Palgrave Macmillan, 2007.

Keck, Margaret E., and Kathryn Sikkink, eds. *Activists beyond Borders: Advocacy Networks in International Politics*. Ithaca: Cornell University Press, 1998.

Kinsella, Helen. *The Image before the Weapon: A Critical History of the Distinction between Combatant and Civilian*. Ithaca: Cornell University Press, 2011.

Kishwar, Madhu. "The Bandit Queen." *Manushi* 84 (September–October 1994): 34–37.

Kozol, Wendy. "Domesticating NATO's War in Kosovo/a: (In) Visible Bodies and the Dilemma of Photojournalism." *Meridians* 4, no. 2 (2004): 1–38.

Kumar, Amitava. "Slumdog Millionaire's Bollywood Ancestors." *Vanity Fair*, December 23, 2008. http://www.vanityfair.com/online/oscars/2008/12/slumdog-millionaires-bollywood-ancestors.html (accessed July 15, 2012).

Kumar, Radha. *The History of Doing: An Illustrated Account of Movements for Women's Rights and Feminism in India*. New York: Verso Press, 1993.

Lal, Jayati, Kristin McGuire, Abigail Stewart, Magdalena Zaborowska, and Justine Pas. "Recasting Global Feminisms: Toward a Comparative Historical Approach to Women's Activism and Feminist Scholarship." *Feminist Studies* 36, no. 1 (2010): 13–39.

Lamont, Michèle. *Money, Morals, and Manners: The Culture of the French and American Upper-Middle Class*. Chicago: University of Chicago Press, 1994.

Lewis, Michael. *Boomerang: Travels in the New Third World*. New York: Norton, 2011.

Lipset, Seymour Martin. *American Exceptionalism: A Double Edged Sword*. New York: Norton, 1997.

Lorenz, Helen Shulman. "Thawing Hearts, Opening a Path in the Woods, Founding a New Lineage." In *This Bridge We Call Home: Radical Visions for Transformation*, ed. Gloria Anzaldúa and AnaLouise Keating, 496–505. New York: Routledge, 2002.

Ludlow, Jeannie. "The Things We Cannot Say: Witnessing and the Traumatization of Abortion in the United States." *Women's Studies Quarterly* 36, nos. 1 and 2 (2008): 28–41.

MacKinnon, Catharine. *Are Women Human? And Other International Dialogues*. Cambridge: Harvard University Press, 2006.

Mahmood, Saba. "Feminism, Democracy and Empire: Islam and the War on Terror." In *Women's Studies on the Edge*, ed. Joan Scott, 81–114. Durham, NC: Duke University Press, 2008.

————. *Politics of Piety: The Islamic Revival and the Feminist Subject*. Princeton: Princeton University Press, 2005.

Mani, Lata. *Contentious Traditions: The Debate on Sati in Colonial India*. Berkeley: University of California Press, 1998.

Mankekar, Purnima. *Screening Culture, Viewing Politics: An Ethnography of Television, Womanhood, and Nation in Postcolonial India*. Durham, NC: Duke University Press, 1999.

Mapping Women's and Gender Studies Data Collection. http://www.nwsa.org/PAD/database/index.php (accessed August 1, 2010).

Marciniak, Katarzyna, Aniko Imre, and Aine O'Healy, eds. *Transnational Feminism in Film and Media*. New York: Palgrave, 2007.

Marx, Karl, and Friedrich Engels. *The German Ideology: Including Theses on Feuerbach and Introduction to the Critique of Political Economy*. Amherst, NY: Prometheus Books, 1998.

Massey, Doreen B. "Geographies of Responsibility." *Geografiska Annaler* 86, no. 1 (2004): 5–18.

———. *Space, Place and Gender*. Cambridge, UK: Polity Press, 1994.

May, Vivian M. "Disciplinary Desires and Undisciplined Daughters: Negotiating the Politics of a Women's Studies Doctoral Education." *NWSA Journal* 14, no. 1 (2002): 134–159.

McCall, Leslie. "The Complexity of Intersectionality." *Signs: Journal of Women in Culture and Society* 30, no. 3 (2005): 1771–1800.

McClintock, Anne. *Imperial Leather: Race, Gender, and Sexuality in the Colonial Contest*. New York: Routledge, 1995.

McClintock, Anne, Aamir Mufti, and Ella Shohat. *Dangerous Liaisons: Gender, Nation, and Postcolonial Perspectives*. Minneapolis: University of Minnesota Press, 1997.

Messer-Davidow, Ellen. *Disciplining Feminism: From Social Activism to Academic Discourse*. Durham, NC: Duke University Press, 2002.

Mies, Maria. *Patriarchy and Accumulation on a World Scale: Women in the International Division of Labour*. London: Zed, 1999.

Migdal, Joel. *State in Society: Studying How States and Societies Transform and Constitute One Other*. Cambridge: Cambridge University Press, 2001.

Mitchell, Timothy. "The Limits of the State: Beyond Statist Approaches and Their Critics." *American Political Science Review* 85, no. 1 (1991): 77–96.

———. *Rule of Experts. Egypt, Techno-Politics, Modernity*. Berkeley: University of California Press, 2002.

Miyoshi, Masao, and Harry D. Harootunian, eds. *Learning Places: The Afterlives of Area Studies*. Durham, NC: Duke University Press, 2002.

Mohanty, Chandra Talpade. *Feminism without Borders: Decolonizing Theory, Practicing Solidarity*. Durham, NC: Duke University Press, 2003.

———. "Under Western Eyes: Feminist Scholarship and Colonial Discourses." *Feminist Review* 30 (Autumn 1988): 61–88.

Moin, Syed. "Disciplinarity and Methodology in Intersectionality Theory and Research." *American Psychologist* 65, no. 1 (2010): 61–62.

Moraga, Cherríe, and Gloria Anzaldúa. 1981. *This Bridge Called My Back: Writings by Radical Women of Color*. New York: Kitchen Table: Women of Color Press, 1981.

Moreau, Ron, and Sami Yousafzai, "We Never Kidnapped Greg Mortenson." *Daily Beast*, April 18, 2011. http://www.thedailybeast.com/blogs-and-stories/2011-04-18/mansur-khan-mahsud-greg-mortenson-is-a-liar/# (accessed July 14, 2012).

Morgan, Robin. *Sisterhood Is Global: The International Women's Movement Anthology*. New York: Feminist Press at City University of New York, 1996.

Mortenson, Gregg. *Stones into Schools: Promoting Peace with Books, Not Bombs, in Afghanistan and Pakistan*. New York: Viking, 2009.

———. *Three Cups of Tea: One Man's Mission to Promote Peace . . . One School at a Time.* New York: Penguin, 2006.

MSNBC. "We Have Ways of Making You Talk." August 22, 2003. http://www.msnbc.com/news. Now accessible through http://newsmine.org/content.php?ol=security/terror-suspects/coerced-confessions/interrogation-techniques.txt (accessed July 14, 2012).

Muñoz, Carolina Bank. *Transnational Tortillas: Race, Gender, and Shop-Floor Politics in Mexico and the United States.* Ithaca: Cornell University Press, 2008.

Najmabadi, Afsaneh. "Teaching and Research in Unavailable Intersections." In *Women's Studies on the Edge,* ed. Joan Scott, 69–80. Durham, NC: Duke University Press, 2008.

Naples, Nancy A., and Manisha Desai, eds. *Women's Activism and Globalization: Linking Local Struggles and Transnational Politics.* New York: Routledge, 2002.

Narayan, Uma. *Dislocating Cultures: Identities, Traditions, and Third-World Feminism.* New York: Routledge, 1997.

Nash, Jennifer. "Un-disciplining Intersectionality." *International Feminist Journal of Politics* 11, no. 4 (2009): 587–593.

Nelson, Cary, and Dilip Parameshwar Gaonkar. *Disciplinarity and Dissent in Cultural Studies.* New York: Routledge, 1996.

Nelson, Dean, and Barney Henderson. "Slumdog Child Stars Miss Out on Movie Millions." *The* Telegraph, January 26, 2009. http://www.telegraph.co.uk/news/worldnews/asia/4347472/Poor-parents-of-Slumdog-millionaire-stars-say-children-were-exploited.html (accessed July 14, 2012).

Newman, Jane. "The Present and Our Past: Simone de Beauvoir, Descartes, and Presentism in the Historiography of Feminism." In *Women's Studies on Its Own,* ed. Robyn Wiegman, 141–176. Durham, NC: Duke University Press, 2002.

Niranjana, Tejaswini. "Cinema, Femininity, and Economy of Consumption." *Economic and Political Weekly* 26, no. 43 (1991): WS85–WS86.

———. "Integrating Whose Nation? Tourists and Terrorists in 'Roja.'" *Economic and Political Weekly* 29, no. 21 (1994): 79–82.

Nnaemeka, Obioma, ed. *Female Circumcision and the Politics of Knowledge: African Women in Imperialist Discourses.* Westport, CT: Praeger, 2005.

Nussbaum, Martha. "Patriotism and Cosmopolitanism." *Boston Review* 19, no. 5 (1994): 1–12.

O'Barr, Jean F., and Stephanie A. Shields. "The Women's Studies Ph.D.: An Archive." *NWSA Journal* 15, no. 1 (2003): 118–131.

Oldenburg, Veena Talwar. *Dowry Murder: The Imperial Origins of a Cultural Crime.* New York: Oxford University Press, 2002.

Oliver, Kelly. *Women as Weapons of War: Iraq, Sex, and the Media.* New York: Columbia University Press, 2007.

Ōmae, Kenichi. *The End of the Nation-State: The Rise of Regional Economies.* New York: Free Press, 1995.

Ong, Aihwa. *Flexible Citizenship: The Cultural Logics of Transnationality.* Durham, NC: Duke University Press, 1999.

———. *Spirits of Resistance and Capitalist Discipline: Factory Women in Malaysia.* Albany: State University of New York Press, 2010.

Orr, Catherine M., and Diane Marilyn Lichtenstein. "The Politics of Feminist Locations: A Materialist Analysis of Women's Studies." *NWSA Journal* 16, no. 3 (2004): 1–17.

Parreñas, Rhacel Salazar. *Servants of Globalization: Women, Migration and Domestic Work.* Stanford, CA: Stanford University Press, 2001.

Pathak, Zakia, and Rajeswari Sunder Rajan. "Shahbano." In *Feminists Theorize the Political,* ed. Judith Butler and Joan Wallach Scott, 257–279. New York: Routledge, 1992.

Peterson, V. Spike. *A Critical Rewriting of Global Political Economy: Integrating Reproductive, Productive and Virtual Economies.* London: Routledge, 2003.

Phillips, Barbara. *Dignity and Human Rights: A Missing Dialogue a Report of a Meeting at the Rockefeller Foundation's Bellagio Center, Bellagio, Italy, April 7–10 2009.* New Delhi: Programme on Women's Economic Social and Cultural Rights, 2011.

Phoolan Devi. *I, Phoolan Devi.* Boston: Little, Brown, 1996.

Poster, Winifred. "Who's on the Line? Indian Call Center Agents Pose as Americans for U.S.-Outsourced Firms." *Industrial Relations: A Journal of Economy and Society* 46, no. 2 (2007): 271–304.

Poster, Winifred, and Zakiya Salime. "The Limits of Micro-Credit: Transnational Feminism and USAID Activities in the United States and Morocco." In *Women's Activism and Globalization: Linking Local Struggles and Transnational Politics,* ed. Nancy Naples and Manisha Desai, 189–219. New York: Routledge, 2002.

Pratt, Geraldine, in Collaboration with the Philippine Women Centre of BC and Ugnayan NG Kabataang Pilipino Sa Canada/The Filipino-Canadian Youth Alliance. "Seeing beyond the State: Toward Transnational Feminist Organizing." In *Critical Transnational Feminist Praxis,* ed. Amanda Swarr and Richa Nagar, 65–86. Albany: State University of New York Press, 2010.

Puar, Jasbir K. *Terrorist Assemblages: Homonationalism in Queer Times.* Durham, NC: Duke University Press, 2007.

Pulido, Laura. "Frequently (Un)asked Questions about Being a Scholar Activist." In *Engaging Contradictions: Theory, Politics, and Methods of Activist Scholarship,* ed. Charles Hale, 341–366. Berkeley: University of California Press, 2008.

Rajagopal, Arvind. *Politics after Television: Religious Nationalism and the Reshaping of the Indian Public.* Cambridge, UK: Cambridge University Press, 2001.

Ranchod-Nilsson, Sita, and Mary Ann Tetreault. *Women, States, and Nationalism: At Home in the Nation?* New York: Routledge, 2000.

Razack, Sherene. "Geopolitics, Culture Clash, and Gender after September 11." *Social Justice* 32 no. 4 (2005): 11–31.

Reid, Pamela Trotman, and Ramaswami Mahalingam. "Dialogue at the Margins: Women's Self-Stories and the Intersection of Identities." *Women's Studies International Forum* 30, no. 3 (2007): 254–263.

Reilly, Niamh. "Cosmopolitanism, Feminism, and Human Rights." *Hypatia* 22, no. 4 (2007): 180–198.

Riley, Robin L., Chandra Talpade Mohanty, and Minnie Bruce Pratt, eds. *Feminism and War: Confronting US Imperialism.* London: Zed, 2008.

Rony, Fatimah. *The Third Eye: Race, Cinema, and Ethnographic Spectacle.* Durham, NC: Duke University Press, 1996.

Rothstein, Edward. "Attacks on U.S. Challenge the Perspectives of Postmodern True Believers." *New York Times*, September 22, 2001. http://www.nytimes.com/2001/09/22/arts/connections-attacks-us-challenge-perspectives-postmodern-true-believers.html?pagewanted=all (accessed July 14, 2012).

Roy, Arundhati. "The Great Indian Rape Trick." August 22, 1994. http://www.sawnet.org/books/writing/roy_bq1.html (accessed July 14, 2012).

Rudolph, Susanne Hoeber, and James P. Piscatori, eds. *Transnational Religion and Fading States*. Boulder, CO: Westview Press, 1996.

Safarik, Lynn. "Feminist Transformation in Higher Education: Discipline, Structure, and Institution." *Review of Higher Education* 26, no. 4 (2003): 419–445.

Said, Edward W. *Orientalism*. New York: Pantheon Books, 1979.

Saldivar-Hull, Sonia. *Feminism on the Border: Chicana Gender Politics and Literature*. Berkeley: University of California Press, 2000.

Sandoval, Chela. *Methodology of the Oppressed*. Minneapolis: University of Minnesota Press, 2000.

Sangtin Writers and Richa Nagar. *Playing with Fire: Feminist Thought and Activism through Seven Lives in India*. Minneapolis: University of Minnesota Press, 2006.

Sassen, Saskia. *Territory, Authority, Rights: From Medieval to Global Assemblages*. Princeton: Princeton University Press, 2006.

Schaffer, Kay, and Sidonie Smith. *Human Rights and Narrated Lives*. New York: Palgrave Macmillan, 2004.

Scott, Joan Wallach. "Experience." In *Feminists Theorize the Political*, ed. Judith Butler and Joan Wallach Scott, 22–40. New York: Routledge, 1992.

———. *Gender and the Politics of History*. New York: Columbia University Press, 1988.

———. *Women's Studies on the Edge*. Durham, NC: Duke University Press, 2008.

Sen, Krishna, and Maila Stivens. *Gender and Power in Affluent Asia*. London: Routledge, 1998.

Shapin, Steven, and Simon Schaffer. *Leviathan and the Air-Pump: Hobbes, Boyle, and the Experimental Life*. Princeton: Princeton University Press, 1985.

Shehabuddin, Elora. *Reshaping the Holy: Democracy, Development, and Muslim Women in Bangladesh*. New York: Columbia University Press, 2008.

Shields, Stephanie A., Rebecca L. Schuberth, and Danielle R. Conrad. "The Women's Studies Ph.D. in North America: Archive II." *NWSA Journal* 18, no. 1 (2006): 190–206.

Shinko, Rosemary. "Agonistic Peace: A Postmodern Reading." *Millennium: A Journal of International Studies* 36, no. 3 (2008): 473–491.

———. "Ethics after Liberalism: Why (Autonomous) Bodies Matter." *Millennium: A Journal of International Studies* 38, no. 3 (2010): 723–745.

Shohat, Ella. *Israeli Cinema: East/West and the Politics of Representation*. Austin: University of Texas Press, 1989.

———. *Taboo Memories, Diasporic Voices*. Durham, NC: Duke University Press, 2006.

———. ed. *Talking Visions: Multicultural Feminism in a Transnational Age*. Cambridge: MIT Press, 2001.

Shohat, Ella, and Robert Stam, eds. *Multiculturalism, Postcoloniality and Transnational Media*. New Brunswick, NJ: Rutgers University Press, 2003.

Smith, Barbara. "Racism and Women's Studies." In *All the Women Are White, All the Blacks Are Men, but Some of Us Are Brave*, ed. Gloria T. Hull, Patricia Bell Scott, and Barbara Smith, 48–51. Old Westbury, NY: Feminist Press, 1982.

Smith, Sidonie, and Julia Watson. "Introduction: De/Colonization and the Politics of Discourse in Women's Autobiographical Practices." In *De/Colonizing the Subject: The Politics of Gender in Women's Autobiography*, xiii–2. Minneapolis: University of Minnesota Press, 1992.

———. *Women, Autobiography, Theory: A Reader*. Madison: University of Wisconsin Press, 1998.

Smooth, Wendy. "Intersectionality in Electoral Politics: A Mess Worth Making." *Politics and Gender*, 2 no. 3 (2006): 400–414.

Spivak, Gayatri Chakravorty. "Can the Subaltern Speak?" In *Marxism and the Interpretation of Culture*, ed. Cary Nelson and Lawrence Grossberg, 271–313. Urbana: University of Illinois Press, 1988.

———. *A Critique of Postcolonial Reason: Toward a History of the Vanishing Present*. Cambridge: Harvard University Press, 1999.

———. *Other Asias*. Malden, MA: Wiley-Blackwell, 2008.

Steinmetz, George. "The State of Emergency and the Revival of American Imperialism: Toward an Authoritarian Post-Fordism." *Public Culture* 15, no. 2 (2003): 323–345.

Stoler, Ann Laura. "Carnal Knowledge and Imperial Power: Gender, Race, and Morality in Colonial Asia." In *Gender at the Crossroads of Knowledge: Feminist Anthropology in the Postmodern Era*, ed. Micaela di Leonardo, 51–101. Berkeley: University of California Press, 1991.

———. *Carnal Knowledge and Imperial Power: Race and the Intimate in Colonial Rule*. Berkeley: University of California Press, 2002.

Sudbury, Julia, and Margo Okazawa-Rey, eds. *Activist Scholarship: Antiracism, Feminism, and Social Change*. Boulder, CO: Paradigm, 2009.

Swarr, Amanda Lock, and Richa Nagar, eds. *Critical Transnational Feminist Praxis*. Albany: State University of New York Press, 2010.

Swarup, Vikas. *Q & A*. London: Doubleday, 2005.

Szanton, David L. *The Politics of Knowledge: Area Studies and the Disciplines*. Berkeley: University of California Press, 2004.

Tai, Emily S. "Women's Work: Integrating Women's Studies into a Community College Curriculum." *NWSA Journal* 17, no. 2 (2005): 184–191.

Tapia, Ruby. *American Pietàs: Visions of Race, Death and the Maternal*. Minneapolis: University of Minnesota Press, 2011.

Tarrow, Sidney G. *The New Transnational Activism*. New York: Cambridge University Press, 2005.

Thayer, Millie. *Making Transnational Feminism: Rural Women, NGO Activists, and Northern Donors in Brazil*. New York: Routledge, 2010.

Thussu, Daya Kishan. *Media on the Move: Global Flow and Contra-Flow*. New York: Routledge, 2006.

Toor, Saadia. "Between Neoliberal Globalization and the War of/on Terror: Why Understanding Pakistan Is Crucial to Understanding the World Today." Paper presented at the "Global South Asia Conference," New York University, February 14, 2009.

———. *The State of Islam: Culture and Cold War Politics in Pakistan.* New York: Pluto Press, 2011.

Trinh, T. Minh-Ha. *Woman, Native, Other: Writing Postcoloniality and Feminism.* Bloomington: Indiana University Press, 1989.

Tripp, Aili Mari. "Challenges in Transnational Feminist Mobilization." In *Global Feminism: Transnational Women's Activism, Organizing, and Human Rights,* ed. Myra Marx Ferree and Aili Mari Tripp, 296–312. New York: NYU Press, 2006.

Valentine, Gill. 2007. "Theorizing and Researching Intersectionality: A Challenge for Feminist Geography." *Professional Geographer* 59, no. 1 (2007): 10–21.

Varma, Ram Gopal. *Satya.* Eros Entertainment, 1998.

Vasudevan, Ravi. "Film Studies, New Cultural History and Experience of Modernity." *Economic and Political Weekly,* November 4, 1995, 2809–2814.

Visweswaran, Kamala. *Fictions of Feminist Ethnography.* Minneapolis: University of Minnesota Press, 1994.

———. "Gendered States: Rethinking Culture as a Site of South Asian Human Rights Work." *Human Rights Quarterly* 26, no. 2 (2004): 483–511.

Ward, Kathryn, ed. *Women Workers and Global Restructuring.* Ithaca: ILR Press/Cornell University Press, 1990.

Waters, Neil L. *Beyond the Area Studies Wars: Toward a New International Studies.* Hanover, NH: Middlebury College Press, 2000.

Weinbaum, Alys E., Lynn Thoman, Priti Ramamurthy, Uta Poiger, and Madeleine Yue, eds. *The Modern Girl around the World: Consumption, Modernity, and Globalization.* Durham, NC: Duke University Press, 2008.

Welch, Sharon. *A Feminist Ethic of Risk.* Minneapolis: Fortress Press, 1990.

Weldon, S. Laurel. "The Structure of Intersectionality: A Comparative Politics of Gender." *Politics and Gender* 2, no. 2 (2006): 235–248.

Wiegman, Robyn. "Academic Feminism against Itself." *NWSA Journal* 14, no. 2 (2002): 18–34.

———. "Feminism, Institutionalism, and the Idiom of Failure." In *Women's Studies on the Edge,* ed. Joan Wallach Scott, 39–68. Durham, NC: Duke University Press, 2008.

———. *Women's Studies on Its Own: A Next Wave Reader in Institutional Change.* Durham, NC: Duke University Press, 2002.

Wilcox, Lauren. "Gendering the Cult of the Offensive." *Security Studies* 18 (2009): 214–240.

Winddance Twine, Francine. *Racism in a Racial Democracy: The Maintenance of White Supremacy in Brazil.* New Brunswick, NJ: Rutgers University Press, 1997.

Wolf, Diane L., ed. *Feminist Dilemmas in Fieldwork.* Boulder, CO: Westview Press, 1996.

Wright, Melissa W. *Disposable Women and Other Myths of Global Capitalism.* New York: Routledge, 2006.

Yuval-Davis, Nira. *Gender and Nation.* London: Sage, 1997.

Zayani, Mohamed, ed. *The Al-Jazeera Phenomenon: Critical Perspectives on New Arab Media.* Boulder, CO: Paradigm, 2005.

Zinn, Maxine Baca, Lynn Weber Cannon, Elizabeth Higginbotham, and Bonnie Thornton Dill. "The Costs of Exclusionary Practices in Women's Studies." In *Making Face, Making Soul/Haciendo Caras: Creative and Critical Perspectives by Feminists of Color,* ed. Gloria Anzaldúa. San Francisco: Aunt Lute Books, 1990.

Index

Abortion, 50, 129–30
Abu Ghraib prison, 48, 51
Abu-Lughod, Lila, 25
Academic programs. *See* Universities and colleges, U.S.
Activism: as global, 38, 42; for human rights, 54; by transnational feminists, 14, 20–22, 102, 157–58, 174; for women's rights, 34, 36–40, 102, 203n6, 204n19. *See also* Ethics; Feminists of color; Research and scholarship
Adoption, as transnational, 64
Affective economy, 25, 63–65, 67, 72, 80, 99
Afghanistan, 3, 32, 36, 38, 40, 43, 45, 54, 57, 143, 193
Africa, 5, 15, 99–100
Agency, of women, 14, 103, 117, 133
Agential realism, 106–7, 120, 125, 130
Ahmed, Sara, 25, 63–64
Aikau, Hokulani, 169
Ajayi-Soyanki, Omofolabo, 218n55
Alarcon, Norma, 171–72, 216n21
Alexander, Jacqui, 13, 132, 161, 163, 167, 175–76, 215n6
Alexander-Floyd, Nikol, 187
American Political Science Association, 143
Anderson, Benedict, 191, 210n8
Anthropology, 34, 66, 73, 89, 143–45, 150, 158
Anzaldúa, Gloria, 105–7, 157, 173, 183–85, 216n20, 216n28
Appadurai, Arjun, 7–8, 10
Ashtiani, Sakineh Mohammadi, 20–21
Authenticity, 62–63, 70, 73, 75–78, 85–86, 89, 91, 176
Al-Awlaki, 57, 206n70

Bachchan, Amitabh, 86
Bandit Queen (film), 68–75, 77, 81–84, 86–88, 90, 101, 118, 208n54, 208nn49–51
Barad, Karen, 28, 105–7, 119–20, 130–31, 180
Basu, Amrita, 33
de Beauvoir, Simone, 184
bell hooks, 173
"Between Neoliberal Globalization" (Toor), 206n69
Bishop, Ryan, 109
Bohr, Niels, 106–7, 120
Bollywood industry, 61, 86
Bolter, Jay, 76
Boomerang: Travels in the New Third World (Lewis), 100
Border-crossing: as cultural, 108; effects of, 124, 191; globalization and, 2, 199n4; politics of, 108, 110; relevance of, 122; as socioeconomic, 108, 114; stereotypes of, 111; territorialization and, 7–8, 103–4; third wave feminism and, 28, 31, 157–58, 170–73, 216n28; transnational feminism and, 14, 105–8, 110–11, 114–15, 123; violence in, 106, 111, 185, 196; as visible, 30, 104, 108, 122
Borderlands (Anzaldúa), 106, 183
Boundaries: of civilian space, 37–38, 44–48, 52, 57–59, 144, 204n23, 205n40; for state, 37; of Third World, 71, 73–74, 207n34; war on terror and, 39, 44, 59; for women's studies, 148. *See also* Affective economy
Bourdieu, Pierre, 196, 202n74
Boxer, Barbara, 32
Boyle, Danny, 79–80

Philippines, domestic labor from, 109
Pierce, Jennifer, 169
Pluralism, in U.S., 8
Political economy: of emotions, 64; inequalities of, 65–66; knowledge and, 101, 104–5, 112, 115, 153; structures of, 67–69, 80, 112; transnational feminism and, 109–10. *See also* India
Politics: of border-crossing, 108, 110; of citationality, 125, 211n43; context of, 11, 197; of crisis, 3, 35, 193; for cultural production, 69, 81–82; of disidentification, 172, 185, 218n53; ethics in, 29; of fear, 63; of fieldwork, 127; as gendered, 14, 36, 168–69, 207n35; of globalization, 38, 43–44, 110, 192; of human rights, 38; of identity, 21, 170, 172–73, 188, 216n16; of incarceration, 48, 51, 53–54, 161–62, 183; of inclusion, 178–79, 217n37; inequalities in, 34; media and, 24; of nationalism, 14; as neoconservative, 18, 22; of otherness, 111; participation in, 14, 32; power and, 10; as racialized, 168–69, 207n35; transnationalism in, 10, 192; of U.S., 168–69, 207n35; of violence, 34, 54, 183. *See also* Representation
Positivism, 66–67
Postcolonial feminism, 33, 150–52, 174, 182
Poststructuralist feminism, 173–74, 181, 216n21
Poverty: in India, 75–77, 79–80, 85, 94; in U.S., 100; violence of, 54, 77
Power: academia and, 22–23, 37; citizenship and, 39; in colonialism, 70, 121; context of, 30; of corporations, 102; as domestic, 54; ethics and, 4, 24, 29; inequality in, 10, 14, 104, 117; as law enforcement, 39; of nationalism, 210n8; politics and, 10; representation and, 62; resistance to, 14, 51, 109, 154; of state, 37–39, 102, 138, 204n32; of surveillance, 39; technology as, 26; by U.S., 39–42, 44. *See also* Knowledge; Relationships; Resistance
Pratt, Geraldine, 104
Prison system, U.S., 48, 51, 53–54, 161–62, 183

Production of knowledge: as academic, 22, 24, 141, 145, 153, 156, 195; analysis of, 9, 108, 140; approaches to, 2–4, 28, 101, 105–7, 123, 130; context for, 105, 117, 125, 135; ethics of, 24, 28–29, 106–8, 127–28, 130–34, 195–97; by Europeans, 124–25; as interdisciplinary, 27, 104, 132, 152–53; politics of, 30, 115, 192; power relationships and, 12, 28, 117, 119; practices for, 29, 107, 116, 119–20; risks in, 15, 19, 27–30, 101, 107, 110, 195–96; state and, 141–45, 196; for transnational feminism, 103, 116–20, 127, 197
Profiling, 52–53, 205n61
Puar, Jasbir, 35
Pulido, Laura, 132

Q & A (Swarup), 68, 94–98, 97–98
al-Qaeda, 36, 39, 205n40

Race and racism: collaboration on, 189; domination of Black women as, 177–78; exclusion by, 216n28; Identity by, 5, 21, 182; inequalities of, 25–26; interdisciplinarity and, 170; intersectionality and, 53, 170, 177–78, 186–87; profiling by, 52–53, 205n61; relations of, in film, 73, 207n33; research on, 180; second wave feminism and, 173–74; state and, 30; third wave feminism and, 176, 216n28; as transnational, 168, 182, 215n1; transnationalism and, 86, 186; violence as, 177; war on terror and, 52, 205n61; against women, 177–78. *See also* Sexuality; Violence
Rahman, Saeed, 34
Reagan, Ronald, 76
Reid, Pamela Trotman, 164
Relationships: under colonialism, 73, 121, 207n33; gendering of otherness in, 36; as global economic, 80; inequity of, 35, 203n13; of power, 10, 12, 15, 26, 28–29, 65, 111, 117, 127, 132; of power in transnationalism, 65; with Third World, 66, 72, 116

Religion, 37, 54, 183
Representation: context of, 4, 34, 68, 118; of cultural production, 66–67, 69, 86, 99; economies of, 118; feminist ethnographers and, 206n8; forms of, 117; of historical images, 74; of intellectualism, 22, 202n58; intervention and, 58; location and, 87, 118, 128; as media visuals, 25, 37, 43, 71–72; of non-Western women, 15, 27, 36–38, 201n41, 204n16, 204n19; of other, 127, 158; politics of, 25, 37–38, 41–42, 44, 58, 62, 69, 101, 117; in post-9/11 period, 35, 37–40; power and, 62; of research and writing, 30, 104–5; strategies of, 29, 54, 116–17; transnational feminism and, 62, 101; by U.S., 26, 34–38, 41–42, 54, 56
Representational economy, 64
Research and scholarship: activism and, 127; affective economy for, 64; anti-intellectualism and, 22; bias in, 111, 114–15; on consumption, 114, 126; on cultural production, 61, 63, 65–66, 74; on culture, 10, 66, 104; discipline of, 12, 24, 31; as empirical, 12, 19, 27–28, 31, 97, 106, 108, 110–12, 121, 123–25; on ethnicity, 12–14, 102–3; on feminism, 12–14, 102–3, 196; by feminists of color, 182–83; feminist waves and, 176–77; funding for, 141; on gender, 102, 114; on globalization, 102, 109; on identity, 5, 173, 216n17; as interdisciplinary, 2–3, 5–12, 14–15, 65–66, 107; on intersectionality, 178; on labor, 109, 178; on location, 6, 24, 118, 123, 131; methodology for, 9, 114–16, 126; National Women's Studies Association for, 24, 202n62; on political issues, 14; possibilities of, 9; as postcolonial, 12, 111; on race and racism, 180; on religious formations, 199n6; representation in, 30, 104–5; on sociocultural formations, 3, 12, 143, 199n6; on socioeconomic issues, 14; on spheres of influence, 6; on Third wave feminism, 28, 157, 184, 188; on

transnational feminism, 2, 11–14, 27, 62, 65, 102–3, 106–8, 110, 114–15, 126–27, 190–91, 199n6; on transnationalism, 3, 6–8, 10–12, 27, 62, 102–3, 115, 154, 191, 199n6, 209n3, 213n31; U.S. nationalism in, 5, 7, 141; visual issues for, 27. See also Women's studies
Resistance, by women, 14, 51, 109, 154
Robinson, Lillian S., 109
Rousseau, Jean-Jacques, 150
Roy, Arundhati, 81

Said, Edward, 124–25, 155, 212n9
Saldivar-Hull, Sonia, 183–84
Sandoval, Chela, 170, 175, 179–80, 188, 216n21, 217nn38–39
Sassen, Saskia, 64
Saudi Arabia, 1
Scattering, 65
Schaffer, Kay, 34, 89
Scott, Joan, 16, 18–19, 173–74
Second wave feminism, 158–59, 169, 171–74, 178, 183, 185, 217n35
Security, culture of, 39–40, 42, 47, 54
September 11, 2001 (9/11), 3, 21, 26, 35–42, 44, 49, 56, 59, 206n68
Sexuality: feminist writers and, 2; gender and, 14; identity by, 5; nationalism and, 36, 204n16; as racialized, 35; sex tourism and, 109; state and, 13; subjectivity of, 111; visual representation of, 208n49
Shinko, Rosemary, 67
Shohat, Ella, 5, 24, 74, 171
Slumdog Millionaire (film), 68, 75–81, 85–86, 101, 118, 209n87
Smith, Sidonie, 34, 88–89
Social Science Research Council, 143
South Asia, area-based studies of, 2, 11, 145, 199n3, 200n28, 213n14
Soviet Union, 58
Spivak, Gayatri C., 29, 62, 78, 116, 216n21
State. See Nation-State
Steele, Michael, 86
Stones into Schools (Mortenson), 194

Subalternity, 29, 62, 78, 114, 117–18, 133,
206n8
Subjectivity: alternative theories of,
174; as consumer, 114; difference in,
171; as empowered, 88; as gendered,
111; identity for, 27; inequalities for,
157; for mestiza, 183–85; of subaltern
woman, 29, 62, 78, 114, 117–18, 133,
206n8
Swarup, Vikas, 68

Tai, Emily, 137–38
Taliban, 36, 45, 51, 55
Technology, 15, 24–27, 30, 36, 102, 114, 191.
See also Visual technology
Terrorism, 37–38, 40, 44, 47–49, 52, 54, 57,
205n40, 206n70
Thailand, 109
Third wave feminism: construction of,
30–31, 170–74; intersectionality and,
181; intervention for, 215n6; racism in,
176, 216n28; scholarship on, 28, 157, 184,
188; as transnational, 157–58
Third World: boundaries of, 71, 73–74,
207n34; cultural production from, 66,
69; globalization and, 8, 69; historical
memory in, 99–100; relationships by,
66, 72, 116; representation of, 34, 70,
99–100; as violent, 73–74, 100, 207n35;
women in, 88–89, 116, 122
Third World America (Huffington), 100
"Third World America" (*Huffington Post*),
100
This Bridge Called My Back (Anzaldúa,
Moraga), 157, 171, 175
This Bridge Called My Home (Keating),
176
Three Cups of Tea (Mortenson), 194
Tiananmen Square massacre, 73
Toor, Saadia, 206n69
Torture, use of, 48
Tourism, 14, 27, 109
"Transcending the Boundaries" (Ajayi-
Soyanki), 218n55
Transdisciplinarity, 21, 152

Transforming Feminist Practice (Fernandes), 218n53
Transnational feminism: as academic,
1–2, 103, 209n3; accountability for, 123,
130–31; agendas for, 51; approaches by,
26, 40; bias of, 18; collaboration for,
189; complexity of, 14; conceptions of,
18, 108, 119–20, 174–75; evolution of,
179–80; feminist thought and, 24, 115,
169; history of, 115–16, 174, 176, 181–82,
216n28; human rights and, 33–34,
37–38, 42, 50–51, 54; inequalities in,
13–14, 116, 157; institutionalization of,
30, 60, 137–40, 146, 151, 153, 155–56, 161,
166, 168, 212n8; knowledge production
in, 103, 116–20, 127, 197; as multicultural, 168, 171; as nation-centric, 14,
50; as other, 158; political economy
and, 109–10; private sphere and, 59;
representation and, 62, 101; terms of,
174; U.S. Third World feminism and,
179, 217n38; visibility of, 103, 107–8;
visual technologies for, 24. *See also*
Activism; Border-crossing; Ethics;
Interdisciplinarity; Perspectives;
Research and scholarship; Second
wave feminism; Third wave feminism;
United States
Transnationalism: collaboration for, 189;
context for, 99; diaspora and, 3–4, 8,
18, 61–63, 186, 200n40; difference and,
186; flow of, 102; materiality and, 120;
as outside U.S., 15, 201n40; perspective
of, 2, 10, 107, 168, 186, 199n4; as political, 10, 192; power relationships in, 65;
as racialized, 86, 186; state *versus*, 6–7,
9, 24, 190; as territorial, 123. *See also*
Affective economy; Border-crossing;
Research and scholarship; United
States
Treason (Coulter), 46
Tripp, Aili Mari, 20

"Under Western Eyes" (Mohanty), 116
United Nations, 33, 41–42, 47

United States (U.S.): characterization of, 203n12; colonialism and, 35; decline in, 100; diasporic communities in, 4, 35, 61, 200n40; domination by, 33, 38, 49, 178; economy of, 3, 7, 100, 113, 199n8; exceptionalism of, 8–9; feminists of color and, 173, 182–83, 186, 216n16; foreign policy of, 7, 32, 123, 196; gender in, 2, 119–20, 196, 207n35; globalization and, 2, 75, 154, 213n31; hypernationalism in, 3, 199n7; identity of, 48; immigration policies of, 34, 52–53, 56, 100; knowledge for, 2–3, 5–6, 125, 141; middle class in, 75–76, 100; nationalism in, 5, 7, 141; nation-building by, 44, 205n39; ontology of, 120, 123; outsourcing from, 4, 11, 75, 78, 80, 109, 112, 120; Patriot Act for, 38, 44; perspective of, 2, 196; pluralism in, 8; politics in, 39, 168–69, 207n35; as postnational, 8; poverty in, 100; representation by, 26, 34–38, 41–42, 54, 56; security of, 39–40, 54; surveillance by, 39, 52–53, 161; theory/practice debate in, 22, 141, 142, 212n9; transnational feminism in, 101, 119, 166, 190; transnationalism and, 4–5, 7, 10, 18, 26, 35, 42, 57, 186. *See also* Cold War; Power; Terrorism; War on terror

Universities and colleges, U.S.: academic programs at, 1–2, 103, 209n3; area studies in, 2, 11, 123, 125, 145, 160, 199n3, 200n28, 213n14; bureaucracies of, 37; contestation in, 141–42, 212n9; curricula in, 2–3. *See also* Perspectives; Women's studies

U.S. *See* United States

U.S. Third World feminism, 179, 217n38

Vasudevan, Ravi, 84

Violence: accountability for, 54; in border-crossing, 106, 111, 185, 196; caste for, 70–75, 83, 87–88, 177, 208n50; against civilians, 44, 47, 49, 55, 59, 205n40; as cultural, 32, 34; as domestic, 13, 49, 54, 96, 98, 110–11, 126; as epistemic,

62; feminist perspective on, 50, 54, 188; as gendered, 54–55, 70–75, 83; Geneva Conventions and, 48, 50; in India, 49–50, 72–74, 82–83, 110–11, 126; nationalism and, 54; as political, 34, 54, 183; of poverty, 54, 77; as racial, 177; redress for, 34; as sexual, 96–97; subjectivity and, 171; terrorism and, 44, 47, 49; in U.S., 53, 110–11, 126; visual representation of, 25, 35, 73, 82–83, 86, 194. *See also* Prison system, U.S.; Profiling; September 11, 2001 (9/11); Terrorism; War on terror

Visual technology, 15, 24–27, 30, 36–38, 43, 71–72

Visweswaran, Kamala, 34, 117–19

Walker, Alice, 218n55

War on terror: civilian casualties in, 44–46, 56–57, 205n40, 206n69; cooperation for, 39; culture of security by, 54; drone attacks by, 45, 57; gender and race in, 52, 54–55, 58, 205n61; human rights and, 30, 35, 37, 40, 45, 48, 58; after 9/11, 3, 18, 26, 30, 35, 39; power and, 38–42, 44; public and private spheres in, 59; surveillance for, 52–53; torture in, 48; transnational perspective on, 37. *See also* Afghanistan; Boundaries; Iraq; al-Qaeda; Terrorism; Violence

Watson, Julia, 88

Weinbaum, Alys E., 164

Welch, Sharon, 131

Westphalian system, 192

White, Mark, 45

Wiegman, Robyn, 145

WikiLeaks, 193–95

Wilcox, Lauren, 43

Woman, category of, 173–74, 184, 215n12

Women: agency of, 14, 103, 117, 133; equality for, 33; international aid for, 108–9; as marginalized, 29, 119; in NGOs, 27; oppression of, 15, 34, 51; organization of, 102; otherness of, 36; racism against, 177–78; resistance by, 14, 51,

About the Author

LEELA FERNANDES is professor of women's studies and political science at the University of Michigan, and author of *India's New Middle Class: Democratic Politics in an Era of Economic Reform*; *Producing Workers: The Politics of Gender, Class and Culture in the Calcutta Jute Mills*; and *Transforming Feminist Practice*.